Kitchen Planning Guide for Builders and Architects

Kitchen Planning Guide for Builders and Architects

by Patrick J. Galvin

STRUCTURES PUBLISHING COMPANY
Farmington, Michigan
1972

Manufactured in the United States of America.

Book designed by Richard Kinney.

Current Printing (last digit)

10 9 8 7 6 5 4 3 2 1
International Standard Book Number: 0-912336-03-X
Library of Congress Catalog Card Number: 72-86396

Structures Publishing Company
Box 423, Farmington, Michigan 48024

Jacket and Frontispiece Photos by Hedrich-Blessing, Chicago.

Contents

Foreword

The kitchen is now the most important and expensive room in the house.

In the homes in which we over fifty folk were brought up, the kitchen was a necessary evil, closed off from the rest of the house. The only requirement for its location was proximity to the dining room, unless servants were involved, and then the kitchen could even be on another floor. The room had to be close to a rear or side door so that the "icebox" could be replenished by the messy "iceman who cometh" nearly every day. The kitchen was equipped by the builder with a sink and little else. Cabinets were frequently an item of furniture to be supplied by the occupant. The gas range was obviously an item to be moved when the family moved and you could have any color you wanted so long as it was stove black. The garbage disposer was a smelly pail under the sink which we had to carry out to the garbage can in the alley.

Today the kitchen is a thing of beauty, a joy to work in, and a proud possession. It is efficient, easy to clean, safe, well lit, sound conditioned, and well ventilated. Equipment includes one or more built-in ovens, ranges, refrigerators, a garbage disposal and lots of factory-built cabinetry styled to suit a variety of tastes. No longer is this room masked from the rest of the house, but other rooms are allied to it by open planning, folding doors and pass-throughs. The kitchen frequently accomodates table-type eating space or a snack bar. A wet bar, a cooled wine cellar, a trash compactor, menu planning desk, built-in mixing center, a communication center (intercom), and a color TV are increasingly incorporated.

In addition to all of this, it has to be economical to build. Per square foot or per room it is by far the most expensive room in the home.

The need has long been recognized for an authoritative kitchen guide that will bring order out of conflicting rules, suggestions, and customs. As with our other books in the structures field, this has been our objective in bringing you the *Kitchen Planning Guide*. Pat Galvin is the most experienced and competent author available and he has ably demonstrated his command of the subject.

How To Use the Guide

First, scan the book from cover to cover so that you are generally aware of its contents. At the same time, get rid of any misconceptions you may have had about kitchen design criteria.

Then, when you need answers to a kitchen problem, from a complete design to selection of a ceiling material or appliance, consult the index and then the book for your answers.

For better kitchens . . . .

R. J. Lytle, Publisher
Structures Publishing Company

September, 1972

A kitchen with a country air, where the mellow fruitwood cabinets are styled with ageless Provincial detailing. The dishwasher, sinks and cooktop are along one wall and a preparation counter surfaced with a hardwood cutting board is convenient to both wall ovens and the refrigerator-freezer. Floor and backsplash are of mosaic tile. (American Olean Tile Co., photo)

1

Introduction: The Room that Makes the House

Decorating the interior of his home offers a person an opportunity to express a distinctive life style. While people can decorate or rearrange bedrooms, living rooms, and family rooms as they wish, they must accept the kitchen pretty much the way it was originally designed. Appliances cannot be moved around because of their utility connections, and built-in cabinets must fit between appliances.

With the exception of the bathroom, the kitchen is the only room that comes fully furnished, but unlike the bathroom, it is an important socializing center.

The kitchen, then, is the one room in the house that is most resistant to change and yet one of the most lived-in areas during the daytime. This is why the architect must consider the kitchen the most important room in any home or apartment.

Buyers and renters may not be aware of the importance of the kitchen, even though they have owned homes themselves. But let us consider two typical situations that every builder will understand.

Mr. and Mrs. X visit Model Home A. They wander through, probing for features they like, whispering to each other, avoiding salesmen, and considering its price as they depart for the next model. But when Mr. and Mrs. Y visit model Home B, the first thing they notice is the interesting peninsula separating—and yet connecting—the dining area and the kitchen. They open a kitchen drawer that glides smoothly and noiselessly. They open the refrigerator door, where the builder has placed a sign that reads: "You will *Never* have to defrost this beautiful refrigerator." Next they open the cabinets and see the certification seal of the American National Standards Institute. Above

the range hood is the Home Ventilating Institute seal certifying air delivery and sound rating. The dishwasher, disposer, and built-in appliances are there, as well as lighting over all the work areas. They note the extras—a chopping board, inserts in the counters for hot pans, etc. Everywhere the builder has put little signs calling attention to the advantages of this "living kitchen."

Here is no furtive whispering. Mrs. Y's eyes light up as she discovers all the special features, and Mr. Y is already thinking, "It's $3,000 more, but maybe we can swing it if . . ."—*and they haven't even looked at the rest of the house!*

This is how a great kitchen makes a great difference whether the unit is for sale or rent. Mr. and Mrs. X may have seen a very nice home, and it may have been a good buy, but there was nothing striking about it. Mr. and Mrs. Y did see something striking—and the deal was already started.

A good kitchen can bring a family closer during the hours they are home together, but if poorly designed it can be a source of annoyance. It can separate them psychologically as well as physically, by a series of minor frustrations.

The builder invariably pays for poor kitchen design. When he cuts corners and fails to engineer a kitchen for human needs, he is losing his customer for a second home in years to come. He is also losing word-of-mouth referrals that could presell his homes before he gets them on the drawing board.

When there is little in a kitchen design to excite the wife, the couple will settle for something adequate. Price will be the determining factor. But when the kitchen excites her, the wife will use all her powers of rationalization to justify the price the builder sets. She will do the sales job.

The purpose of this book is to make builders and architects more aware of what it takes to make an exciting kitchen.

Of course, many builders and architects already have kitchen departments that make it their business to find out what kitchen features appeal to the buyer. But in this rapidly changing field an architect must know about new products and materials on the market.

Split cooktop, with two 2-burner units on either side of drop-in barbecue, adds a unique touch to this bright and airy kitchen. Ceiling windows brighten the room with daylight. (Hedrich-Blessing, photo)

Butcher-block top on island cooking center is increasingly popular both for utility and textural contrast. Bright blue plastic laminate of regular counters continues up backsplash area for ultimate in cleanability. Lighting for task areas is provided by recessed fixtures under wall cabinets, in this Wood-Mode kitchen.

Another Wood-Mode kitchen offers variety of textures with drainboard model stainless steel sink running into butcher block section, and cooking island covered with artificial brick veneer.

Shingled soffits and walls add interesting texture to this kitchen, which has carpeted floor and plastic laminate backsplash all the way to wall cabinets. (Wood-Mode photo)

Sheer elegance results from this wedding of wood and metal. Fully open to the living area, it becomes a showplace in the home. Sliding tambour doors in the island cooking-eating center, in the peninsula cleanup center and on the walls help retain the character of this kitchen. Island top is stainless steel to harmonize with brushed chrome of wall appliances—twin refrigerators on left, twin ovens on right. Island doubles as food preparation center, with refrigerators and sink equally handy. Circular vent hood is above. (Julius Shulman, photo) ——→

Almost all surfaces are of durable, cleanable plastic laminate in this flush, contemporary indoor-outdoor kitchen by Formica. Even the ceiling, which is glass, admits the western sky.

Straight lines and light, balanced proportions are the essence of the Colonial styling of Mutschler. Full plastic laminate backsplash preserves the clean look.

Strategic island adds needed counter space and storage in kitchen that otherwise might be too compact. Total built-in convenience includes double oven, cooktop, paper caddy behind sink and a true built-in refrigerator. Accessories above take the place of a soffit, and a skylight adds both natural light and visual appeal. (Hedrich-Blessing, photo)

Graceful blending of materials makes a showplace of this St. Charles steel kitchen, softened by pastel blue of the cabinets. Big wooden hood vents both barbecue and glass-ceramic cooktop to its right. Cooking center counters are topped with ceramic tile, but cleanup center (sink area) has plastic laminate. And softening it all, carpet underfoot.

Styled for family which loves antiques, this kitchen has soft-toned brick on floor and cooking wall, ceramic tile countertops all around, maple chopping-block island. Antique-styled lighting fixture is suspended from weathered beam. Cabinets are Colonial by Wood-Mode.

Steel cabinets by St. Charles hardly look like steel when they get Provincial moldings. This compact kitchen has everything, including good counter space. Backsplash and wall is ceramic tile, and paper caddy is built into wall. (Hedrich-Blessing, photo) ⟶

Clinically modern when floor-to-ceiling folding doors are closed, this kitchen suggests the cupboards of great-grandmother's day when open for use. Shelving is shallow for each reach. All appliances except built-in refrigerator are in the island. (Formica photo)

Simple, compact kitchen packs individuality into
small space through use of color and by staying open
to adjacent dining area. Avocado woodgrain on
cabinets and patterned wall covering are both plastic
laminates by Formica.

The same kitchen from the dining side shows brunch
space at counter, a more natural woodgrain backing
the wall cabinets, and more use of matching plastic
laminate on other interior walls.

Form rules this kitchen design with geometrics of ceiling above and highly-useful half-circle island below. Island does multiple duty as cooking center, phone center, brunch counter, tray and utensil storage center, and has maple top for cutting or chopping operations. High hood needs extra power.

Shelving takes the place of wall cabinets in this Western Hemlock kitchen by Edgar Wilson Smith, AIA, and shelving is fulling adjustable.

Artistry of Charles Cressent, 18th century French cabinet maker and sculptor, inspired this Country French cabinetry by Mutschler, and Cressent's combinations of wood and metal were emulated in kitchen design. Protruding countertop angles at sink add a design element, but also add work space.

Luminous ceiling adds most modern touch to kitchen in which Wood-Mode's Lexington cabinets and old-style wall covering suggest earlier era. Corner sink in far corner is for cleanup, near diswasher. Island sink with built-in mixer (near corner) makes this a food preparation center.

Provincial styling has a different look when created with darker, contrasting molding on light wood. Gold color tones throughout add an elegance to this kitchen. White on island top is glass ceramic inlay for cutting or for hot pans. (Wood-Mode photo)

Airy, pretty, gay, with muted greens and cheerful yellow, this kitchen has mobile serving cart with maple top, hides in the island when not in use. Island cook center has extra sink to provide water used in cooking or to serve as bar sink when work area in kitchen is busy, or for youngsters' drinks when they dash in from outdoors. (Wood-Mode photo)

Carpeted, single U-shaped kitchen with wall and base cabinets of peninsula opening on both sides. Impulse line by Del-Mar.

Interchangeable panel inserts in wall cabinets enable changes of mood in this Mutschler Mediterranean kitchen. The blue panels can be changed easily by the housewife for any other insert 1/8" thick. Arched entry, beamed ceiling extend the Mediterranean flavor.

Swiss Chalet is the style of this kitchen with pitched, beamed ceiling, brick walls and blue bottled glass inserts in cabinet doors. Special cabinet encloses countertop microwave oven in far corner.
(Wood-Mode photo)

Indoor-outdoor kitchen has glass walls in backsplash area and above wall cabinets. Black and white cabinets are Del-Mar's Overture line. Red countertop matches red dishwasher and refrigerator.

Kitchen with everything has double wall oven, built-in refrigerator, food-warming drawer in cooking center island, barbecue alcove (red) in far wall, lots of glass to let the outdoors in. Here all yellow and red surfaces, including refrigerator front, are plastic laminate. (Formica photo)

Lighting is a major element in this kitchen, starting with the unusual octagonal cabinet overhanging dining area. Interior lighting accents fine crystal, under-cabinet light shines through amber bottled glass on dining area. Ceiling is fully luminous. (Wood-Mode photo)

An "Elbow-Room Kitchenette" is the name given this kitchen, designed by Western Wood Products Association in 6×14' of space. Appliance at left is Modern Maid's unique combination of eye-level oven, cooktop and dishwasher underneath. Cabinets are of Western Hemlock.

Complete entertainment center can be a stunning adjunct to the kitchen. This includes bar sink, under-counter refrigerator, and the small metal plate to right of sink is built-in mixing center. Fluorescent tubes under wall cabinets cast light down to work space, up through bottom of cabinets to illuminate glassware. Plastic laminate on counter simulates maple butcher block. (Mutschler photo)

This kitchen was designed to relate to the outdoors. It overlooks a lake at Chelsea, Mich. This adds meaning to the hand-split fieldstone on wall, brick floor, wood cathedral ceiling, century-old barnside paneling on pantry in far wall. (Wood-Mode photo)

Variations of brown integrate all elements of this kitchen, brightened by the pattern of backsplash and soffit. Counter lighting is recessed under wall cabinets, and a hydronic heating unit is almost hidden in kick space under sink. (Formica photo)

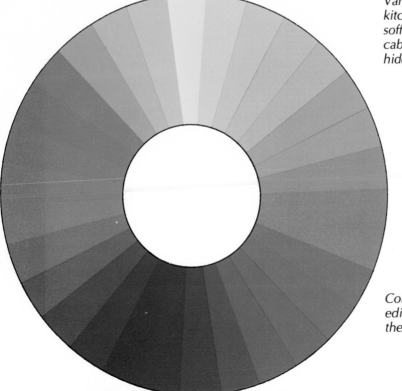

Color wheel from The Oxford Companion to Art, edited by Harold Osborne, 1970, by permission of the Clarendon Press, Oxford.

Carolina Oak kitchen by IXL (division of Westinghouse) gains added interest with peninsula and by carrying same wall covering through backsplash area and on soffit.

Indoor-outdoor kitchen first popularized on West Coast is open to outside living area both above and below wall cabinets. These cabinets are Del-Mar's Overture line.

Modernistic kitchen at Horizon House, Lake Lindera, Cal., has eye appeal and total cleanability. Note the modern hanging lighting fixtures, supplemented by valance light at top of ventilating hood housing.

Even a one-wall kitchen can be distinctive. This one by Connor has pass-through at sink area to adjacent room and decorative opening over wall cabinets. And floor covering is duplicated on backsplash.

26

With all of the new things builders and architects must learn, it is difficult for them to be aware of the more than 10,000 items available from even one single kitchen range manufacturer. Furthermore, there are more than 500 items available from a single cabinet builder. Keeping track of the names and locations of the more than 1,500 basic suppliers to the kitchen industry is a monumental task itself. The interior furnishing and design of modern kitchens is thus a complicated endeavor. Vast resources of kitchen expertise are available to builders and architects. Most major cabinet and appliance manufacturers, for example, supply design services for builders.

But probably the best source for the large builder is a good, local independent distributor. Many kitchen distributors not only bid jobs as specified, but also are prepared to suggest alternate kitchen plans to contractors.

Custom-home builders often prefer to deal with local retail kitchen specialists. Many such specialists are available, but the more reliable ones will probably be members of the American Institute of Kitchen Dealers, an association with extremely high standards for membership and with about 500 members in the United States. Builders will also find individuals who use the initials CKD after their names. These individuals are not necessarily members of the American Institute of Kitchen Dealers. CKD, for Certified Kitchen Designer, indicates certification of the individual by a certifying branch of the American Institute of Kitchen Designers.

The expertise of the specialists mentioned above may not be readily available to you as an architect or builder in your locality, but the services of these individuals can indeed be valuable. This book will help you in working with the professional kiichen designer.

An attempt has been made to include all the information required to design modern kitchens for single and multiple family dwellings. This book is meant to aid you, the architect and builder, in designing, specifying, and installing the kinds of kitchens desired by modern home buyers.

This book will be of value to architects in designing and specifying components. It will be of value to certified kitchen designers as a valuable reference to supplement their professional knowledge. It should be of special value to busy contractors and builders faced either with designing their own kitchens or in working with kitchen designers.

The warmth of redwood brings both elegance and a country flavor to this highly individual kitchen. augmented by good artificial lighting and a skylight that admits daylight. (Architect, Don Batchelder; Photo, Karl Riek; Courtesy California Redwood Association)

2

Basic Kitchen Measurements

The kitchen has no basic measurement standards that cannot be varied for cause. But unless there is cause, everything will work out better if the standardized measurements are followed. For example, the 84-inch total height of a kitchen installation from floor to top of wall cabinets squares off approximately with the top of the door trim, and it squares off precisely with the height of tall cabinets such as those used for broom storage, appliance enclosures, and pantries.

Basic Kitchen Dimensions. Here are the basic dimensions:

1) *Base cabinet*—height is 34-1/2 inches.
2) *Countertop*—1-1/2 inches thick.
3) *Blacksplash attached to countertop*—4 inches high, minimum, can be 5 or 6 inches, or can extend upward all the way to the wall cabinets.
4) *Blacksplash area from countertop to bottom of wall cabinets*—15 or 18 inches, depending on height of wall cabinets.
5) *Wall cabinets* are 30 or 33 inches high. The preferred height is 33 inches, but the most common is 30 inches.

All of these measurements combined will total 84 inches, from floor to the top of the wall cabinets.

Some multiple-housing builders, particularly in New York City, Chicago, scattered other cities, and the West Coast, have begun using 42-inch wall cabinets extending all the way to the ceiling. They claim they do this for esthetic reasons—for a cleaner look—and to gain added storage space in small kitchens.

It should be noted, however, that the minimum property standards do not accept storage space in the kitchen above the 74-inch line, and from a practical point of view such space is simply too hard to reach. Other standard kitchen dimensions are listed below:

1) *Wall cabinets*—12 inches deep, varying to 13 inches. Standard heights progress in 3-inch increments from 12 to 42 inches. Standard widths progress in 3-inch increments from 12 to 60 inches.
2) *Wall cabinets for general storage*—30 or 33 inches high.
3) *Wall cabinets over a range*—18 to 21 inches high.
4) *Wall cabinets over a refrigerator*—12 to 18 inches high, with 15 inches preferable.
5) *Wall cabinets over the sink*—if present these should be 21 to 27 inches high.
6) *Base cabinets* will be 24 to 24-1/2 inches deep, and will have a 4-inch kick-space. Height will be 34-1/2 inches, and widths will vary in 3-inch increments from 9 to 60 inches.
7) *Base cabinets used for kitchen desks or for buffets*—28-1/2 inches high. Units used for bathroom vanities are 30 inches high.
8) *Tall utility cabinets (84 inches)*—usually 24 or 24-1/2 inches deep, although some are half-sized at 12 inches or more. Width ranges from 12 to 42 inches in 3-inch increments. These come in variable configurations. Some have space for upright broom storage in addition to open shelving and/or drawers. Those used for pantries might have a series of revolving shelves or vertical shelving systems that fold out into the room.

HUD Minimum Property Standards. The Minimum Property Standards of the U.S. Department of Housing and Urban Development furnish a starting point in kitchen space planning, because these standards must be met or exceeded in any housing units where federally insured mortgages are involved.

Through 1971 and 1972 these standards were totally rewritten (for the first time since 1956), and builders and architects will probably find the new standards much easier to work with. As a whole, they recognize more fully the environmental factors in the home and in the urban area, are oriented more toward perfor-

Table 2.1.

| Work Centers | Minimum Frontage | | |
	Two Bedrooms	Three Bedrooms	Four or More Bedrooms
Sink	24″	32″	32″
counter and base cab. at each side	20″	24″	30″
Range	24″	30″	30″
counter and base cab. at one side	20″	24″	30″
Refrigerator (space)	36″	36″	36″
counter at latch side	15″	15″	18″
Mixing (base and wall cabinet)	36″	36″	42″

Table 2.2.

| Work Centers | Minimum Frontage | | | | |
	Efficiency	One Bedroom	Two Bedrooms	Three Bedrooms	Four or More Bedrooms
Sink	18″	24″	24″	32″	32″
counter and base cab. at each side	15″	18″	20″	24″	30″
Range	21″	21″	24″	30″	30″
counter and base cab. at one side	15″	18″	20″	24″	30″
Refrigerator (space)	30″	30″	36″	36″	36″
counter at latch side	15″	15″	15″	15″	18″
Mixing (base and wall cabinet)	21″	30″	36″	36″	42″

mance, and tend to encourage design innovations and improved building technologies.

The new MPS are in four volumes: for *One and Two Family Dwellings*, for *Multifamily Housing*, for *Care-Type Housing* (nursing homes and the like), and a fourth publication called *Manual of Acceptable Practices*, which contains back-up material for the three volumes of mandatory standards.

The paragraph numbering system is the same for all three volumes and is similar to the system used in the old MPS, so a builder or architect can easily check differences between requirements for one-family houses and multifamily by checking the same sections and paragraph numbers in the two appropriate volumes.

Following are all requirements pertinent to kitchens in one- and two-family houses with, where appropriate, the differences in multifamily housing.

Table 2.3

Material	Minimum Thickness	Material	Minimum Thickness
Asphalt tile	0.09 in.	Unfilled vinyl sheet	0.065 in. or 0.055 in.
Homogenous vinyl tile	0.050 in. (3/64 in.)	Vinyl-asbestos tile	0.0625 in. (1/16 in.)
Linoleum tile or sheet	0.090 in. (std. gage)	Vinyl sheet (backed) Grade B Grade C	0.070 in. 0.065 in.
Rubber tile	0.80 in. (5/64 in.)		

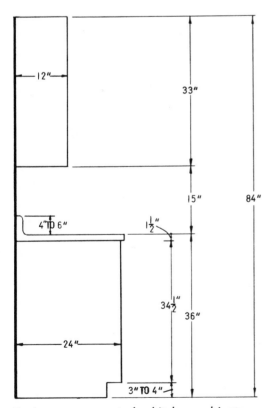

Basic measurements for kitchen cabinets.

Chapter 4, Building Design. Paragraph 401-1.2 applies to the dining area, regardless of whether it is a separate room or combined with living room or kitchen. It specifies:

Space for accommodating the following size table and chairs with proper circulation space in the dining area shall be provided, according to the intended occupancy, as shown:

(2 bedrooms)	4 persons	-2'6"×3'2"
(3 bedrooms)	6 persons	-3'4"×4'0" or 4'0"round
(4 bedrooms)	8 persons	-3'4"×6'0" or 4'0"×4'0"
(5 bedrooms)	10 persons	-3'4"×8'0" or 4'0"×6'0"
(6 bedrooms)	12 persons	-4'0"×8'0"
	Dining chairs	-1'6"×1'6"

In multifamily, this paragraph is the same except for the addition of this specification: "(Efficiency or 1 bedroom) 2 persons -2'6"×2'6"."

Paragraph 401-2.1 applies to the kitchen specifically, with the following provisions:

The kitchen design shall provide for efficient food and utensil storage, and serving, as well as cleaning up after meals.

The kitchen shall be directly accessible to the dining area and shall be conveniently located near the living area.

Circulation space in food preparation areas shall not be less than 40" in width.

Kitchen cabinets shall be provided according to Table 4.1. (Reproduced here as Table 2.1.)

Specific provisions. The following specific provisions are included:

1) Work centers may be combined; the kitchen multiple-use space shall at least equal the largest frontage of any one of the work centers being combined, plus 6 inches.
2) Provide a drawer at each base cabinet, or equivalent group of drawers.
3) Frontage may continue around a corner, except a space less than 12" may not be counted.
4) Frontage of wall cabinets shall equal the required frontage for base cabinets.
5) The frontages are based on typical cabinets. Base cabinet approximately 24 inches deep by 36 inches in height with one shelf and drawer. Wall cabinet approximately 12 inches deep by 30 inches in height with two shelves.

6) Provide at least 9 inches from the edge of the sink or range to any adjacent corner cabinet, and 16 inches from the latch side of the refrigerator to any adjacent corner cabinet.
7) Refrigerator space may be 33 inches when a refrigerator is provided and the door opens within its own width.
8) Where dishwashers are provided, 24-inch sinks are acceptable.

Differences for multifamily housing. A number of differences exist. These are shown in Table 2.2.

Work centers are basically the same except that when requirements for work centers are combined for efficiency and one-bedroom units the combined work centers must at least equal the largest work center being combined, i.e., dropping the extra 6 inches. A 72-inch compact kitchen with adequate wall cabinets may be substituted in efficiency apartments.

Light and ventilation. Paragraph 402-3.1 is a table with minimum requirements for natural light and ventilation in the various house areas. There is no requirement for natural light in the kitchen, but the ventilation requirement is for natural ventilation as 4 percent of the floor area or, if mechanical ventilation is substituted, 15 air changes per hour.

In multifamily housing, the natural ventilation requirement is the same. But for mechanical ventilation the table specifies 15 air changes per hour with a room-controlled exhaust fan or, with other mechanical means such as central system, 10 changes per hour.

Chapter 5, Materials. Paragraph 509-4.3 specifies that walls in kitchens, bathrooms and laundries shall be resistant to grease, water, detergents, and normal household chemicals.

Hardboard. When hardboard is used for interior walls in the kitchen or bath, it must be Class I Decorative grade.

Flooring. When resilient flooring is used, minimum thickness of various materials are as specified in Table 2.3.

Wall coverings. Wall covering requirements are as follows:

509-8.1 Wall coverings shall be of such kind and quality for a given material to assure (a) intended

Specifications page by the National Kitchen Cabinet Association shows typical wall, base, and tall cabinets with their customary sizes as made by most stock cabinet manufacturers.

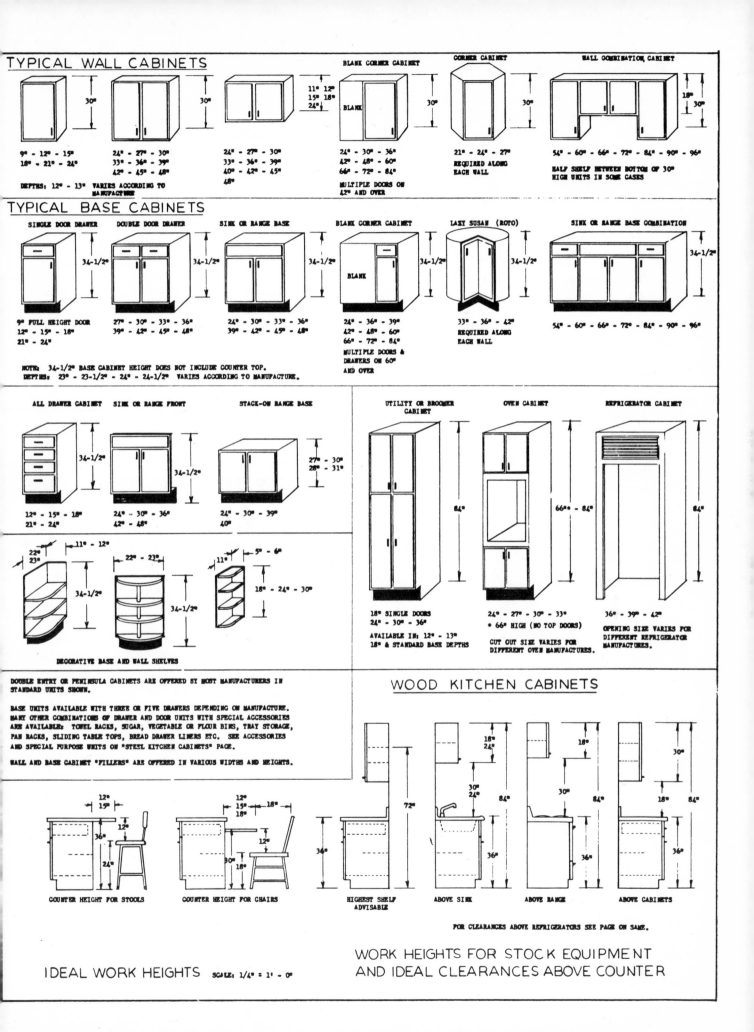

TYPICAL WALL CABINETS

BLANK CORNER CABINET · CORNER CABINET · WALL COMBINATION CABINET

30" | 30" | 11" 12" 15" 18" 24" | BLANK | 30" | 30" | 18" 30"

9" - 12" - 15"
18" - 21" - 24"

24" - 27" - 30"
33" - 36" - 39"
42" - 45" - 48"

24" - 27" - 30"
33" - 36" - 39"
40" - 42" - 45"
48"

24" - 30" - 36"
42" - 48" - 60"
66" - 72" - 84"

MULTIPLE DOORS ON
42" AND OVER

21" - 24" - 27"

REQUIRED ALONG
EACH WALL

54" - 60" - 66" - 72" - 84" - 90" - 96"

HALF SHELF BETWEEN BOTTOM OF 30"
HIGH UNITS IN SOME CASES

DEPTHS: 12" - 13" VARIES ACCORDING TO
MANUFACTURE

TYPICAL BASE CABINETS

SINGLE DOOR DRAWER · DOUBLE DOOR DRAWER · SINK OR RANGE BASE · BLANK CORNER CABINET · LAZY SUSAN (ROTO) · SINK OR RANGE BASE COMBINATION

34-1/2"

9" FULL HEIGHT DOOR
12" - 15" - 18"
21" - 24"

27" - 30" - 33" - 36"
39" - 42" - 45" - 48"

24" - 30" - 33" - 36"
39" - 42" - 45" - 48"

24" - 36" - 39"
42" - 48" - 60"
66" - 72" - 84"

MULTIPLE DOORS &
DRAWERS ON 60"
AND OVER

33" - 36" - 42"

REQUIRED ALONG
EACH WALL

54" - 60" - 66" - 72" - 84" - 90" - 96"

NOTE: 34-1/2" BASE CABINET HEIGHT DOES NOT INCLUDE COUNTER TOP.
DEPTHS: 23" - 23-1/2" - 24" - 24-1/2" VARIES ACCORDING TO MANUFACTURE.

ALL DRAWER CABINET · SINK OR RANGE FRONT · STACK-ON RANGE BASE

34-1/2"

12" - 15" - 18"
21" - 24"

24" - 30" - 36"
42" - 48"

27" - 30"
28" - 31"

24" - 30" - 39"
40"

UTILITY OR BROOMER CABINET · OVEN CABINET · REFRIGERATOR CABINET

84" | 66" - 84" | 84"

18" SINGLE DOORS
24" - 30" - 36"

AVAILABLE IN: 12" - 13"
18" & STANDARD BASE DEPTHS

24" - 27" - 30" - 33"
* 66" HIGH (NO TOP DOORS)

CUT OUT SIZE VARIES FOR
DIFFERENT OVEN MANUFACTURES.

36" - 39" - 42"

OPENING SIZE VARIES FOR
DIFFERENT REFRIGERATOR
MANUFACTURES.

22" 23" | 11" - 12" | 22" - 23" | 11" 5" - 6"

34-1/2" | 34-1/2" | 18" - 24" - 30"

DECORATIVE BASE AND WALL SHELVES

DOUBLE ENTRY OR PENINSULA CABINETS ARE OFFERED BY MOST MANUFACTURERS IN
STANDARD UNITS SHOWN.

BASE UNITS AVAILABLE WITH THREE OR FIVE DRAWERS DEPENDING ON MANUFACTURE.
MANY OTHER COMBINATIONS OF DRAWER AND DOOR UNITS WITH SPECIAL ACCESSORIES
ARE AVAILABLE: TOWEL RACKS, SUGAR, VEGETABLE OR FLOUR BINS, TRAY STORAGE,
PAN RACKS, SLIDING TABLE TOPS, BREAD DRAWER LINERS ETC. SEE ACCESSORIES
AND SPECIAL PURPOSE UNITS ON "STEEL KITCHEN CABINETS" PAGE.

WALL AND BASE CABINET "FILLERS" ARE OFFERED IN VARIOUS WIDTHS AND HEIGHTS.

WOOD KITCHEN CABINETS

12" 15" | 12" 36" | 36" 24"

COUNTER HEIGHT FOR STOOLS

12" 15" 18" | 30" 18" | 12" 36"

COUNTER HEIGHT FOR CHAIRS

72" 36"

HIGHEST SHELF
ADVISABLE

18" 24" | 30" 24" | 84" 36"

ABOVE SINK

18" | 30" 84" 36"

ABOVE RANGE

18" 30" 84" 36"

ABOVE CABINETS

FOR CLEARANCES ABOVE REFRIGERATORS SEE PAGE ON SAME.

IDEAL WORK HEIGHTS   SCALE: 1/4" = 1' - 0"

WORK HEIGHTS FOR STOCK EQUIPMENT
AND IDEAL CLEARANCES ABOVE COUNTER

life, (b) renewability, and (c) walls in kitchens, bathrooms and laundries resistant to grease, water, detergents and normal household chemicals.

509-8.2 Vinyl covering shall be cotton cloth coated with plasticized polyvinyl chloride resin or copolymer thereof conforming to applicable requirements of Federal Specification CCC-A-700. Minimum weights and thickness shall be:

Total weight per square yard . . . . . .7 ounces
Coating thickness . . . . .5 mils

When *wallpaper* is used, of course it must be sunfast, waterfast and of waterproof type.

Mechanical Ventilation. Mechanical ventilation is covered in 515-2.1 and 2. It states:

Ventilating equipment shall comply and be tested and rated in accordance with the "Air Flow and Sound Test Procedures of the Home Ventilating Institute" dated October, 1968. Evidence of compliance shall be a Home Ventilating Institute or manufacturer's label showing capacity and sound characteristics. Sound levels on kitchen exhaust and range hood fans rated 500 cfm or less shall not exceed 9.0 sones. Bathroom fans not to exceed 6.5 sones. Electrical equipment shall comply with the National Electric Code.

Kitchen range hoods must be labeled and listed by Underwriters Laboratories.

Construction (Chapter 6). The 611-1 paragraphs cover kitchen cabinets and countertops. The requirement is that all manufactured factory-finished cabinets must comply with ANSI A161-1, "Recommend Minimum Construction and Performance Standards for Kitchen and Vanity Cabinets," or an equivalent standard. Further, they must bear a label of an independent inspection agency acceptable to HUD, and the label must indicate compliance with the standards.

Cabinets. Custom or job-built cabinets must be equivalent in quality and construction.

Countertops. Countertops must be securely bonded "to reinforced steel core or to 3/4-inch plywood or other equivalent material. Top material shall be phenolic laminate, vinyl plastic covering, linoleum, ceramic tile, stainless steel or other material suitable for the intended use. Also required is at least a 3-inch back and end splash against all abutting vertical surfaces.

All edges, including sink and built-in surface units, must have non-corrodible metal molding or other suitable edging installed.

Kitchen and bathroom ventilation. The 615-2 paragraphs outline requirements for kitchen and bathroom ventilation. Following are the kitchen requirements:

1) *Fan capacity* in cfm, based on air changes per hour, shall be calculated by this equation:

$$cfm = \frac{\text{cu. ft. room vol.} \times \text{no. air changes per hr.}}{60}$$

2) *Discharge openings* to exterior must be protected against rain entry, and have automatic backdraft dampers or louvers.

3) *Kitchen air* must be exhausted directly to outdoors, either by vented range hood or a ceiling or wall fan, if natural ventilation is not provided.

4) A *range hood* must be at least as long as the range, at least 17 inches wide, and the bottom of the hood rim must not be more than 30 inches above range top.

5) *Range hood fan* must have a minimum capacity of 40 cfm of hood length, increased to 50 cfm when in island or peninsula location.

In the multifamily book, the specifications change drastically because of the nature of the central vent systems normally used. But for low multifamily walk-ups, such as townhouse complexes, the multifamily book refers to the one-family requirements.

Electrical requirements. These are spelled out in the 616 paragraphs. Demand for the various needs in the home, including all kitchen appliances, is listed in the Table 2.4.

As for lighting, the MPS requirement first is that there must be permanent lighting fixtures, controlled by wall switches, in dining areas, kitchens and all other habitable areas.

No point along a floorline can be more than 6 feet from a convenience outlet, and there must be at least two duplex receptacle outlets over counter work spaces in kitchens.

Recommended Kitchen Measurements. The HUD Minimum Property Standards are workable, and they represent a tremendous improvement over those used for the previous 15 years. But they are minimums, and even for dwellings intended for small families the prudent builder would do well to expand the

Table 2.4.

Electrical Equipment Demand	
	Diversified demand (KW)
Basic demand	4.0
Clothes washer	.8
Dishwasher	1.2
Range	12.
Oven, built-in	4.5
Top, built-in (4 units)	6.0
Clothes dryer:	5.0
Water heater: (high recovery)	5.5
Food freezer	.6
Food waste disposer	.4
Water pump	.4
Attic fan	.4
Electric bathroom heater (each)	1.3
Central heating system (1)	.5
Room air conditioner (each)	1.2
Central air conditioner (1)	(2)

(†) Only the larger of the heating or cooling load need be considered.
(2) Rated wattage.

Table 2.5

	Counter (Lineal)	Base Cabinets (Lineal)	Wall Cabinets (Lineal)
1 or 2 bedrooms			
(HUD minimums)	52″	68″	68″
(Generous)	84″	96″	96″
3 bedrooms			
(HUD minimums)	60″	72″	72″
(Generous)	96″	120″	144″
4 bedrooms			
(HUD minimums)	72″	84″	84″
(Generous)	108″	120″	168″

countertop and cabinet capacities. And since they leave more open to interpretation than the old standards, it is possible to make them even more minimal. For example, by combining work areas it would be possible to get off with as little as 52 inches of lineal counter space in a two-bedroom house. But in this instance a little added cost can add a great deal of appeal and usefulness.

The countertop is for the purpose of serving the sink and appliances, and thus basic countertop needs do not change greatly as the size of the family increases.

Basic cabinet requirements do change as the size of the family increases because of the need for increased food storage and the necessity of storing additional dishes. Other requirements, such as storage for utensils and small appliances, remain largely the same.

In Table 2.5 the HUD minimums (by the wildest possible interpretation) are compared with other figures more in line with what a kitchen expert might recommend.

In augumenting the minimums for larger kitchens for larger houses and larger families, there are the following recommendations:

1) *Dry vegetable storage* is best accommodated by a 3-drawer base cabinet (no shelves).
2) *Bread and cake* storage is best accommodated by a 3-drawer base cabinet.
3) *Sink area* (within easy reach of sink) is best accommodated by a 2-drawer base cabinet (which will have one shelf). This augments the storage provided by the floor of the sink cabinet.
4) *General storage* is adequately accommodated by 1-drawer 2-shelf base cabinets. This includes pots and pans.
5) *Small appliance storage* is best accommodated by pull-out shelves.

For basic needs and measurements in the distribution of countertop space and for kitchen brunch and dining areas, see Chapter 6.

3

Everything You Should Know about Kitchen Cabinets

Kitchen cabinets are manufactured in such a variety of sizes, shapes, styles, finishes, colors, and materials that classification becomes difficult. Perhaps we should stop calling them "kitchen" cabinets. Nearly all major cabinet manufacturers now manufacture and promote cabinet assemblies for nearly every room in the house. All of these other-room applications utilize standard or scaled-down "kitchen" cabinets with the fine "furniture finishes" that were developed in the 1960s.

Two types of cabinet manufacturers with whom the builder and architect may be involved may be identified: stock and custom manufacturers.

The stock cabinet manufacturer is most commonly used for new home construction, for several good reasons:

1. He manufactures to stock, to fill his own warehouse and the warehouses of his distributors. Delivery often is available almost immediately from local supply points.

2. Sales are usually handled through the local distributor. Although shipments are often made direct to the building site, particularly in large projects, the builder does have a direct local line to the factory through the distributor. The distributor will schedule shipments according to the progress of the building job and may even coordinate the various trades involved in kitchen installation, a chore most builders are happy to be rid of.

3. Stock manufacturers usually offer lines ranging from lowest to upper medium price, a range usually most consistent with new construction needs.

4. Stock cabinet manufacturers must, of necessity, tailor their lines along the broad lines of general customer preference. They follow the results of their own marketing research and of current developments in the furniture field. While there will seldom be a unique color or finish in a stock line, a speculative builder will find that all of these lines are "safe."

5. Freight or other damages are immediately rectifiable from local distributor stock.

The custom cabinet manufacturer is quite different from the stock manufacturer. He usually is local or regional, although some operate on a national basis. He does not start making cabinets until the kitchen floorplan is in his plant.

This normally means a delivery period of from six to eight weeks. Prices here range from upper medium to high. Sales to builders in the field are made through factory representatives (who are independent businessmen) or through local dealers who often act as representatives on builder jobs.

Custom home builders especially like the advantages of dealing with custom manufacturers because:

1. The quality ranges from very good to superb.

2. Exotic woods, style, finishes, and variations are available and can be specified for unique cabinets and kitchens. These manufacturers can supply teak, cherry, pecan, solid wood, or even a "five-quarter" door as opposed to the usual 3/4-inch or 7/8-inch thickness.

3. Many builders have gained real competitive advantages by using the design service of the local custom kitchen dealer.

The builder has a few other options, particularly if he is risk-oriented. He can build the cabinets himself, on-site. This used to be common practice. Now only about 100,000 kitchens a year are built on this basis as more and more builders discover that they cannot afford this kind of work. Also, it can be very difficult to prove that site-built cabinets meet the new ANSI construction and performance standards without taking them through the established testing procedures at a recognized testing laboratory.

There also are numerous small plants and shops set up in various parts of the country specifically to serve the builder. Some may be very good. They usually

Typical of well-planned cabinetry is this pantry next to the cooktop. Spices and condiments are easy to reach without fumbling, a real convenience for a gourmet cook who is stirring a sauce with one hand, groping for the garlic with the other. *American Olean Tile Photo.*

Next to planning desk is this specially-fitted linen storage cabinet. Roll-out trays make placemats, napkins and tablecoths readily accessible, minimize creases. *American Olean Tile Photo.*

DESIGN-A-WALL COMPONENTS

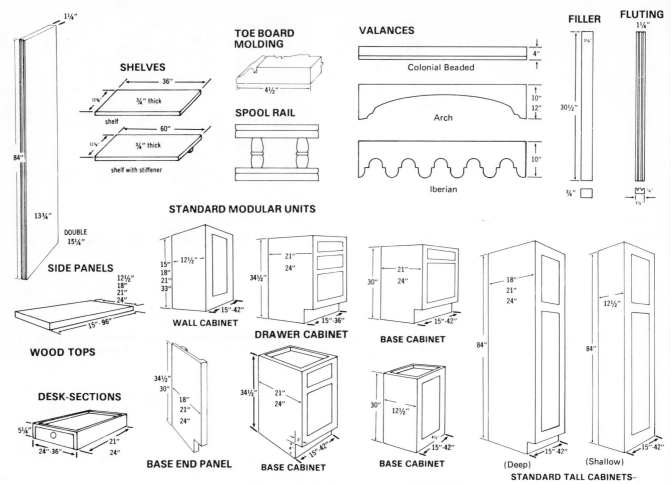

SHELVES

36"
3/4" thick
shelf

60"
3/4" thick
shelf with stiffener

TOE BOARD MOLDING

4 1/2"

SPOOL RAIL

VALANCES

4"
Colonial Beaded

10"
12"
Arch

10"
Iberian

FILLER

30 1/2"

3/4"

FLUTING

1 1/4"

1 1/4"
84"

13 3/4"

DOUBLE
15 1/4"

SIDE PANELS

12 1/2"
18"
21"
24"

15"-96"

WOOD TOPS

DESK-SECTIONS

5 1/4"
24"-36"
21"
24"

STANDARD MODULAR UNITS

15"
18"
21"
33"
12 1/2"

15"-42"

WALL CABINET

21"
24"
34 1/2"

15"-36"

DRAWER CABINET

21"
24"
30"

15"-42"

BASE CABINET

18"
21"
24"

84"

15"-42"
(Deep)

12 1/2"

84"

15"-42"
(Shallow)

STANDARD TALL CABINETS–

34 1/2"
30"
18"
21"
24"

BASE END PANEL

34 1/2"
21"
24"

15"-42"

BASE CABINET

30"
12 1/2"

15"-42"

BASE CABINET

ALL BASE CABINETS AVAILABLE WITH FULL HEIGHT DOORS

are neither stock nor custom in the sense previously described. They often make an 8-ft. or 10-ft. run of wall or base cabinets as one unit for a specific builder floorplan, and turn them out by the hundreds with consequent economies. These cabinets may be good, but the builder must be sure of what he is buying. When the housewife climbs up to put some plants on top of the wall cabinets and finds raw wood with nails sticking out, she will certainly be upset.

Cabinets set the kitchen style

There are four basic kitchen styles: Colonial, Traditional, Provincial and Contemporary.

There also are special styles such as Mediterranean, Oriental, Nautical, Pennsylvania Dutch, Swiss Chalet or others that the imaginative merchandiser might want to feature.

Whatever the style, basic or special, the motif is

set by the cabinets. That means the style of the whole kitchen really is set by only two elements, the cabinet doors and the drawer fronts, since these are the most visible elements in the kitchen.

Appliances are visible, but they have no particular influence on style. They simply "go with" the cabinets. Their colors might be varied to blend or highlight certain styles, but their role in kitchen styling always is either supplementary or complementary.

There is wide latitude in the definitions of styling. If a manufacturer wants to call his new line Colonial, Colonial it is, no matter how provincial or contemporary it looks.

With that in mind, let us review the various styles.

Traditional—This is the leader. More manufacturers offer it, and it accounts for 33 percent of all U.S. cabinet production. But many manufacturers include colonial in this category because they are relating to American tradition.

36

The term "kitchen cabinets" has become a misnomer as builders increasingly spread them throughout the house. Most manufacturers assist with components to adapt them. These pages showing adapting components and how to use them are from a booklet of Rutt Custom Kitchens. The photos that follow show what can de done with them.

Characteristically, traditional is a somewhat dignified and conservative style featuring a recessed or a raised panel, or at least a false raised panel. Oak carries this style well.

Colonial—This might be called Early American or Country Western, or other similar names. A pegged, board-and-batten door possibly is the ultimate in this styling. V-grooves are common, but pegs alone are usually enough to establish the style even on an otherwise plain door. On the west coast and in the southwest, knotty pine is enough to establish the style, or knotty cedar where a redder look is desired. Colors will be mellow.

Provincial—This might be French or Italian, with the Italian being somewhat more ornate. Provincial is characterized by moldings on the face of door and drawer front, with arcs at the corners. In cost-cutting versions, the moldings are replaced by a routed groove. Routed grooves also are commonly used on plastic surfaced doors.

Birch and maple are commonly used in provincial styling.

Contemporary—This style, often called modern, is characterized by clean lines and flush or overlay doors.

In all other styles, lip doors are more common. Contemporary doors often are overlay, with a reverse lip to eliminate the need for pulls and knobs. It is in this styling that we often find the solid color cabinetry. It also is a common style used by manufacturers of plastic laminated cabinets.

Mediterranean—This is so popular that perhaps it is inaccurate to call it a special style. It is also difficult to define, because the Mediterranean region includes Greek, Italian, Moorish, French and many other possible styling influences.

Generally speaking, Mediterranean style is dark and heavy (although it might be light), and quite ornate (although it might be simple). Some builders simply use a dark-toned avocado wood-grain plastic laminated cabinet and call it Mediterranean.

Here cabinetry changes a bedroom to a room that can be used all day.

In the same Colonial styling, cabinets adapt the bathroom and also furnish a design tie-in with the adjacent bedroom.

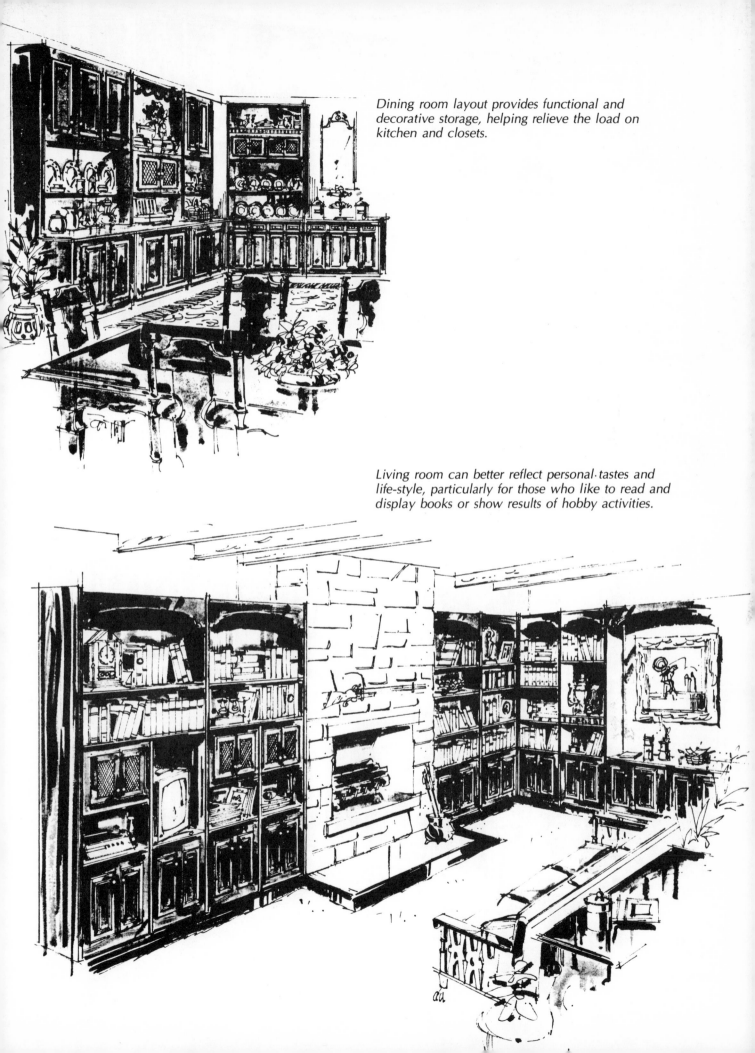

Dining room layout provides functional and
decorative storage, helping relieve the load on
kitchen and closets.

Living room can better reflect personal·tastes and
life-style, particularly for those who like to read and
display books or show results of hobby activities.

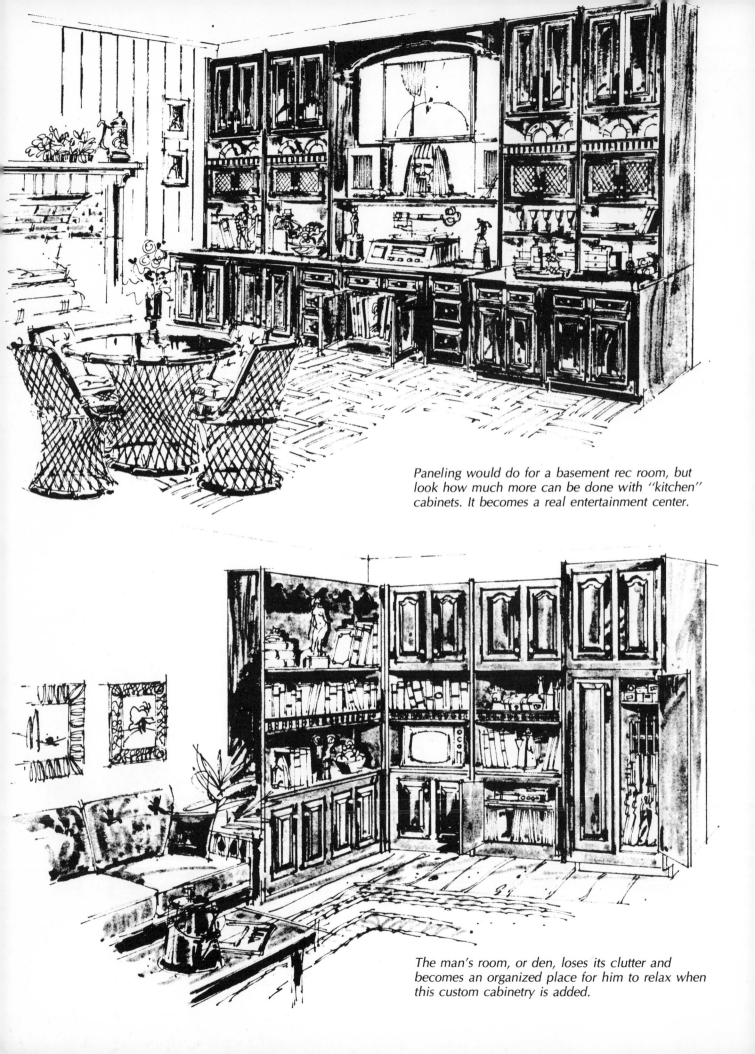

Paneling would do for a basement rec room, but look how much more can be done with "kitchen" cabinets. It becomes a real entertainment center.

The man's room, or den, loses its clutter and becomes an organized place for him to relax when this custom cabinetry is added.

Other special styles, such as Oriental or Nautical, are good for model homes where the kitchens are being merchandised. They get talked about and they can draw crowds. But it isn't good business to install them before a home is sold, because the more special the style the more it cuts down the number of prospects. When the customer desires a special kitchen style, builders usually give the customer the kitchen allowance and refer him to a local kitchen specialist who handles it on a separate contract.

Wood, steel or plastic—and which plastic?

Wood cabinets lead in popularity with home buyers. Plastic laminated cabinets are making slow, steady gains. Steel, a strong leader in the mid-1950s, is no longer a major factor in the residential market although it continues to show some strength in apartments. In fact, at least one widely-respected custom manufacturer still specializes in steel (with wood and plastic options for the doors and drawer fronts).

New plastics are making an impact. These include foamed polyurethane, polystyrene, nylon, and other types manufactured for surfacing.

SOFTWOODS are more popular in the west and southwest. They include:

Pine—most common, creamy white and very workable. Both Ponderosa and Sugar varieties are used.

Fir—Douglas variety is most widely used, but western cabinet manufacturers also use White.

Knotty pine—again, either Ponderosa, Sugar, or Idaho, but characterized by numerous knots for distinctive styling.

Knotty cedar—quite similar to pine, but reddish in color.

Hemlock—a variety of spruce.

HARDWOODS are more numerous in variety and much more common in cabinetry in the east and midwest where most nationally-distributed cabinets are made. They include:

Birch—the leader by far, heavy, strong and hard with great texture variety, and very inexpensive. White, red, and European are used.

Particleboard used for corestock is a finely engineered product relating little to the familiar floor underlayment. This demonstration by Georgia-Pacific shows its versatility and machinability.

Oak—second in popularity only to birch, it is more expensive but has great appeal to homeowners. It is used in all styles but is especially good for traditional. While the wood itself has a wide color range, it usually is finished dark.

Maple—an excellent, straight-grained material but often with good markings and widely used in colonial styles.

Walnut—strong, with varied patterns, almost always finished medium to dark, but quite expensive.

Birch, beech, alder, ash, cherry, pecan, hickory and red or white lauan (often called Philippine mahogany) are used to varying extents by an appreciable range of manufacturers.

Before moving on to other materials, it should be noted that some of the prettiest teaks and sandalwoods you'll ever see are not that at all, but birch.

Some major manufacturers take an inexpensive birch and print an exotic finish on it. This is done with big 4-color presses that print full rich coloring on drab birch and impress the grain markings. This technique is also widely used for stereo and television cabinets. It requires very expensive tooling, but the end result is the appearance of exotic woods at bargain-basement prices. The price, naturally, must be a function of volume.

WALL UNITS

First Two Digits Indicate Width in Inches. Second Two Digits Indicate Height in Inches. All Wall Units Are Reversible.

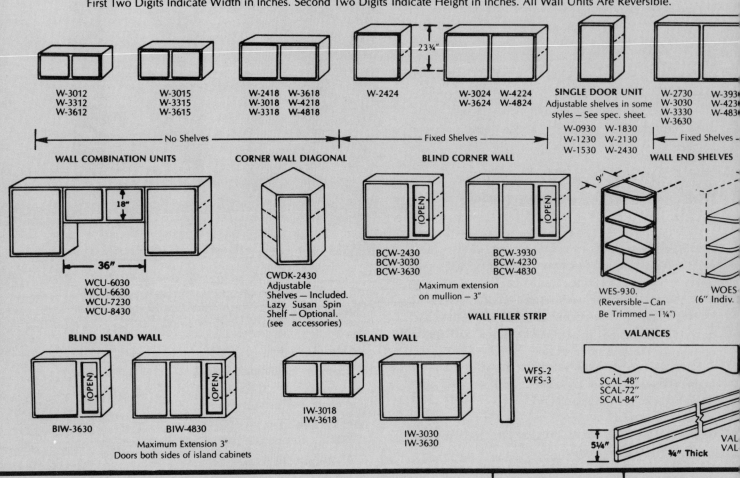

W-3012
W-3312
W-3612

W-3015
W-3315
W-3615

W-2418 W-3618
W-3018 W-4218
W-3318 W-4818

23¾"

W-2424

W-3024 W-4224
W-3624 W-4824

SINGLE DOOR UNIT
Adjustable shelves in some
styles — See spec. sheet.

W-2730 W-393●
W-3030 W-423●
W-3330 W-483●
W-3630

── No Shelves ──   ── Fixed Shelves ──

W-0930 W-1830
W-1230 W-2130
W-1530 W-2430

── Fixed Shelves ──

WALL COMBINATION UNITS

18"

36"

WCU-6030
WCU-6630
WCU-7230
WCU-8430

CORNER WALL DIAGONAL

CWDK-2430
Adjustable
Shelves — Included.
Lazy Susan Spin
Shelf — Optional.
(see accessories)

BLIND CORNER WALL

(OPEN)

BCW-2430
BCW-3030
BCW-3630

(OPEN)

BCW-3930
BCW-4230
BCW-4830

Maximum extension
on mullion — 3"

WALL END SHELVES

9"

WES-930.
(Reversible — Can
Be Trimmed — 1¼")

WOES
(6" Indiv.

BLIND ISLAND WALL

(OPEN)

(OPEN)

BIW-3630

BIW-4830

Maximum Extension 3"
Doors both sides of island cabinets

ISLAND WALL

IW-3018
IW-3618

IW-3030
IW-3630

WALL FILLER STRIP

WFS-2
WFS-3

VALANCES

SCAL-48"
SCAL-72"
SCAL-84"

5¼"

¾" Thick

VAL
VAL

ACCESSORIES

SLIDING TRAY KIT

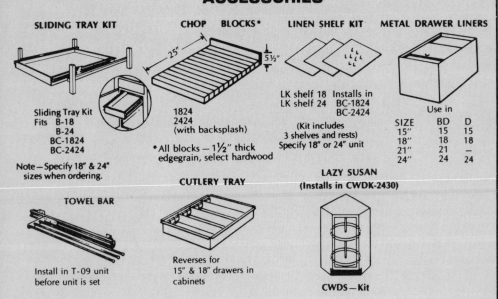

Sliding Tray Kit
Fits B-18
       B-24
       BC-1824
       BC-2424

Note — Specify 18" & 24"
sizes when ordering.

CHOP BLOCKS•

25"

5½"

1824
2424
(with backsplash)

•All blocks — 1½" thick
edgegrain, select hardwood

LINEN SHELF KIT

LK shelf 18 Installs in
LK shelf 24 BC-1824
             BC-2424

(Kit includes
3 shelves and rests)
Specify 18" or 24" unit

METAL DRAWER LINERS

Use in

SIZE	BD	D
15"	15	15
18"	18	18
21"	21	—
24"	24	24

CUTLERY TRAY

Reverses for
15" & 18" drawers in
cabinets

LAZY SUSAN
(Installs in CWDK-2430)

CWDS — Kit

TOWEL BAR

Install in T-09 unit
before unit is set

DESK UNIT
CAN BE USED WITH
VANITY CABINETS

Not available in all styles
DSK-18

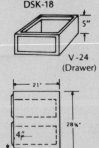

5"

V-24
(Drawer)

21"

28¾"

4"

5"

BROOM
AND
LINEN
CLOSETS

BC-1812 BC-1824
BC-2412 BC-2424

The walls of the Broom Units
are bored to receive LK-18
and LK-24 shelf kits.

Sliding 18" and 24" tray kits
can be used for canned goods
storage, and for a variety of
other household supplies.

SEE ACCESSORIES

BASE UNITS

First Two Digits Indicate Width in Inches—Base Cabinet is 34½" High and 24" Deep from Face of Frame.
Single Door Base Units Reversible. Except Diplomat Style.

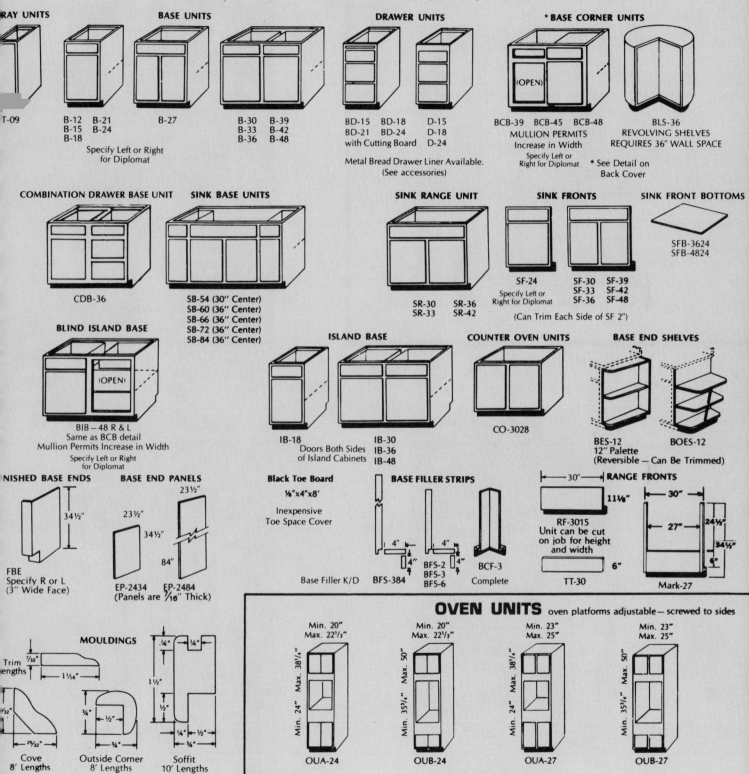

RAY UNITS

T-09

BASE UNITS

B-12 B-21
B-15 B-24
B-18

Specify Left or Right
for Diplomat

B-27

B-30 B-39
B-33 B-42
B-36 B-48

DRAWER UNITS

BD-15 BD-18   D-15
BD-21 BD-24   D-18
with Cutting Board   D-24

Metal Bread Drawer Liner Available.
(See accessories)

* BASE CORNER UNITS

BCB-39 BCB-45 BCB-48
MULLION PERMITS
Increase in Width
Specify Left or
Right for Diplomat

BLS-36
REVOLVING SHELVES
REQUIRES 36" WALL SPACE
* See Detail on
Back Cover

COMBINATION DRAWER BASE UNIT

CDB-36

SINK BASE UNITS

SB-54 (30" Center)
SB-60 (36" Center)
SB-66 (36" Center)
SB-72 (36" Center)
SB-84 (36" Center)

SINK RANGE UNIT

SR-30 SR-36
SR-33 SR-42

SINK FRONTS

SF-24
Specify Left or
Right for Diplomat

SF-30 SF-39
SF-33 SF-42
SF-36 SF-48

(Can Trim Each Side of SF 2")

SINK FRONT BOTTOMS

SFB-3624
SFB-4824

BLIND ISLAND BASE

BIB—48 R & L
Same as BCB detail
Mullion Permits Increase in Width
Specify Left or Right
for Diplomat

ISLAND BASE

IB-18
Doors Both Sides
of Island Cabinets

IB-30
IB-36
IB-48

COUNTER OVEN UNITS

CO-3028

BASE END SHELVES

BES-12
12" Palette
(Reversible — Can Be Trimmed)

BOES-12

NISHED BASE ENDS

34½"

FBE
Specify R or L
(3" Wide Face)

BASE END PANELS

23½"

23½"

34½"

84"

EP-2434   EP-2484
(Panels are 7/16" Thick)

Black Toe Board
⅛"x4"x8'

Inexpensive
Toe Space Cover

Base Filler K/D

BASE FILLER STRIPS

4"

4"

BFS-384

BFS-2
BFS-3
BFS-6

4"

4"

BCF-3
Complete

30"

11⅛"

RF-3015
Unit can be cut
on job for height
and width

6"

TT-30

RANGE FRONTS

30"

27"

24½"

34½"

6"

Mark-27

MOULDINGS

Trim
engths

7/32"

1 1/16"

Cove
8' Lengths

¾"

½"

32"

25/32"

¾"

Outside Corner
8' Lengths

¼" ¼"

1½"

½"

¼" ½"

¾"

Soffit
10' Lengths

OVEN UNITS oven platforms adjustable — screwed to sides

Min. 20"
Max. 22½"

Min. 24" Max. 38¼"

OUA-24

Min. 20"
Max. 22½"

Min. 35¾" Max. 50"

OUB-24

Min. 23"
Max. 25"

Min. 24" Max. 38¼"

OUA-27

Min. 23"
Max. 25"

Min. 35¾" Max. 50"

OUB-27

*Typical specifications sheet of a cabinet manufacturer
(in this case, Connor) shows cabinets available with
nomenclature and sizes available. Line drawing of
each item helps eliminate confusion.*

Cabinet style sets the kitchen style—Traditional, Colonial, Provincial, Contemporary, Mediterranean or special. And cabinet style is set by the door, but door style is named by the manufacturer and so variations are obvious and confusing. Sometimes a change in hardware makes it a different style. This door is Classic by White-Meyer Wood Products.

c

Colonial styling is exemplified here by, upper right, Provincial Type C by George C. Vaughan and Sons, and below, Colonial by Scheirich, left, and Williamsburg by Wilson, right.

a

b

a

b

Provincial is characterized by the curves at the corners of the design. Shown here are Royal Coach

by Grabill, left above, and Mission Oak by Raygold, right above.

a

b

Contemporary styles are clean, uncluttered, often have no knobs or pulls on doors and drawers, as with the drawers of the first example here. Left,

Luxuria by Long-Bell; right, Contemporary Walnut by Wilson.

Mediterranean styles derive from all of the many cultural influences that border that sea, and so generally are more decorative than other styles, as these examples indicate. Shown here are, left to right above, Espana by Yatron Bros., Granada by Keystone, and Venetian Oak by Springfield Cabinet.

PLASTIC LAMINATES are particularly favored by apartment developers, especially those who keep the property as an investment, because of their great durability, cleanability and visual attractiveness.

They nearly always are wood-grained and the variety is almost infinite. A builder can choose, for example, not just a walnut but from a dozen different walnuts in almost any of the major brands. Or he can choose any exotic woodgrain and it will be almost as true as the natural wood. It should, because it will be precisely printed from an actual color photograph.

The "high pressure" plastic laminates, more or less familiar to builders for the last 25 years, actually are made up of several sheets of heavy Kraft paper, the top sheet printed with the woodgrain or other pattern, and then covered with a transparent melamine plastic which gives the material its great hardness. Traditionally this has been 1/16" thick, and in this thickness it is by far the most common material for kitchen countertops.

Responding to a charge of "over-engineering" (which means "too expensive"), the laminate manufacturers have offered a 1/32" material specifically for vertical surfacing. This is less expensive and highly suitable for kitchen cabinets as well as for walls and table or desk tops that do not receive the wear of a kitchen countertop.

National high-pressure laminate brands are Formica, Pionite, Melamite, Wilson-Art, Parkwood, Micarta, Textolite, DuraBeauty (Consoweld), Enjay Nevamar, and Reliance Panelyte.

Wood lovers charge that these laminates can never really look like wood because of their uniformity of pattern. This is right, perhaps, when one looks at a full 5×12 sheet of plastic laminate, but in a finished cabinet door very few people can tell the difference.

For the plastic laminate manufacturers, competition is not really coming from wood cabinet manufacturers. It is coming from the manufacturers of "poor boy" laminates. This new trend is led by the rigid vinyls, which come in sheet or roll form. This material is much less expensive and provides a reasonably competent substitute for laminates. Its woodgrains are printed by the same type of sophisticated color presses used for the more expensive laminates. Other materials, somewhat similar, include polyesters, used by some cabinet manufacturers, and ABS (acrilonitrile butadiene styrene).

All of these plastic laminates must be adhered to a substrate, or corestock. The substrate might be plywood, styrofoam, or even a honeycomb paper, but more often it will be particleboard. Particleboard as a corestock is not the rough material familiar to builders as floor underlayment. It is a superbly engineered combination of wood particles and resins, almost infinitely variable (to spec) for surface smoothness, weight, screw-holding quality and any other characteristics the cabinet manufacturer might order.

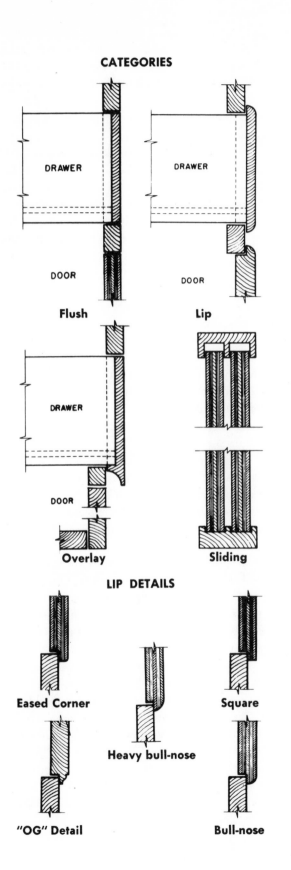

CATEGORIES

Flush

Lip

Overlay

Sliding

LIP DETAILS

Eased Corner

Heavy bull-nose

Square

"OG" Detail

Bull-nose

Detail drawings show the different ways cabinet doors might be constructed. Drawings are by the Southern California Assn. of Wood Cabinet Manufacturers.

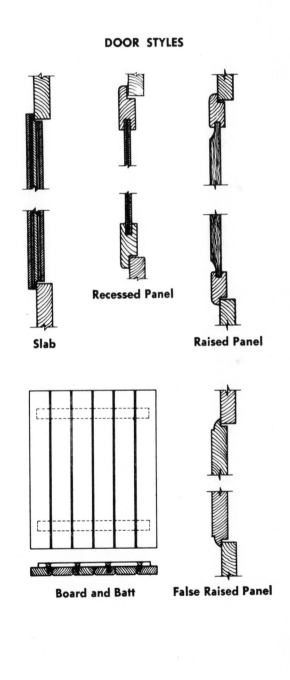

DOOR STYLES

Recessed Panel

Slab

Raised Panel

Board and Batt

False Raised Panel

Plastic Laminates for Durability

All of these plastic laminates are good materials for cabinets, as are all of the corestocks mentioned, but there are some traps the builder must avoid.

Any plastic laminated cabinet door needs a backing sheet. Otherwise, the construction is out of balance and warping can follow. The flocking or cheap paint sometimes applied to the back will not do the job.

Also, in any market area there always is a peripheral assortment of suppliers who prey on the builders who want the cheapest price. These are the ones who will offer unbalanced doors. Their vinyl surfacing often does not have proper adhesives. The result of this is that the vinyl, which has been molded to the door with heat, attempts to revert back to its original form. This is called "creep," a term a housewife might also use to describe the builder when she sees the vinyl shrinking from the corners of her cabinets and leaving the wood exposed.

This is a common problem, because vinyl itself is so inexpensive that it attracts the kind of cabinet maker who cuts corners. The solution is to stick with reputable manufacturers.

In recent years, the texture of high pressure plastic laminates has been expanded to true 3-dimensional surfaces. Nevamar pioneered this development with a "Cameo" pattern, and now several manufacturers offer 3-dimensional slate patterns in either white or black.

The 3-dimensional feature always has been available with the other laminates. A great advantage of vinyl, for example, is that it can be vacuum-formed to conform to any mold. In this process the sheet of vinyl is heated to a point of pliability, then sucked down by vacuum not only to cover the mold but to surround it. This yields a shell that is fully edged with corners turned, all one piece with no joining problem. This shell then needs only to be slipped over the corestock, adhered, and backed for balance.

The mold might be a specially carved or built-up wood master. It might be the cabinet door of a competitor that is being copied. Whatever it is, if the vacuum-forming is done properly the resultant vinyl shell will be a precise copy, mirroring all 3-dimensional aspects. Since the woodgrain or other pattern will already have been printed on the underside (so it will be protected against scratches by the vinyl on top) the door will need no further finishing except for the back.

This practice of printing the woodgrain or other pattern on the underside is called "reverse printing." Its only disadvantage is that the adhesive that bonds the vinyl shell to the corestock does not grip the vinyl itself, but the ink on the underside of the vinyl. Modern adhesives and bonding techniques make this a minor problem. But it does mean the job must be done right.

Some vinyls are surface-printed, so the bond is direct from corestock to vinyl. This helps the bond, but makes the surface more susceptible to scratching. Some suppliers now are solving both of these problems by surface-printing the vinyl and overlaying it with another sheet of clear vinyl. It solves the problems, but raises the cost.

Some cabinet manufacturers take different options. They buy prelaminated stock from their suppliers, then cut this to size for their cabinets. The prelamination can be done by various other methods, even to impregnating the corestock with a melamine plastic to make what might be called a fully plasticized board. These other processes are not of particular interest to the builder or architect, but they are worth checking when there are variations in bids. A little stepup in price sometimes can add many years of serviceability.

STEEL, as has been mentioned, is no longer a major factor in residential kitchen cabinets. As of this writing, there are only two quality custom steel manufacturers in the field, and there are several others who specialize in the apartment market. The apartment market, of course, is a price market.

Low-priced steel cabinets find it very hard to compete on a price basis with low-priced wood cabinets.

At the expensive end of the steel market, cabinet manufacturers offer a strong steel framework with options of steel, wood, plastic laminated or all-plastic doors and drawer fronts.

At the other end of the market there is a steel framework with steel doors, but sometimes the steel doors have vinyl plastic inlays to give them a semblance of wood. These inlays not only make the cabinets more acceptable to homeowners, they also permit modernization of the doors in later years through exchange of the inserts for new ones.

Steel is structurally rigid, strong, durable, and warp-free. Everything good that the steel people say about steel as a cabinet material is true.

a

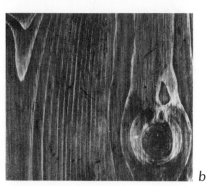

b

c

Anyone who thinks plastic looks like plastic can try their eyes out on these examples of plastic laminates. *a. Formica's Mozambique, an African woodgrain similar to Teak or Rosewood, grained with 4-color Quatramatic printing; b. Parkwood's Spectrographic Pine, a 5-color printing process; c. Cameo, in bright colors and the first 3-dimensional high pressure laminate, by Enjay Nevamar; d. Formica's Silver Slate, a decorative metallic plastic laminate; e. Castilian, a plastic laminate by Union Carbide; f, g, h, i. Four examples of polyurethane doors—solid plastic—by the Faultless division of Bliss & Laughlin.*

d

e

f

g

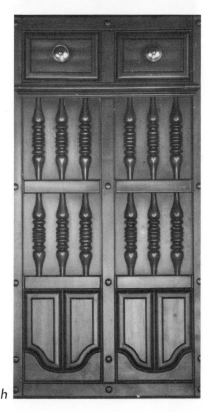

h

i

How Plastic Laminates are Made

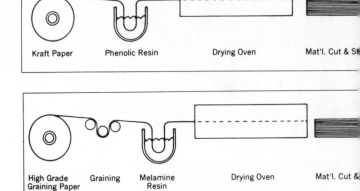

SHEET BUILD-UP

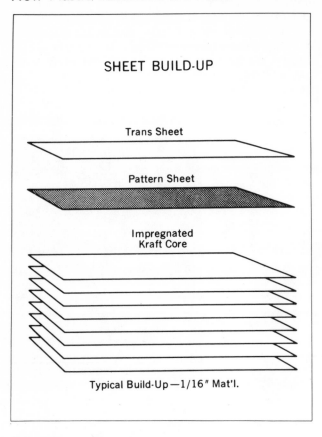

Trans Sheet

Pattern Sheet

Impregnated
Kraft Core

Typical Build-Up—1/16″ Mat'l.

| Kraft Paper | Phenolic Resin | Drying Oven | Mat'l. Cut & St |

| High Grade Graining Paper | Graining | Melamine Resin | Drying Oven | Mat'l. Cut & |

High pressure plastic laminates gain their durability from a transparent sheet of melamine resin on top. A pattern sheet is just underneath, which might be woodgrained or have some other pattern printed on it, and the bulk (thickness) then comes from several sheets of Kraft paper underneath.

Sketches show manufacturing process for making high pressure plastic laminates, used for cabinets, wall paneling and the most common material for countertops. The decorative paper which gives the pattern or woodgrain is grained (printed) for the appearance that shows through the transparent sheet on top. Other layers of paper are resin inpregnated, but there is no need for graining.

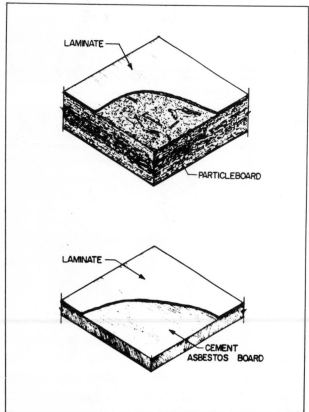

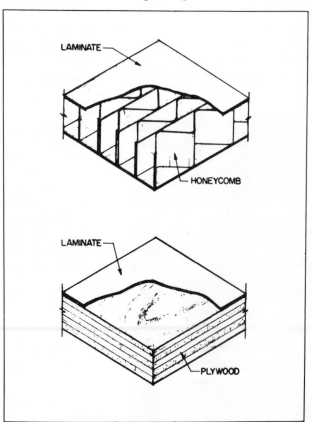

Most common substrate for high pressure plastic laminate is particleboard. But other materials are used, such as paper honeycomb, plywood or even foamed plastics.

There is nothing wrong with steel, except that most customers want wood.

THE NEW MOLDED PLASTICS have just commenced their invasion of the cabinet market. They include polyurethane, polystyrene, and nylon, and there undoubtedly will be others. These materials are formulated in the Research & Development labs of the petrochemical companies who develop combinations of resins and binders, and then start scrambling for applications. In the scramble, the cabinet market always shows up because it offers a potential annual market of some 100,000,000 cabinet doors, plus drawer fronts.

Generally, polyurethane is best for relatively short production runs, polystyrene for long runs, nylon for very long runs. This evaluation is related directly to tooling costs. Tooling for polyurethane is quite cheap. For the other materials it is very expensive. Quality of the end product, for all three, is excellent.

True value of these plastics is in the stylistic effects that can be achieved at a reasonable price.

If considered as a price product, they cost about 50% more than birch. Styles that would be impossible with any wood because of dimensional instability, such as in an interwoven cane door, can be achieved easily with any of these molded plastics with realism that defies detection. When the difference is only about $1 per door, the high style of the cane often is desirable.

These plastics are finished like wood, using the same equipment and materials. They are getting to be very common on bathroom vanities, because only four or five molds can supply an entire vanity line. Their success has been more limited in kitchen cabinets because the mold needs multiply. It is not unusual for a cabinet manufacturer to have as many as 400 or 500 variations in size and style, and this would mean that many different molds for a plastic line.

Marriages of wood and plastics are becoming common—plain wood doors are decorated with plastic moldings to create Provincial, Mediterranean, or other styles. This is a low-priced way to get a highly-styled cabinet.

CABINET CONSTRUCTION varies among manufacturers to some extent, but it is fairly well standardized for stock cabinets.

The main components are *front frames, doors, drawers and drawer fronts, end panels, backs, bottoms, shelves* and *hardware.*

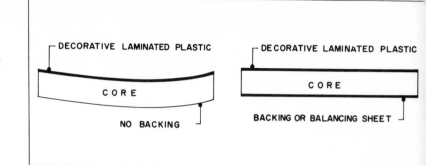

Plastic laminate, when used for cabinet doors or any other unsupported application, must have a backing sheet to balance the substrate for dimensional stability. Otherwise it will warp. Countertops do not need backing sheets because they are held stable by the base cabinets.

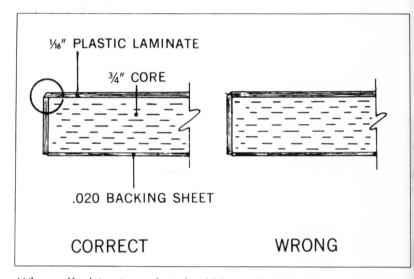

When self-edging is used, it should be applied first, before top surface, so top surface covers the edge-band.

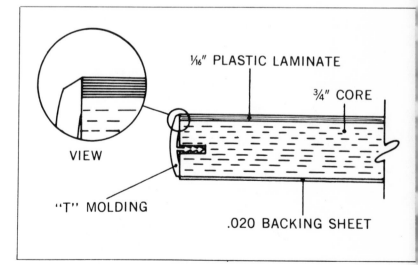

If T-edging is used it is applied after top surface. It must be precisely indexed with top of laminate.

Cabinet Construction Detail

Horizontal members of the *front frame* are called *rails*. Vertical members of the front frame are *stiles*. Interior horizontal framing members are *subrails,* and interior vertical framing members are *substiles*. A kick rail at the bottom of the base cabinet, recessed 3″ behind the front frame, is called the *toe kick.*

Front frames are usually made of 1/2″ to 3/4″ hardwood, and the rails and stiles usually are doweled or mortise-and-tenoned, with both glue and staples added for rigidity.

End panels are usually constructed of hardwood plywood, 3/16″ or 1/4″, glued to 3/4″ side frames. Sometimes a 1/2″ or thicker end panel is used without a side frame, and usually tongue-and-grooved into the front frame.

Doors typically are 3/4″ or 7/8″ but this is subject to wide variation. They might be hollow or have cores of particleboard, wood, high density fiber, plastic, paper honeycomb, or other material. As mentioned before, doors set the style, and drawer fronts match the doors, so this is the area where manufacturers are creative.

Backs usually are 1/8″ hardboard or 3-ply plywood, and the backs have *mounting rails* or *hanging strips* at top and bottom for screwing cabinets into the wall.

Tops and *bottoms* generally are made of 3-ply or 5-ply hardwood plywood, 1/4″ to 1/2″ thick, dadoed into the sides and interlocked into the hanging strips of wall cabinets.

Shelves are 1/2″ to 3/4″ thick and might be lumber, plywood or particleboard. Increasingly they are vinyl-laminated for easy cleaning. They usually are adjustable.

Conventional *drawers* have hardwood lumber sides and backs with plywood bottoms. Sides usually are connected to the front and back with a lock or rabbeted joint, although more expensive cabinets go to multiple dovetailing. Drawer bottoms are dadoed into the sides, front, and back.

Some cabinet companies now are using molded polystyrene drawers, all one piece except for the front, with rounded corners for easy cleaning.

A few companies offer cabinets unfinished, but most are finished, some in very sophisticated equipment systems. Fundamentally, all surfaces are well sanded before a penetrating stain is applied. After the stain is dry, one or more coats of sealer are applied and then all nail holes are filled with a suitable putty. A thorough sanding follows, and then one or more finish coats. In finishing, some factories use spray gun systems, some use curtain coaters which lay on the finish in controlled mil thickness, while others use immersion systems. Finishing lines usually are conveyorized with the lines carrying finished parts directly through heat tunnels for drying.

TYPES OF CABINETS can be grouped into three categories: *Base, wall* and *miscellaneous.* The standard base cabinet is 34-1/2″ high, so the addition of the countertop will bring it to an even 36″. Depths vary from 23″ to 24-1/2″, depending on the manufacturer. Base cabinets are offered in 3″ modules from 12″ to 24″ for a single door cabinet, and 27″ to 48″ for a double door cabinet. Special cabinets for the sink or a built-in cooktop range from 24″ to 48″ wide. Also relatively standard is a sink base combination with four doors and a drawer over the door on either end, with the center section blank, of course, for sink or cooktop, and these vary from 54″ to 96″ in width.

The standard *wall cabinet* is 30″ high and 12″ or 13″ deep, depending on the manufacturer. Wall filler cabinets, designed to fit above the refrigerator or window or for other special purposes, might be 11″, 12″, 15″, 18″ or 24″ high. There also are wall combination cabinets with 30″ doors on the ends and 18″ doors in between. All of these match the widths of the base cabinets.

Two other fairly common cabinets are revolving-shelf (or lazy susan) cabinets, base or wall, and blank corner cabinets. The revolving shelf cabinets require 21″, 24″ or 27″ along each wall for the wall cabinet, or 33″, 36″, or 42″ along each wall for a base cabinet.

Blank corner cabinets are for turning a corner where another run of cabinets will join at a right angle. They are blank (no door or drawer) in the area where the other cabinets must butt up against them. Base blank corner cabinets might be 24″, 36″, 39″, 42″, 48″, 60″, 66″, 72″ or 84″. There is one door and drawer in sizes over 24″, multiple doors and drawers at 60″ and over. Wall blank corner cabinets run in 6″ modules from 24″ to 48″ and from 60″ to 84″.

Miscellaneous cabinets include:

A *refrigerator cabinet,* 36″, 39″ or 42″ wide with the opening varying according to the size of the refrigerator;

An *oven cabinet* for built-in ovens, in widths of 24″, 27″, 30″, or 33″, with cutout sizes that must vary according to the countless specifications of oven manufacturers;

Hardware is available for a wide variety of interior fittings for kitchen cabinets. These are only a few that bring much greater convenience to the new kitchen.

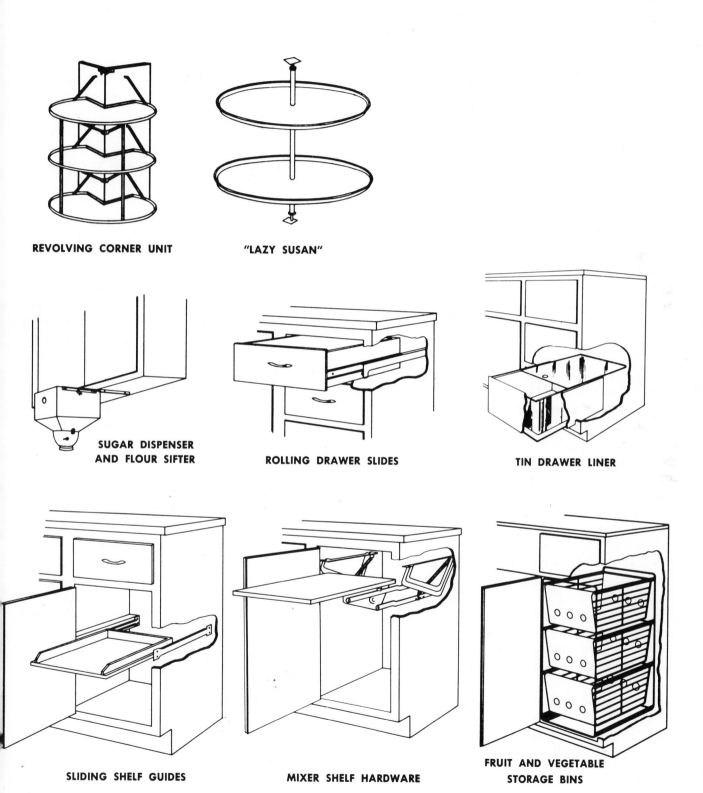

REVOLVING CORNER UNIT

"LAZY SUSAN"

SUGAR DISPENSER AND FLOUR SIFTER

ROLLING DRAWER SLIDES

TIN DRAWER LINER

SLIDING SHELF GUIDES

MIXER SHELF HARDWARE

FRUIT AND VEGETABLE STORAGE BINS

Types of Cabinets

Utility or broom cabinets in widths of 24", 30" and 36", and depths of 12", 13" and 18" as well as standard base depths.

All of these come in the standard 84" height, but oven cabinets also come in 66" height without doors at the top. The broom cabinets also are often outfitted with hardware for lazy susan shelves or special fold-out pantry cabinets.

Base cabinets may be obtained without drawers, with one drawer, or with all drawers and no door. Sink or range fronts also are available, without full cabinets. Both wall and base cabinets are available with doors on both sides for entry from either side, for use in peninsulas such as between the kitchen and the dining or living area.

INTERIOR FITTINGS are to cabinets what accessories are to cars—all the little options that add function, organization, utility, and convenience and that make the difference between ordinary and great. Unfortunately, builders pass them up because they add to cost and homeowners never know about them.

These fittings are much more widely used in Europe. Builders, architects and homeowners often return from abroad raving about these little kitchen conveniences and wondering why U.S. kitchens don't copy them, actually they always have been available here from both stock and custom cabinet manufacturers, and there are indeed many, many options.

There are towel racks, sugar bins, flour bins, vegetable bins, vertical tray storage cabinets, bread drawer liners, pan racks, slide-in table tops that disappear into the cabinetry, lazy susan assemblies for both base and wall units, electric mixer shelves counterbalanced with springs to pop up into place, slide-out maple cutting boards, to name just a few. There are even wheeled serving carts that roll into the cabinet run where they look like just another cabinet, silver drawer organizers, cup and plate storage organizers, in-cabinet or under-cabinet spice racks, and bar organizers, etc.

All of these are fitted into the cabinets or into the drawers by the cabinet manufacturer. In some cases he provides a special cabinet or special shelving for them, in other cases it is a matter of finding appropriate hardware and correctly installing it. In all cases these fixtures add special appeal to the kitchen and make it much more convenient for the housewife who will use it.

HARDWARE, generally, is a tremendously varied part of the kitchen cabinetry that performs many functions, both utilitarian and decorative.

Some of the possibilities of utility hardware are indicated in the previous section on options. There are many more. For example, drawers of low cost cabinets often operate with wood sliding on wood. They will work all right when new, but will be far less than satisfactory when humidity is high or as they get older.

In contrast, both simple and elaborate slides are available. These might have nylon sliding on nylon, low-priced but with excellent results, or finely engineered ball-bearing wheels in metal channels. It is a small part of the total kitchen, but a big factor in customer satisfaction as the years go by.

The pulls and knobs, and sometimes the hinges on cabinet doors, are decorative as well as functional. In fact, one hardware manufacturer calls its line "Cabinet Jewelry." And it is.

Knobs and pulls, for the drawers and doors, usually are metal and might be finished as brass, bronze, brushed chrome, antique pewter, or enamel. Some knobs and pulls are ceramic while others are plastic. The latter usually are finished to resemble ceramics. They might be solid colors or they might have delicate inlays. One hardware manufacturer has a "Mod" line with colored knobs with square or circular backplates with mondrian designs, geometrics, or swirls. These can work chromatic magic in brightening up a run of cabinets that otherwise might be dull.

Cabinets usually come with standard hardware selected by the manufacturer. However, the builder, architect or customer can ask to see options, and usually some options are available at no extra cost. In some cases the hardware is an integral part of the cabinet design, and the cabinet manufacturer will be reluctant to change it. In these cases, the manufacturer usually is right. He has spent a lot of money developing a design and he doesn't want to see it changed.

CABINET INSTALLATION is the true key to success in any kitchen.

If installed properly, the cheapest cabinets available give better service than poorly installed expensive cabinets. Proper installation is the one nonvarying essential, and as a precept it also is the most abused.

Cabinets must be installed level, plumb and true.

1

Cabinets must be attached to studs for full support. Studs are usually located 16″ on center. Locate studs with stud finder, tapping with hammer or nail driven through plaster at height that will be hidden by cabinets. Cabinets must always be attached to walls with screws. **Never use nails!**

2

Cabinets must be installed perfectly level — from a standpoint of function as well as appearance. Find the highest point of floor with the use of a level.

3

Using a level or straightedge, find the high spots on the wall on which cabinets are to be hung. Some high spots can be removed by sanding. Otherwise, it will be necessary to "shim" to provide a level and plumb installation.

4

Using the highest point on the floor, measure up the wall to a height of 84″. This height, 84″, is the top height of wall cabinets, oven and broom cabinets. 84″ cabinets can be cut down to 81″.

The most expensive cabinets made will be failures if not properly installed. And the cheapest cabinets can give good service if they are installed right. Cabinet manufacturers realize this, and all give

5

On the walls where cabinets are to be installed, remove baseboard and chair rail. This is required for a flush fit.

6

Start your installation in one corner. First assemble the base corner unit, then adding one unit on each side of the corner unit. This — as a unit — can be installed in position. Additional cabinets are then added to each side as required.

7

"C" clamps should be used in connecting cabinets together to obtain proper alignment. Drill 2 or 3 holes through ½″ end panels. Holes should be drilled through to adjoining cabinet. Secure T-nut and secure with 1½″ bolt. Draw up snugly. If you prefer you may drill through side of front frame as well as "lead hole" into abutting cabinet, insert screws and draw up snugly.

detailed instructions for installation. The accompanying sequence is from the installation manual of Kitchen Kompact, the giant of the industry. (Also overleaf)

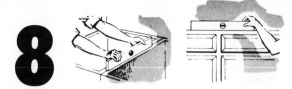

8

Each cabinet — as it is installed to the wall — should be checked front to back and also across the front edge with a level. Be certain that the front frame is plumb. If necessary, use shims to level the cabinets. Base cabinets should be attached with screws into wall studs. For additional support and to prevent back rail from "bowing," insert block between cabinet back and wall. After bases are installed cover toe kick area with material that is provided.

9

Attach counter top on base cabinets. After installation, cover counter tops with cartons to prevent damage while completing installation.

10

Wall cabinets should then be installed, beginning with a corner unit as described in step #6. Screw through hanging strips built into backs of cabinets at both top and bottom. Place them ¾" below top and ¾" above bottom shelf from inside of cabinet. Adjust only loosely at first so that final adjustments can be made.

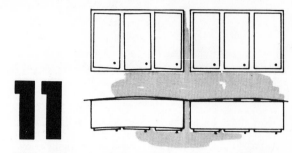

11

Wall cabinets should be checked with level on cabinet front, sides, and bottom to insure that cabinets are plumb and level. It might be necessary to shim at wall and between cabinets to correct for uneven walls or floors. After cabinets and doors are perfectly aligned, tighten all screws.

Problem Doors:

There are very few "perfect" conditions where floors and walls are exactly level and plumb. Therefore, it is necessary to correct this by proper "shimming" so that the cabinet is not racked or twisted and so that cabinet doors are properly aligned.

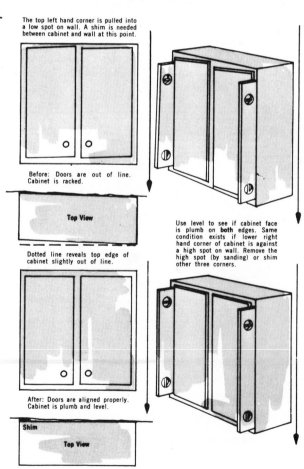

The top left hand corner is pulled into a low spot on wall. A shim is needed between cabinet and wall at this point.

Before: Doors are out of line. Cabinet is racked.

Top View

Dotted line reveals top edge of cabinet slightly out of line.

After: Doors are aligned properly. Cabinet is plumb and level.

Shim

Top View

Use level to see if cabinet face is plumb on **both** edges. Same condition exists if lower right hand corner of cabinet is against a high spot on wall. Remove the high spot (by sanding) or shim other three corners.

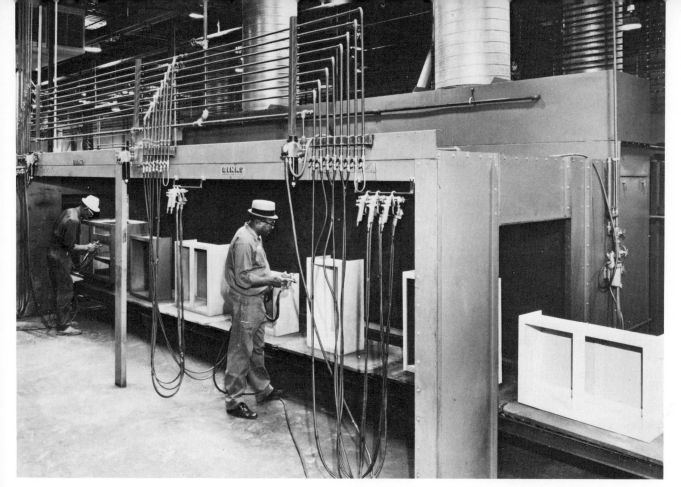

Both stock and custom cabinet manufacturers have achieved high degrees of automation and sophistication in their plants. This is one of several huge Binks installations at Adler-Kay Co., Wayne, Mich. At this station, conveyorized cabinets get stain, sealer and varnish topcoat.

This means the walls and floor must be checked for high spots and low spots, and corners must be checked for square. High spots sometimes can be sanded down. Low spots must be shimmed.

If, on installation, one corner of a cabinet is pulled into a low spot in the wall, the cabinet will be racked and the door will hang crooked. If it is a cabinet with multiple doors, all of the doors will be crooked.

Cabinets should be installed always from a corner, never toward a corner. C clamps should be used to hold them alligned perfectly as they are screwed to each other. They must be attached to the wall with screws, never with nails, and the screws must go into the studs.

Base cabinets should be installed first, and then the countertop should be installed. Cartons then should be placed on top of the installed base cabinets to protect them while the wall cabinets are installed, and wall cabinets also should start with a corner.

(Note: Some inexperienced installers know that a kitchen always is *designed* starting with the sink, which usually is in the center of a run of cabinets. This is one reason why they sometimes try to install them that way, but this is wrong.)

Again, make sure the installers are expert at their work. Poor installation can ruin the highest-quality cabinets, and a bad kitchen can make it a bad house.

4

Major and Minor Appliances

By definition and by function, the major home appliances are the range, the refrigerator, the freezer, the dishwasher, the washer, and the dryer.

The latter two are not kitchen appliances, although they sometimes are placed in the kitchen. More properly they belong in a utility room or a basement or, ideally, in the main bathroom if space permits.

Other very important appliances that belong in any modern kitchen are a ventilating hood over any cooking appliance, and a garbage disposer.

There are some other appliances that can add greatly to homeowner convenience and lift a kitchen far above the ordinary. These include the microwave oven, built-in warming drawer or other food warmer, built-in mixing center, toaster, can opener, and under-the-counter ice maker. There also is the barbecue grill, which might be integral with the range or cooktop or, better, separated from the main cooking area as an added appliance.

And there are, of course, the trash compactors. These are rapidly getting to be standard appliances, but they still are relatively new.

Some communities have challenged them on an ecological basis, fearing that their community incinerating facilities may not be able to handle their compacted "bricks" of trash, and have even gone so far as to legislate against their use.

On the other hand, the compacted trash makes excellent landfill. So where a builder runs into a local incinerator problem, there are alternatives he can investigate.

There's no question on consumer attitudes. They like compactors. And as a family grows to four or more, this appliance becomes much more significant.

There are other areas to be watched on a month-to-month basis. Some water purification systems are already on the market and others might come out at any time. Also check air purification and humidity control systems. As new appliances are introduced, they must be weighed for value, utility, and customer appeal.

Every category of appliances presents its own range of choices and decisions. In this chapter we will consider the available options, category by category.

Ranges

No other category of kitchen appliances enjoys the variety of cooking appliances, in sizes available, configurations, and features.

Free-standing—a range that stands by itself, independent of the wall or cabinets on either side. It can be a single oven model, with broiler, or a double-oven with eye-level oven or broiler, even with a microwave oven. These come now with squared sides so they fit neatly against adjacent countertops. The common size is 30" wide, but choices range from 19" to 40". They can be gas or electric, with or without backsplash, with controls in the front, on top along the side, or on a backsplash.

Built-in—again either single or double cavity for the oven which must be fitted into a wall cabinet built for this purpose, with or without a microwave component. Companion to the wall oven is the built-in cooktop, and these also are offered in a wide variety of configurations, gas or electric, and many sizes. The built-in system offers the greatest flexibility in kitchen design. However, it entails cutting precisely-sized holes in the oven cabinet and the countertop according

Free-standing ranges now have squared corners for a built-in look. They can fit flush against cabinetry or stand by themselves. This, by Modern Maid, has two continuous-clean ovens, "smoothie" glass-ceramic cooking surface, and built-in "Vent-Pak" that vents entire range.

Slide-in ranges might come with or without side panels, and squared corners give a built-in look. With side panels they can be free-standing. This is by Caloric. Some come without backsplash, fit snugly under countertop backsplash for more of a built-in look.

Drop-in ranges must rest on a cabinet at bottom, as these do, or hang from flanges that extend over countertop on either side. The model shown, by Corning, has a backsplash. The model by Jenn-Air must be cut into countertop, has no backsplash of its own. The Jenn-Air has down-draft ventilation through grill in center, needs no hood above. Optional kit available to convert to free-standing, with backsplash.

Built-in installations have most design flexibility. This Tappan glass-top was installed in island. Built-in wall oven is out of traffic area. Corning glass-top also is in island, with double wall-oven showing in background.

to specifications for the particular model being installed, so great care must be taken to check the specs against the model numbers. There are about 60 manufacturers of built-in cooking equipment, each with from two to a dozen models, and specs vary widely.

Slide-in—this is basically a free-standing range, but with the side panels left off and engineered to fit snugly against the countertop, or even overlap it, for a built-in look. Nevertheless, it rests on the floor. It is popular with builders and in less-expensive modernization, and sizes range from a minimal 19" to a more standard 30". It can have one or two ovens and can be either basic or deluxe. It might fit under or against a backsplash that is continuous with the countertops, and some are made to be fitted to the cutout backsplash of the countertop on either side.

Drop-in—a variation of the slide-in, the drop-in does not rest on the floor. Flanges rest on the countertop on either side, and it is supported from there. Special cabinets are available to fit under it for a more built-in look, although it might extend all the way down to the kick space.

Stack-on—a type that might not always be on the market at a given time, the stack-on consists of a built-in cooktop and superstructure with an eye-level oven. Although configuration limits the range to a single cavity oven, one manufacturer has had great success by combining a stack-on with a matching built-in dishwasher that fits directly beneath it, an innovative space-saver.

The specials—There are other models which do fit into the foregoing categories, but they are so different that they require special mention.

One is Pan-O-Matic, a "topless" cooktop. Actually it is a powered panel that rises behind the countertop, in the backsplash area, and into which portable cooking vessels are plugged. The vessels include wired pots and pans, engineered for use with this system, and there also are standard convenience outlets on the panel. The panel is luminous and rises to an eye-level shelf which holds all controls, and the upper surface of which serves as a warming shelf. The wired utensils are stored in cabinets beneath.

The other special product is the Jenn-Air, a cooktop with integral down-draft ventilation which obviates the need for a conventional ventilating hood. There are matching eye-level ovens to go with this, and a slide-in model is available with oven below.

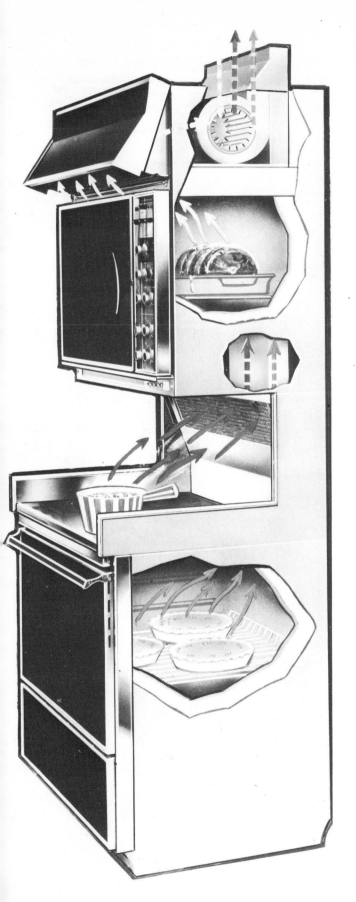

Cleanability of modern cooktops is demonstrated with this Modern Maid model. Top flips up exposing only a shallow pan to be wiped.

Catalytic continuous-cleaning is demonstrated by applying special frit on one side, not on other, then setting oven to baking temperature for a couple of hours.

Drawing shows how blower at top can vent entire Modern Maid range. Hood at top tilts out when in use.

Deluxe version of Thermador's built-in microwave oven includes the microwave at the top, self-cleaning oven in the middle, and warming drawer at the bottom

Yes, this is a cooking range, but behind the countertop! Tappan's Pan-O-Matic is a "topless" cooktop occupying practically no counter space. Matched utensils are stored in cabinet below, have built-in rigid male plug that plugs into black base at bottom. Controls at top match the six outlets at base, and top serves as warming shelf.

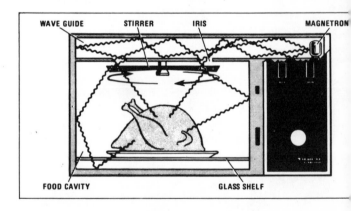

Sketch showing operation of microwave oven.

Another version of drop-in range has non-supporting cabinet below. Range is suspended from flanges that extend over countertop. This is new Tappan model.

Tappan stack-on range is suspended from countertop by flanges, has self-cleaning eye-level oven.

Self Cleaning Ovens: 2 Types

CONVENIENCE FEATURES of cooking appliances are as plentiful and varied as the configurations.

Cooktops, which might come with from two to six burners, often have thermostatic controls on at least one burner.

Cooktops can be purchased with griddle and grill inserts, which might be in the center or along the side.

They feature varying degrees of cleanability. Some detach completely to leave only a smooth-surfaced pan to be cleaned. Many feature top surfaces that can be raised, with a drop bar to hold them upright for cleaning underneath.

Automatic timers are common. It should be noted, though, that many less-expensive models have built-in timers that will signal a lapse of time, but do not control the cooktop or the oven.

Some ovens feature simultaneous over-and-under broiling. Some have their own built-in exhaust systems. Most have optional rotisseries and temperature-sensing probes.

The real aristocrats of ovens will have such complete automatic controls that a housewife can put her meal in the oven, set a time for it to start cooking hours later, set a time for it to stop cooking, and from then on it will hold a keep-warm temperature (about 170 degrees) until she and her family return home in the evening.

The cook-and-hold feature is available even without the more elaborate start-and-stop controls described.

One manufacturer even provides an instant hot water tap on the backplate of the range, so the housewife needn't go to the sink for cooking water.

SELF-CLEANING is probably the greatest oven feature to be developed in recent years. Through the years, cleaning the oven has been the housewife's most-abhorred kitchen chore. Now ovens clean themselves.

There are two types of self-cleaning ovens, pyrolytic and catalytic, and they should be explained.

In the pyrolytic system, the oven is heated to a temperature range between 900 and 1,000 degrees and the mess in the oven is incinerated. This leaves only a fine ash to be wiped off.

The catalytic system employs a coating on inside surfaces which, in effect, lets the oven clean itself in normal cooking ranges through action of the catalytic coating. This system usually is referred to as "continuous clean," or "stay clean."

The pyrolytic system adds about $100 to the selling price of a range. The catalytic system adds only about $25. But there are many other considerations besides cost.

The pyrolytic system, in its infancy, placed serious design demands on the range manufacturer, particularly for gas ranges.

Simply stated, it requires raising interior temperature to the 900–1000-degree range for a period of from 30 to 90 minutes. The heat-up and cool-down time, however, makes this a period of from two to four hours. The time depends on soil density.

The heat must be raised and the burning must take place under fully-controlled conditions, and this means the oven must be brought to full-heat slowly. This is first a matter of safety, and second, a matter of preventing thermal shock to the porcelain which would result in crazing and loosening.

Also, the burning process requires a controlled input of air for proper oxidation. This is done usually through control of the air space under the oven door, or air passages in the lower part of the door. If too much air is admitted the temperature will rise too fast. This is why all pyrolytic oven doors become locked when the temperature is over 625 degrees. Any opening of the door after that point would permit a dangerous inrush of oxygen.

Pyrolytic ovens also have to be made somewhat smaller than others. This is because the usual organic binders in common insulation break down at pyrolytic temperatures. Inorganic high-temperature binders are needed, and this makes the insulation package bulkier.

Conventional control systems will not work in pyrolytic ovens, either. Most common control systems use an organic, oil-type fluid in hydraulic tubes, and expansion or contraction of the fluid in response to heat activates a thermostat. This fluid will not stand up over 750 degrees. This has been solved with matched resistance systems, with inert gas or by utilizing the different expansion properties of dissimilar metals.

There also must be some method of eliminating the smoke that results from the burning of the oven soil.

And as a matter of safety, the manufacturer must insure that the oven cannot be turned on accidentally.

Gas range manufacturers had to solve different kinds of problems in addition. For example, gas combustion requires much air, and in a gas pyrolytic oven there would be about 720 cubic feet of air and gas going through the oven. That is about 12 cubic feet per minute, which at 1000 degrees, cannot be exhausted into a kitchen.

It took a lot of engineering ingenuity, but all of these problems have been solved satisfactorily and pyrolytic ovens are now part of our lives.

In the catalytic process, interior oven surfaces are coated with a porcelain frit that contains a catalyst. This gives the surfaces a porosity that enables them to retain oxygen. At higher (baking) temperatures this results in a slow oxidation that disposes of the oven soil.

Much oven cooking, however, is not baking, so obviously the system does not work as totally and automatically as indicated. Nevertheless, the oven can be set for "bake" for a few hours after cooking is completed, and then it will clean itself.

With either system, excessive food spillage should be wiped up before cleaning.

Both systems are available from most range manufacturers, but because of the lack of design problems and because of the price advantage, the catalytic system probably offers a greater variety of choices among models.

THE NEW SMOOTH GLASS COOKTOPS are an exciting development in cooking appliances. They are attractive, totally uncluttered, effective, and reduce surface cleaning to a minimum.

Actually, the idea of a smooth cooktop is not new. It was common in grandmother's day when much cooking still was done with wood and coal. The only breaks in the smooth metal top of the range were for the slots into which a lifter was placed to remove the burner covers.

Corning Glass brought the idea up to date with the development of a glass ceramic, Pyroceram, in 1957. There now are different versions by several other manufacturers.

The material has interesting features. For example, it transmits heat vertically to the cooking vessel, but heat does not migrate horizontally through the glass ceramic material. While the area of the burners can be hot enough for all cooking operations, at the same time the areas immediately surrounding the burners remain cool to the touch.

As a safety factor, heated areas over the burners turn a yellowish color to warn against careless touching. This coloration disappears as the glass cools. While

some critics have expressed the fear that a hot surface might be touched accidentally by a child, there really is no more danger of this than there is from a conventional electric range burner.

Other critics have worried about breakability. But Corning is so confident of the strength of its unit that it has gone to a single sheet of glass over the full 30-inch width of the range. Other manufacturers, in deference to the worriers, put a separate sheet of glass over each burner so that, in the unlikely event of breakage, only that one part would have to be replaced.

In actual use, the main difference between the Corning product and all others is that Corning provides a matched set of cooking vessels, also of Pyroceram, with bottoms that are perfectly flat and ground to mate with the smooth surface of the cooktop. The recommendation is that no other cooking vessels be used.

The primary reason for this is control. All materials have temperature limitations, and this includes metals as well as glass ceramics. And while these limitations are subject to change according to the progress in the R&D departments, at this writing the limits are around 600 to 700 Celsius (degrees Centigrade.)

A bright aluminum saucepan with a wavy bottom could easily raise the rangetop temperature above the limit, particularly at times when the housewife forgets and lets it boil dry.

Corning uses temperature control on each of the four elements, with a sensor cycling the heat on and off according to the setting. The precise control requires excellent thermal contact with the cooking vessel, hence the special vessels which insure this contact.

The top will cook with other vessels, including metal, but if the bottoms are not flat for good contact, there could be a control problem.

MICROWAVE COOKING is not the newest marvel in the kitchen but it certainly is one of the most exciting. These microwaves are electromagnetic waves of energy, similar to radio waves, light waves, or radar. Microwave cooking was, in fact, discovered in the 1940's by a radar technician who inadvertently left some uncooked popcorn exposed to radar waves. When the corn started popping a whole new system of cooking was conceived.

There are many microwave ovens on the market in countertop, built-in, and free-standing configurations.

Side-by-side refrigerator/freezers are gaining in popularity. This, by Hotpoint, has ice maker that feeds out through door.

Why is it exciting? Because it is instant cooking. Four strips of bacon that take 23 minutes to cook conventionally take four minutes in a countertop microwave. Roast beef medium takes about eight minutes per pound and frozen shrimp is cooked in six minutes.

It is cooking without pots and pans. Cooking can be done on a paper plate or a glass or plastic dish, and these materials do not heat up except from the heat of the food itself.

The waves pass through paper, glass or plastic with no effect. Since they are reflected by metal, metal cannot be placed in a microwave oven. Foods absorb the microwaves, and the waves cause food molecules to rotate 180 degrees with such rapidity that they cause heat from the friction, and this heat causes cooking.

In conventional cooking food is surrounded by heat and heat must penetrate and cook the food through. Microwaves, on the other hand, penetrate into the food and cause heat to happen, so the food cooks all the way through more or less simultaneously, although the rate slows as the microwaves go deeper.

The rapidity of the rotation is according to the frequency. Only two frequency ranges are allocated to microwaves by the Federal Communications Commission and they cannot stray from these ranges because if they do they will interfere with radio communications. One is 890 to 940 megacycles, available only in the Americas but not used much, and the other is 2400 to 2500 megacycles, available world-wide. In a 2400-megacycle oven, the food molecules will rotate 2400 million times a second. Since a little power is used up on each successive layer of molecules, molecules deep inside the food rotate less than 180 degrees, so there is less heat, permitting a rare steak. Cooking does occur deep inside, but at a slower rate.

In an oven the microwaves are generated by a magnetron tube. They are channeled through a wave guide through a stirrer. The stirrer is a metal fan that adds the element of dispersion so the waves will more completely cover the oven cavity. These waves travel only in straight lines, therefore proper functioning depends on the stirrer and on the action of these waves bouncing off the metal sides of the oven.

Are microwave ovens dangerous?

They are dangerous in the same way that the hot sun in Texas is dangerous, or any other hot oven. Unfortunately there have been a lot of wild charges by doctors, bureaucrats, and elected officials that have

been almost totally inadvised.

One medical administrator, for example, created a scare by warning that the microwaves could affect a heart Pacemaker. He neglected to mention (or perhaps he didn't know) that an ordinary pop-up toaster in the kitchen will also do this.

You and I walk through microwaves day and night, wherever there is radio, television, radar, and the sun itself. As with the sun, if microwave emission is too strong you feel the heat. Certainly, there is danger if you stay there and cook yourself. Unknowing children are fully protected by interlocks that must be built into the ovens.

The only factor to restrict use of this great appliance is cost. Most people who have tried it agree that it is more than worth it.

REFRIGERATORS: "OLD FAITHFUL" OF THE KITCHEN

There is probably no other manufactured product that gives as much for the consumer dollar as the refrigerator. It stays on duty every minute of every day and night, often for as long as 15 or 20 years, controlling its own temperature, recycling itself on and off, with very infrequent need for service.

It is such a great appliance that it is unfortunate that it is such a monstrosity. Refrigerators are very handsome per se, but they are too big and inflexible to really fit in with kitchen design. In many cases it's almost like parking your car in your kitchen. The car might be beautiful, but it just doesn't belong.

The best treatment for a refrigerator is to design it into a cabinet run and then use available trim kits to install cabinet paneling to match the cabinets, or plastic laminate to match the countertops, or even wallpaper or fabric. This raises the cost, but it helps integrate the design.

Mechanically, the refrigerator consists of a compressor, or pump, which pumps the refrigerant; an evaporator, or plate, which gets cold and cools the cabinet, and a condenser that transfers heat from the cabinet.

Basic features to be found on any model include shelving, crispers, ice cube trays, a freezing compartment, and light. Special features on better models would include rollers, a 7-day meat keeper, a butter conditioner, an ice maker, egg holders, and convertible doors.

There are some deluxe models that also offer ice cubes and ice water through the door. This, of course, and any ice-maker model, also requires a cold water line. Some models are available that provide for later installation of an ice maker, a good feature for the builder who wants to cut his costs without totally precluding the convenience.

There are four types: The single door, the 2-door top-mount, the 2-door bottom-mount, and the side-by-side.

The *single door* model is the lowest priced, and a spring-type door inside gives access to a freezer compartment that will be 10 to 20 degrees above the desired 0 degrees. So it is not a true freezer.

All other models have two doors with a solid barrier between freezer and refrigerator. So the freezer will hold at 0 degrees while the fresh food compartment will maintain a temperature of between 37 to 40 degrees.

Top-mount models have the freezer above the regular food compartment, and bottom-mounts have the freezer below. *Side-by-sides* have gained fast popularity by eliminating all the bending and stooping, and their gains have been directly in proportion to losses for the bottom-mounts.

Refrigerators may be free-standing or built-in. The built-ins are best from a design viewpoint, and they usually have wood fronts to match the cabinets. They require a refrigerator cabinet, adding to the cost.

There also are many "compact" refrigerators, which might be free-standing or built-in. These usually are found in mobile homes, vacation homes, recreational vehicles, offices, motels, and apartments, but they also are fine for the home as a luxury touch—for the den, rec room, master bedroom, or even to store cold drinks for the kids by the outside door to keep them out of the kitchen traffic patterns.

Conventional refrigerators must be defrosted, usually about once a month. Automatic models have separate freezer and fresh food compartments, and the latter will defrost itself but the freezer must be defrosted about once a year. No-frost models have dual controls for the two compartments and neither compartment should ever need defrosting. This runs about a penny a day more in operating cost.

A separate freezer, which might be upright or chest type, is good for large families or families that like to cut the frequency of their shopping trips. It is good for the budget-conscious person because it permits economies such as buying a half a hog and a half a steer which a butcher would carve up into the appropriate cuts and package and label for storage in the home freezer.

But there must be a place to put a freezer. This should not be in the kitchen. The basement, utility room, or garage would be better, but fewer houses are being built with basements, and, on the average, houses are getting smaller. Space, then, could be a problem.

Where there is a separate freezer, there is no need to have more than a conventional refrigerator except as a luxury.

DISHWASHERS: CHEAP AT TWICE THE PRICE

Washing dishes is the easiest task in the home. It is just a simple matter of applying a little hot water and soap to a succession of plates and glasses, requiring no skill, strength, or concentration, and thus there is little need for an expensive appliance to do the job. Ask any husband.

Home Economist Retta Presby, however, struggled through massive calculations to determine that any average American who lives to the age of 70 will have consumed 150 head of cattle, 2400 chickens, 225 lambs, 26 sheep, 310 pigs, 26 acres of grain, and 59 acres of fruits and vegetables.

Multiply that by the number of people in the family and break it down to the number of plates, dishes, glasses, pots, pans, etc., it takes for individual servings, and communicate it to The Great American Husband. Now he is beginning to wonder about giving the best years of his wife to this senseless job.

Dishwashers are no longer luxuries, they are essentials. It is difficult to rent an apartment that does not have a dishwasher. Builders are including them in their new-home appliance packages. A housewife who gets used to one in her first apartment will never go back to the old method, nor should she.

Dishwashers can be top-loading or front-loading. Top-loaders are "portable," which means free-standing. Front-loaders are built-in or convertible. A convertible comes on wheels, but can be installed under the counter later when the consumer has more money or moves to what she considers her permanent home.

Standard width for a built-in is 24 inches. All other dimensions are standardized to fit under the standard kitchen countertop with the base cabinets. Cabinet

Water-powered dishwasher needs no electric connection, recesses into countertop. In kitchens where there isn't room for regular dishwasher installation, this can be a solution. It is made by Coronet Imperial of St. Louis.

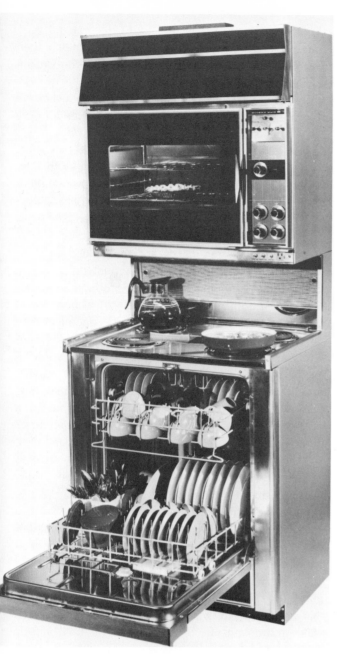

"Cook-n-Clean Center" by Modern Maid solves the space problem in another way. Center includes eye-level oven, a super-thin cooktop and dishwasher below.

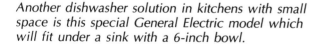

Another dishwasher solution in kitchens with small space is this special General Electric model which will fit under a sink with a 6-inch bowl.

While there are big differences in disposers, their method of operation is substantially the same. Here a cutaway shows interior of Waste King grinding mechanism.

manufacturers offer dishwasher fronts to match their cabinets, so they can be made to blend in with kitchen design.

Some manufacturers of related kitchen products have cooperated to make dishwashers feasible even for very small kitchens.

One sink manufacturer, for example, makes a special double-bowl sink with one bowl deep, the other shallow enough to fit over an undercounter dishwasher. Another manufacturer offers a matching family of cooktop, eye-level oven, vent hood and dishwasher below, so all four fit in 30 inches of space.

One manufacturer makes a different kind of dishwasher that can be sunk into a countertop, over a dead corner, for example. This product is water-powered and therefore needs no electrical hookup.

In operation, a dishwasher is more economical than most people think. In a normal full cycle of two washes and three rinses, the housewife hears the spraying and roiling of about 800 gallons of water. But actually only about 15 gallons of water are consumed, less than she would use when washing by hand. In a dishwasher the water is used, filtered and recirculated, over and over.

In her apartment, the housewife always has had the builder model, the economy model. She turned the knob and it did the job.

The lower-priced single-control dishwasher will do an excellent job. All the fancy pushbutton models will do a lot more, however. They do add to performance.

For example, one pushbutton might be for warming plates for dinner. Another might be for fragile dishes that aren't very dirty, giving gentler action with less water and detergent.

Still another would boost water temperature in the final rinse for greater sanitation. Other buttons would be for pots and pans, or to give dishes a quick rinse after which it automatically waits for her to get the other dishes loaded. And then, of course, there's the regular cycle, the equivalent of the single control on the economy model.

For effective dishwasher operation, water temperature must be between 140 and 160 degrees. The increasing impurities in and hardness of water have not been much of a problem because dishwasher detergents are formulated to cope with a wide range of water conditions. But in some areas of excessive water hardness, a water softener might be needed.

GARBAGE DISPOSAL—A REAL GRIND

Most of us in today's world have mental pictures of women, their noses wrinkled in distaste, emptying garbage from the sink into paper bags to be carried out to a garbage can.

Those mental pictures are justification enough for the modern garbage disposer, an appliance that takes a small bite of electricity, a long drink of water, and then chews up all the garbage you feed it into tiny particles that wash down the drain with the waste water.

There are two types of disposers.

The batch-fed type has a locking cover that also serves as a switch. To operate this type you fill it with waste (just put it in, don't pack it in), lock the cover in place, and the disposer operates.

The continuous-feed type has a separate switch, usually on the wall over the sink. To operate this type the water is turned on, the switch turned on, and food waste is simply fed in until it all is gone.

Both must be operated with running cold water. Both will do the job with the same efficiency. Neither has any advantage over the other. It is a matter of personal preference.

There is, however, another way to categorize disposers, and this way the difference is vast.

There are cheap ones and there are expensive ones.

Buying a cheap disposer is like buying a cheap parachute. It is made of different materials that won't wear nearly as long, performance will not be as good, noise will be worse, and you will be lucky to get more than two or three years of use out of it.

A good one will cost three times more—$70 and up (builder price) as compared with $25 and down. But the good one will be dependable for 10 years, it will install more easily, it will operate more quietly and it will do more.

Anyone who has had an unhappy experience with a disposer in the past should be aware of those big differences. Disposers that builders put into housing developments almost always are bought on a price basis, and that means the consumer gets a cheap disposer. You should be aware also that these "economy" disposers are made by the same manufacturers who make the very finest, so don't condemn a good brand name just because you got stuck with one of their cheapies 10 years ago.

Good disposers will dispose of bones, and fruit pits, and corn cobs, and some will even take normal household quantities of paper napkins and towels. They have trouble with food wastes that are particularly fibrous, such as corn husks or avocado leaves. They will handle these, but it will take longer because of the stringiness, so often it is easier to dispose of such waste with other kitchen trash. Celery and coffee grounds are no problem.

Metal should never be dropped in a disposer, not even small bits like the staples on tea bags.

There was a time when disposer repairmen would drop glass pop bottles into an operating disposer to clean it. This was a good way to clean the disposer, but the glass particles would collect in the plumbing lines, catch food particles and eventually clog the lines. Therefore, glass is not recommended. Bones and fruit pits will do the same cleaning job.

Incidentally, there are about 100 cities in the U.S. that require, by ordinance, disposers in all new residential construction. These cities benefit from improved sanitation and from considerable economies in garbage collection.

And, for those who are not in cities, any septic tank system which meets HUD Minimum Property Standards can handle the slight added load from a disposer.

VENTILATING HOODS—FOR INDOORS ECOLOGY

A ventilating hood provides the gift of fresh air in the kitchen. It stops airborne cooking odors at their source, traps grease and soil that otherwise would end up on walls, ceilings and draperies, and should be considered one of the essentials over every cooking appliance. That means over both the cooktop and wall ovens when these are built-in, over both the cooking surface and the oven in an eye-level range, and over either a microwave oven or barbecue grill when these are present in the kitchen.

There are many things you should know about vent-hoods that affect their performance. There are different types, and performance features, and they must be powered in relation to their distance above the cooking appliance. All vent hoods manufactured by members of the Home Ventilating Institute have performance ratings, and they also have sone ratings that measure their noise levels.

As for types, there are ductless and ducted vent hoods.

Ventilating hoods have become decorative as well as functional. These, the Chuck Wagon series by Broan, have various optional straps and plaques that apply with adhesive and can be changed. These take big dual squirrel cage blower rated for cfm and sones—air movement and sound level. They have solid state controls for light and power.

Ducted types are better. They filter the air as it enters the hood, and then they have ductwork to exhaust it to the outside. Because of the ductwork, their fan units can be remote, out of the kitchen, to minimize noise, and they can have more powerful fan units for greater air movement.

But there are some places where ducted hoods are not practical; in apartments, for example. Here a non-ducted hood is much better than none. These have excellent filter systems that gather the air, clean it and then exhaust it back into the kitchen, commonly from vents in the top that direct it upward. Thus the heat and moisture of cooking is exhausted back into the kitchen rather than being vented to the outside, but grease and odor have been removed.

Some expensive wall ovens are made with attached vent hoods. These are designed to match the ovens. They pull out to protrude a few inches when in operation during cooking, then can be pushed in to fit flush with the oven at other times.

Hoods come in many shapes, colors, and sizes. Some are squared, some angled, some curved. They come in colors to match major appliance colors—mainly the earth colors, such as avocado and harvest—or in white, chrome, or other options.

Some are manufactured with three finished sides

Infra-red heating lamps are incorporated in this Trade Wind hood, so it serves as a food warmer while it vents.

And ventilating fans aren't what they used to be, as these pictures prove. The ceiling model is by Emerson. The wall model is by NuTone. They suck in air around the perimeter. All of these fans and hoods have HVI power and sone ratings.

to project over kitchen peninsulas, or with four finished sides for kitchen islands. One brand has modular sections so it can be made larger or smaller on-site. While most are made of steel, at least one brand is constructed of fiber glass.

In addition, most cabinet manufacturers offer custom hoods of wood to match the cabinets, and most kitchen dealers have local sheet-metal sources for making custom hoods.

The perfect vent hood in one kitchen might be unsatisfactory in another kitchen because the layout of the kitchen can affect the performance of the product. For example, a certain cfm rating in a hood over a built-in cooktop that is installed against a wall might be inadequate over a cooktop installed in a peninsula or island, because of cross-drafts in the kitchen. Added duct run from a peninsula also would require greater power.

In order of importance, there are these four considerations in selecting a vent hood:

1) *Be sure of enough power.* A hood must take out smoke, odors and grease as fast as they are produced, and it must have power to overcome the resisting pressure of the length of duct run with its elbows and end caps. Look first for a Home Ventilating Institute rating. Otherwise, be wary of suspiciously low prices for any power rating.
2) Then consider *noise level.* Again, check HVI sone ratings.
3) Select the right product then on the basis of *style, service,* and *workmanship.*
4) Then consider *price.* There will still be price variations, big ones, even after the first three considerations, but to put price ahead of those other considerations would be a disservice to the housewife who must live with the product.

As for performance, the FHA and the HVI both require a minimum of 40 cfm per foot of hood length. So a 140-cfm fan would be minimum for a 42-inch hood. Most of these are fan type and have retail prices well under $50, but this type is for minimum performance.

For fair performance, a 200-cfm fan could qualify, but it would not get the job done when the cook is using all burners or cooking something exceptionally smoky. Fan type vent-hoods in this range still usually retail for about $50 or less but might be noisy. A centrifugal blower would be more quiet for only about $5 or $10 more.

For good performance, think in terms of 300 cfm and up. These will have several speeds, or with solid state control an infinite range of speeds. You will seldom see a fan-type here. Most will have twin centrifugal blowers (often called "squirrel cage") which will be quiet and might sell at retail for as low as $75 or up to twice that.

In tightly constructed houses, a window might have to be opened slightly to permit a vent hood to do its job. A hood should be 24 inches to 30 inches over the range.

LITTLE EXTRAS FOR BIG DIFFERENCES

The appliances described so far are the routine equipment that might be found in any new kitchen. There might be extra margins of quality—the extra features interpretable into extra convenience or extra function—but still, they are basics.

There are many other appliances that can be built in and that can add up to a super kitchen.

When a housewife moves into her new home, for example, she must go out and buy a toaster, and an electric mixer, blender, and perhaps a knife sharpener. She will go to a housewares department and look for some sort of box that her husband can hang on a wall or attach under a wall cabinet to dispense her foil and plastic wrap and paper towels.

Whatever she buys, she has to find space for the item, both in use and when she wants to put it away. She has a shining new kitchen, but every time she buys something for it she finds she has bought a problem.

It doesn't have to be that way. All of these items can be designed into the kitchen in the first place. No storage problem. No countertop space problem. Here are a few examples.

Built-in toasters are available. They can be wired and recessed into the wall, tilting out for use and then pushing back to their flush position.

Two different manufacturers offer two different built-in mixing systems, combining all mixing, blending, juicing, and other such functions. In both of these, the motor is mounted under the counter, which helps minimize noise, and all attachments go in a base cabinet directly under the appliance, at the point of

Another built-in appliance that helps organize kitchen and eliminate problems is the built-in mixing center. The two shown here are by Ronson (above) and NuTone (below). Both take full range of attachments, and storage of all these and bowls is right at point of use.

use. In one of these systems only a small stainless steel plate shows above the counter, and when lifted it exposes the drive shaft onto which all attachments fit. The other system has a small control panel that protrudes above the counter.

There also are built-in can-openers, electric-powered, that recess into the wall, and built-in knife-sharpeners.

There are either electric or hydronic heating units engineered to recess into the kick-space under a base cabinet.

There are different types of food-warming appliances. One is a slide-out drawer, similar to those used in restaurants but designed for the modern residential kitchen. Wood trim kits are available for these so they accept paneling to match the cabinets. Another food warmer is a wired rectangular glass-ceramic plate that recesses into the countertop. This has the added advantage of providing a place to put hot pans from the cooktop. Other food warmers use infra-red radiation and mount under the wall cabinets, and one ventilating hood incorporates this warming feature.

There are water purification systems that become more relevant in these days of bottled drinking water. One can be mounted on the wall or recessed into the wall near the sink, or mounted on a wall cabinet near the sink. These need a cold water line, of course. There are several others in the developmental stage.

There are musical-intercom systems that can put music throughout the house from a master panel in the kitchen, which also monitor other rooms (such as the baby's bedroom) and incorporate burglar and fire alarms.

Paper caddies can be recessed into the wall. Automatic ice-makers are available and can be free-standing or can be built-in under the counter. There are also instant hot water dispensers.

Trash compactors can be free-standing or they can replace a 15-inch base cabinet under the counter. They require a 3-wire line, and should take a separate 15-amp fuse. But there are a dozen different brands, so specifications will vary and might be changed.

5

Sinks and the Counter-Revolution

Kitchen countertops are playing an increasingly important role in the modern kitchen. Years ago when the sink was recessed in the only countertop in the kitchen, they were called sinktops. Gradually, new materials and new ideas changed this ordinary part of the kitchen. In the middle 1950s, high-pressure plastic laminates were popular as a surfacing for these countertops, but it was difficult to mate sink with sinktop in a way that would prevent moisture seepage and consequent rotting. To answer that challenge a clamp-down rim, the "Hudee" rim, was developed.

At around the same time the technique known as postforming became popular. This is the technique that gives a clean seamless sweep of plastic surface from the front of the countertop to the back, curving up at the back to cover a 4-inch backsplash or more.

And then sink manufacturers started wondering why sinks had to be so ordinary. They started improving their surfaces and materials. They added lights and soap dispensers. They became innovative in configurations.

All of these factors led to the counter-revolution. Sinks and countertops became things of beauty and previously-undreamed-of function. They became parts of the new kitchen concept.

In more recent years, new adhesives and sealants have led to a return of the "self-rimming" sink that does not require a Hudee-type rim. Now either type can be trusted for long years of use.

The most popular sink is of stainless steel. The most inexpensive is made of porcelain-on-steel, often called pressed steel. A more expensive type is porcelained cast iron. The newest material is molded plastic, or artificial marble, commonly used for bathrooms but not kitchens.

Both porcelain-on-steel and cast iron sinks now come in glamour colors and with innovative configurations. But the former can chip easily. The latter is very durable but more expensive.

Stainless steel costs more than either, but its prices vary according to gauge of the steel and nickel and chrome content. Some are shiny, some are not.

All of these differences are more or less academic in new homes where the sink is provided by the builder. The kitchen sink, after all, is a small part of a kitchen and most housewives will accept anything the builder provides.

But the differences are significant in custom homes and in kitchen remodeling, where the housewife is shown the options for added beauty and utility. In stainless steel, she will have a definite preference for either the satin or brilliant finish, and she should be given the opportunity to choose. She might want the bright color of a porcelain finish, or the futuristic design of a particular brand. She might want a deluxe model with three compartments, a fluorescent light attached, soap and lotion dispensers, a separate pull-out spray, a purification device for the drinking water, an instant hot water device for instant soups and beverages, and built-in compartments for ice or for placement of a built-in small appliance.

The new designer styling has pretty much done away with standard measurements in kitchen sinks. Most still are 21 or 22 inches from front to back because the depth of the countertop is standardized, and the bowl itself usually is 16 inches from front to back. But these dimensions vary according to brand and style.

While the usual depth of the bowl is 7-1/2 inches, this too can vary widely. For example, a triple-bowl

How classy a kitchen sink can be is proven by this, the self-rimming stainless steel ''Cuisine Classique'' by Elkay. With the glamorous name go glamorous functions, even to a color-coded temperature control. Back ledge features, from left, include: Separate goose-neck faucet for disposer compartment; pull-out spray; single main faucet; water supply knob; color-coded temperature-control knob (from blue to red, for cold to hot), and then another goose-neck faucet for vegetable-cleaning compartment.

Another example is pie-cut for corner installation and with a fluorescent fixture mounted behind the faucet. This also is by Elkay.

Decorator colors characterize sinks of porcelain-on-steel or cast iron. This cast iron model by Kohler is the Trieste, with two big working bowls and one in the center to take the disposer.

Kohler's Urbanite is unique in that it combines a disposer compartment in a single bowl sink to meet space limitations. It's only 25×22".

sink might have a small vegetable sink between two larger bowls, and this might be only 3-1/2 inches deep. It also might be round, and it might be the ideal place for the disposer. A 3-1/2-inch depth for one bowl of a double-bowl sink allows the housewife to sit while cleaning or preparing vegetables and salads.

While there are many round and oval sinks, they normally are used in bathrooms or hospitality areas rather than in the kitchen.

For corner installation, sink manufacturers offer double-bowl sinks in a pie-cut configuration. For kitchens where space is at a premium, there also are special depths (5-1/2 inches) to permit one bowl to fit over a built-in dishwasher.

Sinks may come with faucets and other attachments, or simply with punched holes so faucets can be purchased separately.

In the latter case, options are limited by the number of holes punched. But it will always be possible to accommodate either the traditional pair of faucets—hot and cold—or the more modern single-handle faucet.

A single-bowl sink is adequate if the kitchen is equipped with a dishwasher. Even with a dishwasher, the double-bowl is desirable.

Stainless steel sinks come in 18-gauge and 20-gauge. The 18-gauge is heavier and much more satisfactory. Two other figures that require interpretation refer to the mix of the alloys. For example, 18-8 would mean 18 percent chrome content and 8 percent nickel content. Chrome relates to the sink's ability to stand up and keep its finish over the years. Nickel gives the steel the ability to withstand corrosion.

There are three basic surfaces for kitchen countertops.

The standard utility surface is decorative high-pressure plastic laminate, such as the well-known Formica. It should be 1/16-inch thick for horizontal applications in the kitchen. The thinner 1/32-inch vertical grade material is not recommended, although it often is used as a cost-cutting measure.

The other two basic materials are for use in conjunction with high-pressure laminates. One is laminated hardwood, the familiar "butcher block," for cutting operations. The other is tempered glass ceramic (or ceramic tile, stainless steel, or marble) used as a counter insert for hot pans direct from the range, or for cutting.

This is not to say that all, nor even that most, kitchens actually have these three types of surfaces. Most have only the plastic laminate surfacing.

And as a consequence, the woman who must take a hot pan from the oven and put it down quickly must put it in the sink, or on the range top if there is a space there. And she cuts bread or meats or vegetables on the plastic laminate and, in the course of only a couple of years, puts thousands of tiny cuts in it. If, in an emergency, she puts a hot pan down on the unprotected countertop, permanent damage can result. Then the top must be replaced, or a kitchen specialist or top fabricator can cut out the damaged part and replace it with the counter insert that should have been there in the first place.

In the far west, ceramic tile is widely used for the entire kitchen countertop. This is an excellent and beautiful material. But it also is much noisier, its hard surface dulls knives, and dishes break more easily on it. The same is true of marble and of the newer artificial marbles so widely used as bathroom vanity tops. Stainless steel is a good material, but it can be dented, it dulls knives, and the scratches and stains on this surface are difficult to remove.

Many kitchen designers will plan whole sections of laminated wood into the countertop, along with a glass ceramic section or insert. Many like to include custom stainless steel sinks in the design with stainless steel drainboards or extensions for the hot pan problem.

Forget linoleum. It went out with running boards and rumble seats. Vinyls, low-pressure polyester laminates, and other plastic alternatives are also poor choices. They are fine for vertical surfaces and good for table tops, but not for kitchen counters.

Since high pressure plastic laminated tops are the standard, from this point on we'll simply call them tops. Two types of tops can be identified: self-edged and postformed. Self-edged tops are flat. They have a square front and the edging is a separate piece of the same material, hence the term self-edged. The backsplash is a separate piece with a square inside corner, but firmly attached at the shop before delivery.

The backsplash can be any height, but the standard is 4 inches. The usual alternative is a backsplash that rises all the way to the bottoms of the wall cabinets, adding much to the overall cleanability of the kitchen. This high backsplash is seldom done with postformed tops because of equipment limitations.

Postformed tops present one clean sweep of plastic surface from the bottom of the front edge to the top of the backsplash.

In a modern postforming line, which can be fully automated, a sheet of corestock is fed in flat. The

Plastic laminated tops have 1/16" high pressure plastic laminate adhered to particleboard. Close-ups show no-drip edge at front, accomplished with plastic T-mold inserted in particleboard and under laminate.

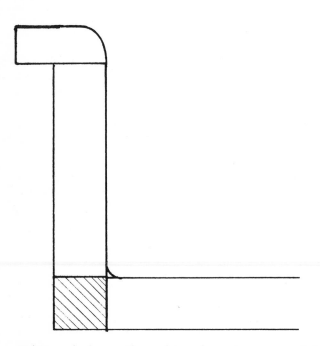

Other end of a postformed top shows how cove stick is placed for 90-degree angle. Small void at radius is not undesirable.

leading edge is machined and grooved for a T-molding, the under side is grooved in the backsplash area, contact adhesive is sprayed onto the corestock and onto a sheet of plastic laminate, and the plastic is indexed onto the corestock. Next the two go through a pinch roller which fuses the plastic to the core permanently. The plastic is then heated along the leading edge and molded down and adhered, and the plastic is heated along the backsplash area. The machine bends it up 90 degrees, and finally a coving stick is inserted in the resultant gap in the core to hold it at 90 degrees. This process produces a fully formed top.

The top just described will have a waterfall leading edge. If a T-molding is inserted in the groove of the leading edge before the plastic sheet is laid on it, the result is a slight rise at the edge before the plastic is bent down. This is a no-drip edge.

Because of the automation, postformed tops, which are better and more attractive products in every way, are often available at about the same price as self-edged. But in high-production shops, self-edged tops can be made on a completely automated basis also.

However they are made, tops are one of the best bargains in the home.

Fabricators usually use 3/4-inch particleboard as a corestock. The finished product must be at least that thickness, and it might vary up to 1-3/4 inches. But there would have to be some special reason for the latter thickness. In normal use it would be sheer extravagance. Depth of the top from front to rear would be 24 inches or 25 inches, enough to extend a minimum of 1/8 inch or a maximum of 1/2 inch over the cabinets beneath. These figures are from the standards of the National Association of Plastic Fabricators.

Regular kitchen countertops, properly attached to the base cabinets, need no backing sheet for dimensional stability. The structure itself will prevent warping.

But peninsulas that extend several feet out from the base cabinets must have backing sheets.

Measuring for tops is critical. When a top is delivered to the home it is complete. There is no way to change it. It has to fit.

Kitchen specialists find a folding 6-foot rule is more accurate than a steel tape. If the measurements are going to be checked by a second person, each makes sure they use the same type and brand of rule. There are differences. Many specialists also check their rules against those being used in the shop where the countertops are fabricated.

Tops that must be positioned tightly between walls

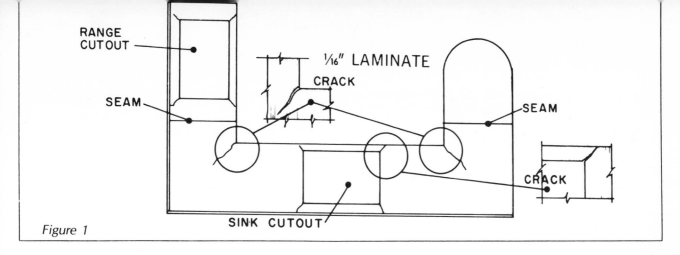

RANGE CUTOUT

SEAM

¹⁄₁₆″ LAMINATE

CRACK

SEAM

CRACK

SINK CUTOUT

Figure 1

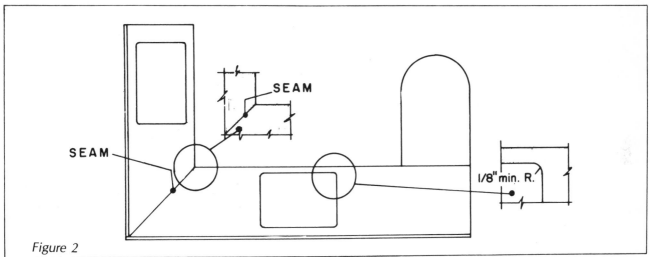

SEAM

SEAM

1/8″ min. R.

Figure 2

Improper placing of laminate seams can cause cracks. When seam is mitered from front to back corner it avoids stresses that come with no miter. Figure 1 shows wrong way, Figure 2 shows right way. All corners of sink or range cutouts should be radiused. Square corners in these places tend to crack. Formica Corp.

must be 1/4-inch to 3/8-inch short. A top that measures the same as the between-walls dimension will not go into position.

Out-of-square walls are always a problem. Theoretically, every wall meets another wall at 90 degrees. In practice it just doesn't happen. So, in practice, tops often must be slightly out-of-square.

The rule-of-thumb used by kitchen specialists on corner squareness is a simple formula: 3 ft. + 4 ft. = 5 ft.

To use it, measure the base wall to a point 3 feet from the corner and mark the point. Then measure along the side wall and mark a point 4 feet from the corner. Now measure the direct distance, point to point. It should be 5 feet.

If it measures less than 5 feet, the side wall is coming in. If it measures more than 5 feet, the side wall is going out.

Communicate the precise measurements to the top fabricator and he can allow for it so that the top will fit.

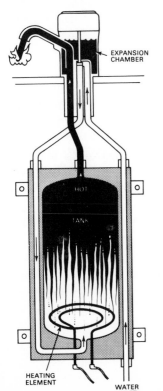

EXPANSION CHAMBER

HOT

TANK

HEATING ELEMENT

WATER INLET

Here's how instant hot water dispensers work. Sketch by In-Sink-Erator shows how turning valve at top allows cold water to enter inlet at bottom right. Water passes through valve assembly, down and enters tank at bottom where heat is. Tank does not operate under pressure since valve controls inlet water, not instant hot water.

6

Kitchen Planning and Design

The primary ingredient in good kitchen design is common sense. You've got to have places to put things. You've got to have places to put things down. It's better to store things near where you use them. You've got to have a little elbow room. And when you're working in the kitchen you don't want to have to step aside whenever somebody else in the house wants to go from the living room to the bathroom.

Those are the basics, but they raise several loaded questions.

For example, you've got to have a place to put things. But how many things? A 2-bedroom house presumes a family of two or three, maybe four. A 4-bedroom house presumes a family of five or six. Obviously a homeowner needs a lot more pots and pans and dishes and space for a family of six than for a family of two.

The concepts of "enough room" and "good kitchen layout" are matters of opinion for most people until they actually start storing foods and dishes and working in a kitchen. Kitchen experts through the years have formularized most kitchen planning principles to remove the subjective guesses and substitute objective facts and measurements that always will work.

The considerations are these:

1. Storage space that is both ample and logical. Ample means enough, but not too much. Too much would be wasteful both of money and of floorspace in the home. Logical means having enough storage space at the proper places.
2. Countertop space that is both ample and in the right places.
3. Well-planned placement and areas for each of the major appliances and their related activities.

4. Reduction of waste motion. (Few of us are naturally efficient, but our inefficiencies can be lessened greatly by good kitchen planning.)
5. Good lighting and good color-matching.

The best way to start planning to satisfy all of those considerations is to consider the activity areas. Each of these relates closely to a major appliance or the sink. And each requires its own cabinetry and work space. These are:

1. The food preparation center, which incorporates the refrigerator. This sometimes is referred to as the mixing center.
2. The cooking and serving center, which includes the range or, in built-in installations, at least the cooktop.
3. The clean-up center, which incorporates the sink. Major appliances found in this area include the dishwasher and disposer.

Many housewives also want an eating area in the kitchen, and there is a growing trend to include a planning center which serves as the housewife's "office." Such a planning center will include at least a desktop with some storage facility for household bills, notes and the like. Well-planned ones will also include a telephone and an intercom which provides communication throughout the house, monitoring of baby's sleeping or play areas, and even burglar and fire alarms.

Other possible centers could include a bar, a hobby center, or sewing center, but these are functions of space.

The ground rule for arranging these three major centers is to form a triangle, and the straight-line

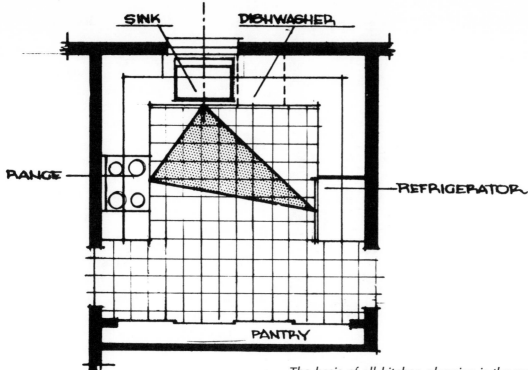

The basis of all kitchen planning is the work triangle. It connects the food preparation center, which includes the refrigerator; cooking center, which includes the range; and the cleanup center with the sink and dishwasher. Total distance from middle front of sink, to range to refrigerator and back to sink, should be from 12 to 22 feet. Within these limits the housewife has sufficient freedom of action but doesn't have to cover tiring distances.

distance between the front center of the sink, refrigerator and cooktop must not total more than 22 feet nor less than 12 feet.

That is called the work triangle, and it is the basis for all kitchen planning.

The distance from the sink to the refrigerator should be from 4 to 7 feet; from sink to range, 4 to 6 feet, and between range and refrigerator, 4 to 9 feet.

Any one-piece range fits into that triangle. A built-in installation, however, adds a fourth element, since there is a separate oven and cooktop. The guideline here is to put the oven outside the triangle since it is used least, although it often can be designed within the triangle.

Both the maximum (22 feet) and the minimum (12 feet) of the work triangle are important. More than 22 feet wastes steps, energy, and time. Less than 12 feet crowds the appliances and activities too close together.

Kitchen planning starts with the sink. A kitchen designer always locates it first, partially because good planning usually centers it with refrigerator to the right of it, or clockwise from it, and the cooking and serving area to the left of it, or counter-clockwise. In addition, the sink must go where the plumbing lines are, and location of the plumbing lines usually is determined by other factors, such as location of bathrooms.

The sink is the center of clean-up activity before as well as after the meal. So plenty of counter space is required.

There should be 36 inches of counter space to the right of the sink, and there should be 30 inches of counter space to the left.

The dishwasher should be adjacent to the sink. If a dishwasher is not included, a 24-inch cabinet should be designed adjacent to the sink for later installation of a dishwasher.

If a dishwasher is not included, a double-bowl sink

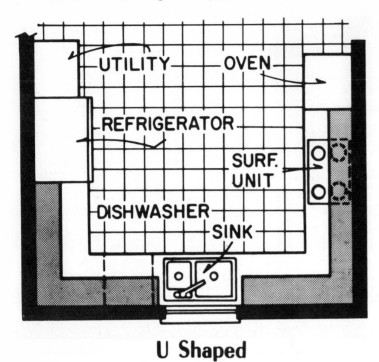

U Shaped

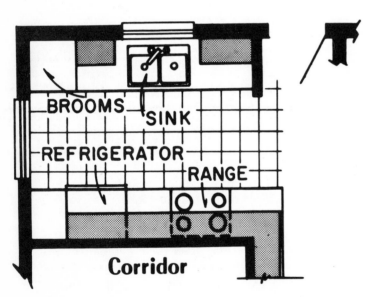

Corridor

The four basic kitchen configurations are the U shape, the L shape, the Corridor, and the One Wall. The U and the L usually afford efficient work triangles without cross traffic. A U or L broken by a door cuts efficiency by permitting cross traffic. The corridor is efficient if it is a closed corridor. If it is open, traffic cuts through. A central island or a peninsula often is used to help form the work triangle.

is needed. Even if there is a dishwasher, a double-bowl sink is desirable.

If fillers are required to make the run of cabinets fit flush to walls to left and right, the best place to put them is to the left and right of the sink cabinet.

Many kitchen activities relate closely to both refrigerator and range so, as stated before, the sink is best placed between those two other centers.

Storage must be provided near the sink for clean-up supplies, for fruits and vegetables that do not require refrigeration, for sauce pans, coffee pot and food preparation supplies, and for foods that require soaking and washing.

If the recommended counter space to the right (36 inches) and left (30 inches) of the sink cannot be provided, the absolute minimums would be 24 inches and 18 inches respectively. But don't be that stingy to the housewife.

A double-bowl sink with one shallow bowl will permit sit-down convenience for the housewife when she is cleaning vegetables or for similar tasks.

The sink does not have to go under a window. This is a matter of personal preference, and the idea that it enabled the mother to watch the kids playing has always been questionable. At best, it leaves a lot of gaps in the surveillance. If there is one window, it might be best to save it for a breakfast-lunch area.

We have referred to the area around the refrigerator as the food preparation area, or the mixing center. Some kitchen designers separate these in different ways, but the functions and needs are closely related.

It is good to localize various types of food storage here—cold foods in the refrigerator and its freezer compartment, canned goods in a pantry unit of some sort. Pantry units can be obtained 84 inches high or as wall or base cabinets, with fold-out vertical racks to hold a maximum number of cans, or with revolving shelves that are particularly good for corners.

The refrigerator door must open into the work triangle, not away from it. And there must be at least 18 inches of landing space where the refrigerator door opens. Side-by-side refrigerator-freezers tend to defeat this principle, but with these models it is the refrigerator door, not the freezer door, that should open to the landing space.

When the food preparation and mixing functions are included in this activity center, there should be 36 to 42 inches of counter space on the door-opening side of the refrigerator.

A maple insert in the countertop is particularly useful here. It could be as small as 12 inches wide, or it could be a whole section of countertop. Women use knives often when preparing food and it is next to impossible to keep from cutting the countertop.

The maple cutting board also can be a pull-out accessory of the base cabinet, positioned over a drawer.

Here, also, is the place for a built-in mixer, with a cabinet below for its many accessories.

The cooking center is the most active area of the kitchen after the sink and cleanup center.

The built-in cooktop should have at least 18 inches of counter space on each side.

A built-in oven needs 24 inches of counter space.

A one-piece range needs at least the minimum 18 inches on each side, but it is much better to provide at least 24 inches on the inside of the work triangle.

Provide a counter insert of either stainless steel or glass ceramic near the range for placing hot pans. The plastic laminate of a countertop should never be subjected to heat over 270 degrees.

Since the oven is the least-used appliance in the kitchen, built-in installations can be out of the work triangle. However, it still will need its counter space.

In their specifications for every model, manufacturers of built-in ovens always list a height above the floor for the bottom of the oven cut-out.

A woman can work with least effort at an oven if the opened door is 3 to 4 inches below her elbow level. The usable range here is from 1 to 7 inches below elbow level. If there is a choice, relate the height of the opened oven door to the user's elbow level.

The cooktop usually will be 36 inches from the floor because it is cut into the countertop and that's the height of the counter. It could be dropped as much as 4 inches, and a lot of housewives would probably appreciate it.

Because both the built-in wall oven and the refrigerator are high appliances, a common design error is to put them together. This should never be done, because both need their own landing space. It does not help to have a landing space on either side when these two are together because that non-solution would put the landing space on the wrong side for either the refrigerator or the oven.

If the range corner of the work triangle is oriented

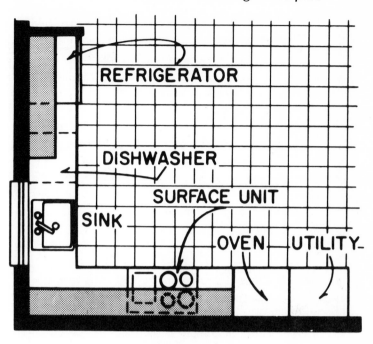

L Shaped

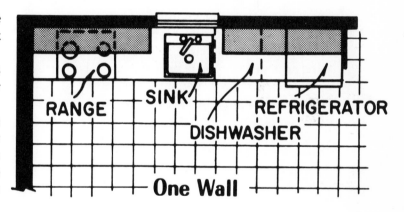

One Wall

toward the dining area, it might be combined with a serving center. This is common, although the serving center need not be in conjunction with any particular appliance.

The serving center needs storage space for the toaster, serving trays, ready-to-eat foods, platters, serving dishes, table linens, and napkins. There should be at least 30 inches of counter space.

Needless to say, the serving center should be near and accessible to the eating area. Since this is where the china and glassware are stored for serving and eating, it also can be considered as a china center.

Families like eating space in the kitchen, supplementary to a separate dining area, and most builders provide this space in most of their homes.

This adds another center to be included in the kitchen plan—the eating center.

This might be along a peninsula, an island, or it might protrude from a wall.

If it is a peninsula, island, or protrusion, allow at least 42 inches clearances from its end to the opposite wall. Do not put the refrigerator or wall oven on that opposite wall where an open door would block traffic.

Allow 24 inches of elbow room for each place for the lunchers.

For breakfast, the minimum depth should be at least 15 inches. For dinner, it should be 24 inches.

A table and chairs require at least 8×6-1/2 feet.

Tables and chairs are simpler and easier. Islands and peninsulas add much to the impact of the kitchen, and they are not complicated.

For about $200 or less a builder can design-in an island with a maple block top that can serve as a food mixing and preparation center on one side, a snack bar on the other. For approximately another $30 he can make this a beautifully textured brick island, then add a built-in barbecue unit and a cooktop.

The peninsula is different only in that it is connected to the cabinets along the wall, extending out into the room to add design interest, give extra storage and counter space, and keep traffic out of the work triangle.

The builder needs a run of 14 feet minimum for a peninsula, which would allow a minimum of 8 feet for the kitchen, including the 24-inch peninsula, and 6 feet for the dining area.

If the opposite side of the peninsula will provide a snack bar instead of a dining area, the 6 feet can be reduced. There must be at least 30 inches from the edge of the snack bar to the wall for seating, and this is a bit tight.

Standard height for island or peninsula would be 36 inches. The snack bar height would drop to 30 inches. If the snack bar is not dropped, high chairs or stools would be needed.

If the snack bar is 36 inches high, the top will have to be extended from 12 to 18 inches for knee space, depending on the type of seating.

If, however, the snack bar is dropped to 30 inches, the minimum for knee space is 15 inches.

The island or peninsula also can be an excellent place for the sink and clean-up center. Unfortunately, this usually will add to plumbing expense.

If possible, the kitchen should be laid out so there will be no traffic crossing any legs of the work triangle. This will not always be possible, but if compromises must be made, the range center should be kept most sacrosanct.

Avoid placing the refrigerator too close to an adjoining wall. If the door cannot be opened far enough, the crisper trays cannot be removed for cleaning.

As a rule of thumb, the kitchen should have at least 10 feet (linear) of base cabinets and 10 feet of wall cabinets. These are absolute minimums.

Allow 27 inches of space along both walls to turn a corner. A base corner filler is the most economical way to turn the corner but gives only dead space. This insures full operation of adjacent doors and drawers.

Other better ways to turn a corner are (1) with corner units that give reach-in storage space; (2) with a lazy susan cabinet that makes all the corner space easily accessible, and which requires 36 inches along each wall; (3) with a sink or appliance cutting the corner on the diagonal, requiring varying amounts of wall space.

For turning a corner above the counter, a wall corner filler (with dead space, so not desirable) takes 15 inches along each wall. Diagonal wall cabinets can be used, or open diagonal shelving, or butted wall cabinets that have reach-in space. A diagonal wall cabinet takes 24 inches along each wall.

In the home-planning stage, the kitchen should be planned before house plans are finalized. Otherwise it can be costly to the kitchen. For example, a door placed in a corner of the kitchen must use both walls of that corner, with a resultant loss of 30 inches of valuable kitchen space. If this door is installed at least 30 inches from the corner, cabinets can be run all the way to the corner and the only loss is the dimension of the door itself, and its framing. And windows should be a minimum of 12-3/4 inches from a corner for the same reason.

In any inside corner of a cabinet installation, watch for clearances. Normally there will be doors and drawers along both sides of the corner. If they are butted precisely, there might not be clearance for the knob or pull. This would call for a filler to create the clearance. Minimum for clearance is 1/2 inch.

When blank base cabinets are used to turn a corner, the blank end of the cabinet does not have to fill the entire space where it is not exposed. In fact, it is better if it does not fill the space because it is very difficult to reach into such a corner and much of the space would, therefore, be wasted.

Diagonal corner cabinets can add much interest to the kitchen design. However, they use up a lot of wall space. For example, a cabinet that has 20 inches of exposed surface along the diagonal requires 39 inches along each wall. A 30-inch diagonal cabinet requires 45-1/2 inches along each wall. (This presumes that the depth of adjacent cabinets is 24-1/2 inches.) This does not waste any space, because all space inside the diagonal cabinet is usable. But it uses wall space that, depending on overall kitchen dimensions, might be needed for other purposes.

For the above reason, kitchen specialists usually advise that no sink or appliance over 32 inches in width be used to turn a corner diagonally.

In a straight-wall assembly, the distance from the front edge of the countertop to the front edge of the sink is usually 2 inches. In a diagonal assembly, this distance must be increased to 3 inches so as not to intrude into adjoining cabinet area on each side.

Conventional cabinets can be positioned diagonally across corners. But this creates big pie-shaped dead spaces on either side, wasting kitchen space.

Putting it all together makes the kitchen—the cabinets, the appliances, the corners, the work centers, the activity areas—with the basic work triangle measuring from 12 feet to 22 feet.

This results in one of four basic configurations, or "kinds" of kitchens.

These are the one-wall kitchen, sometimes called straight-line; the corridor kitchen, sometimes called two-wall or pullman or parallel; the L-shaped kitchen which turns one corner, and the U-shaped kitchen which has two inside corners.

All of these have variations. If, for example, a door interrupts the continuity of an L or a U kitchen, it becomes a broken L, or a broken U. If an island or a peninsula is used to achieve the work triangle, it might be called an island kitchen or a peninsula kitchen.

In the one-wall kitchen, the work centers and the appliances are arranged along one wall. This means,

of course, that there is no work triangle, and usually both storage space and counter space are much too limited for efficiency or convenience. It is, however, the most economical kind of kitchen, and the most easily installed.

For motels, vacation homes, offices and the like, this configuration is available from about a dozen manufacturers in one manufactured piece, usually called a unit kitchen, or a compact kitchen.

A complete unit kitchen will include a sink, two surface burners (or more), and, underneath, an oven compartment and a refrigerator compartment. The smallest such unit is made by Douglas Crestlyn, fitting into only 19 inches of wall space. Larger units, such as those by Crane Chef or Oakland Foundry, range up to six feet or more. Sub-Zero offers them as ornate consoles with furniture finishes, with tops and drawers that close so they look like a buffet.

A corridor kitchen adds the opposite wall, making possible a tight, efficient work triangle and added usable storage and counter space. Where the opposite wall is too distant, a peninsula or island can be added to create one side of a corridor kitchen, and in this case at least one of the work centers will be placed in the created counter space.

The only disadvantage of a corridor kitchen is that through traffic always cuts through two legs of the work triangle. In a family with active children this can be bothersome.

The L-shaped kitchen is the most popular, affords the most efficient work triangle, and is never bothered with through traffic. While the two sides of the L are usually along two walls of the room, in larger kitchens one leg of the L often is formed with a peninsula that affords a snack bar on the other side, outside the work area.

A U-shaped kitchen, as its name indicates, has three sides. Customarily these are three of the walls of the room, but often a peninsula is added to make a U out of what otherwise would be an L. The objective of a U-shape is to place a work area in each side, making a well-balanced equilateral work triangle.

U-shaped kitchens usually go into fairly good-sized rooms, but sometimes there is an effort to squeeze one into dimensions that are too tight. The base wall, or middle leg, of the U must be at least 9 feet to give the desirable 5 feet clearance in the middle after the cabinets are in.

Kitchen Planning Principles

Broken U's or L's are signs of failure in the house design. They happen when a door has been placed without allowing for the kitchen design. Kitchen design still can be good except for the basic flaw of interrupted work from cross traffic. Traffic through the kitchen always will cross two legs of the work triangle.

As noted previously, islands and peninsulas can be used to form the work triangle, provide eating space in the kitchen, or added counter for work space.

Sometimes a peninsular eating area is nothing more than a countertop projecting from a cabinet line or a wall, with a supporting leg at the far end. These can be square, rectangular, kidney-shaped, free-form or in any shape desired. This is a simple, easy installation that, in effect, makes the dinette table a structural part of the house and relieves the home-owner of the need to buy a dinette.

Other peninsulas that also provide storage space are a bit more involved. Projecting from the cabinet line, they will consist of regular base cabinets, a counter which might also hold the sink or cooktop, and a line of wall cabinets overhead which would house the vent hood.

Both wall and base cabinets in such a peninsula can be ordered to open on either side of the peninsula, or on both sides. When they open on both sides it adds greatly to convenience, because then dishes or other items can be stored or removed from either side.

Here are a few pointers for these peninsulas.

The base cabinet at the end of the peninsula should have a kick space on the end side, as well as on the kitchen side, so a person can work at the end. Depending on the use of the peninsula, it might be necessary to have kick space on both sides of all the base cabinets.

The wall cabinet run should be shorter than the base cabinet run. This prevents head bumping and also contributes to a more open appearance to the kitchen.

When ordering wall cabinets for use in a peninsula, the buyer should specify that they are for peninsular use. The cabinet manufacturer will add extra reinforcing at the top of these cabinets—maybe. If they do not come with reinforcing, it will have to be provided by the installer.

The countertop at the end of the peninsula should have radiused corners for safety. Square corners will lead to bruised hands and hips forever.

All of these considerations apply also to islands.

If a cooktop is used in either a peninsula or an island it probably will need some sort of backsplash or other barrier to protect others from grease spatters, hot handles, and the like.

60 SUCCESSFUL KITCHEN FLOORPLANS

The Kitchen Design Studio of General Electric Company and Hotpoint has designed at least 25,000 kitchens for builders and architects in the last 15 years, kitchens which have been installed in hundreds of thousands of new homes.

Specifically for this book, Department Manager George T. Warren and Design Manager William J. Ketcham selected 60 floorplans that represent good design principles well worth emulating.

All are drawn to 1/4" scale.

In some cases extended areas of the house are included because of the way the kitchen inter-relates. In one case, two different floorplans are included for the same kitchen, one in Corridor and the other in L-shape configuration, showing how variations are possible for cause. In this case, the Corridor kept all cross-traffic out of the kitchen, but the L permitted access to the bathroom from the kitchen.

In many cases the laundry area is included in the floorplan. The laundry is never recommended *in* the kitchen, but it often is wanted near the kitchen, with access.

Floorplan abbreviations: REFR—refrigerator; DW—dishwasher; RA—range; COMP—trash compactor; W—clothes washer and D—dryer.

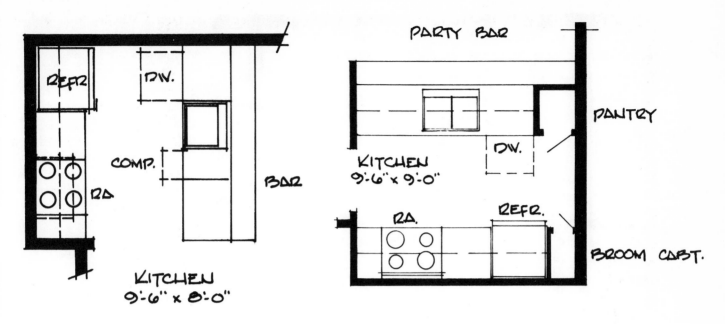

REFR.

DW.

COMP.

RA

BAR

KITCHEN
9'-6" x 8'-0"

1.

PARTY BAR

KITCHEN
9'-6" x 9'-0"

DW.

PANTRY

RA.

REFR.

BROOM CABT.

2.

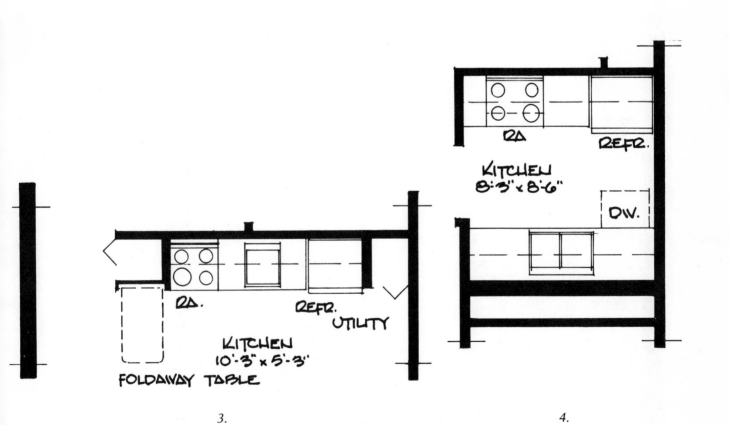

RA.

REFR.

UTILITY

KITCHEN
10'-3" x 5'-3"

FOLDAWAY TABLE

3.

RA

REFR.

KITCHEN
8'-3" x 8'-6"

DW.

4.

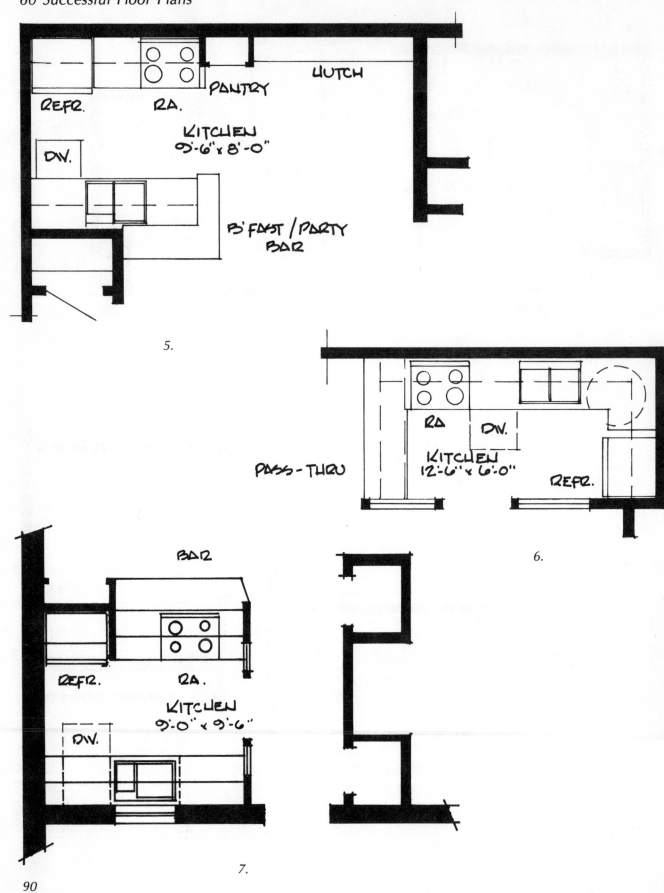

REFR.   RA.   PANTRY   HUTCH

KITCHEN
9'-6" x 8'-0"

DW.

B'FAST / PARTY
BAR

5.

PASS-THRU

RA   DW.

KITCHEN
12'-6" x 6'-0"

REFR.

6.

BAR

REFR.   RA.

KITCHEN
9'-0" x 9'-6"

DW.

7.

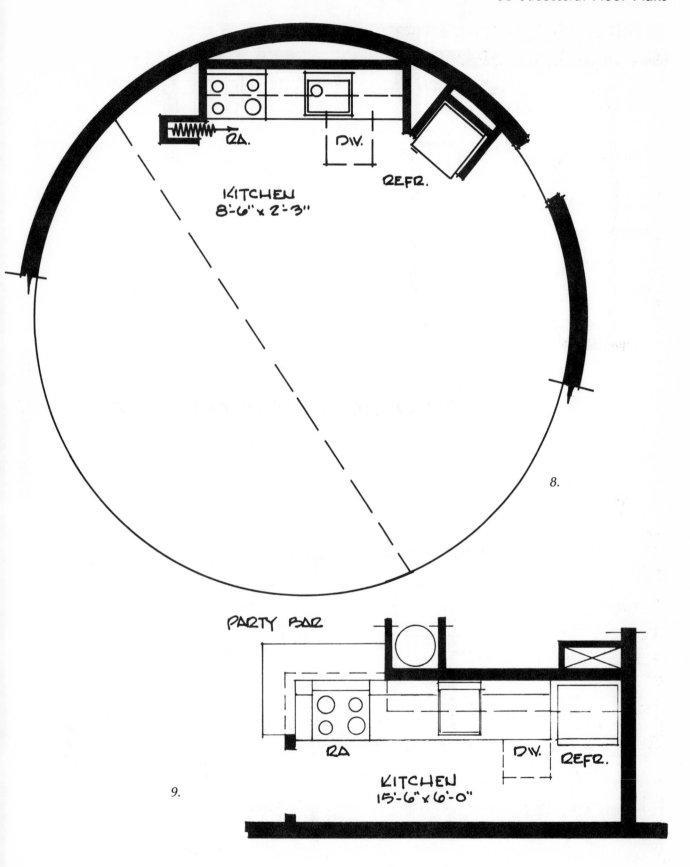

KITCHEN
8'-6" x 2'-3"

RA.

DW.

REFR.

8.

PARTY BAR

9.

RA

DW.

REFR.

KITCHEN
15'-6" x 6'-0"

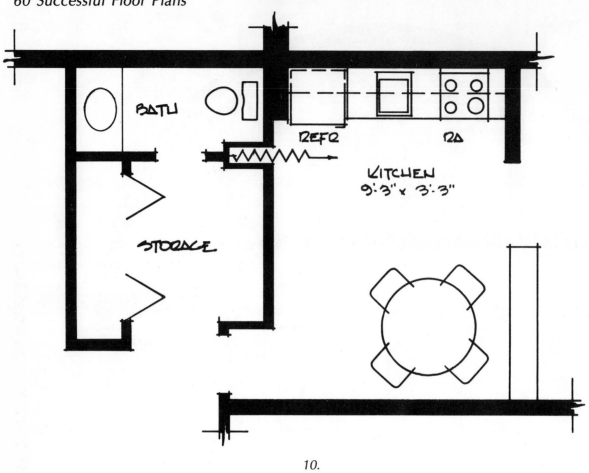

KITCHEN
9'-3" x 3'-3"

REFR

RA

BATH

STORAGE

10.

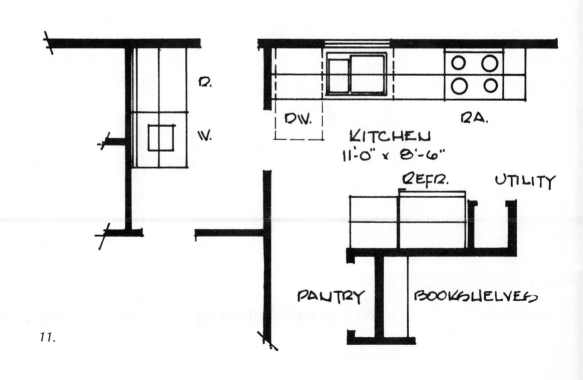

D.

W.

DW.

KITCHEN
11'-0" x 8'-6"

RA.

REFR.

UTILITY

PANTRY

BOOKSHELVES

11.

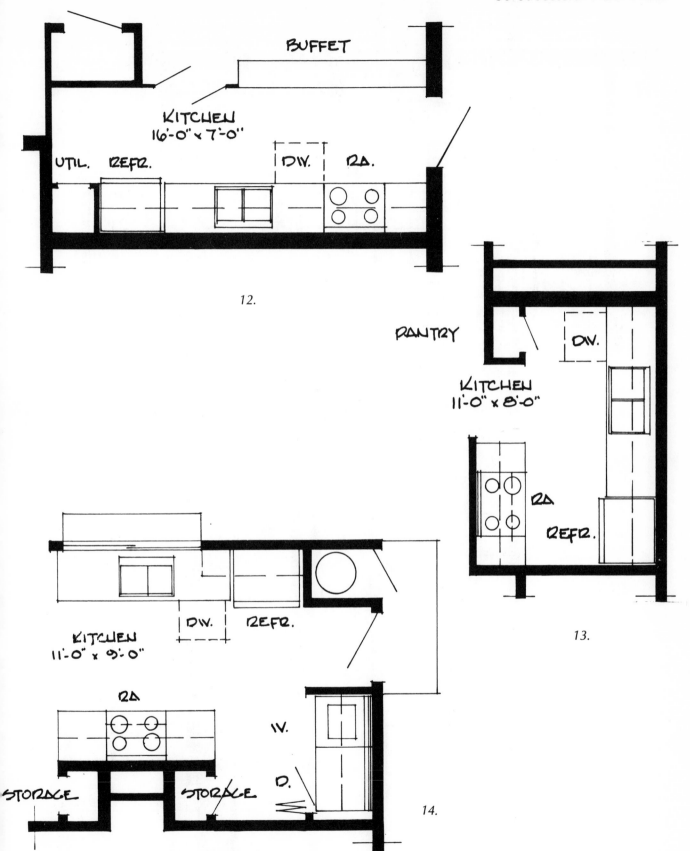

BUFFET

KITCHEN
16'-0" x 7'-0"

UTIL.   REFR.   DW.   RA.

12.

PANTRY   DW.

KITCHEN
11'-0" x 8'-0"

RA

REFR.

KITCHEN
11'-0" x 9'-0"

DW.   REFR.

RA

13.

W.

STORAGE   STORAGE   D.   14.

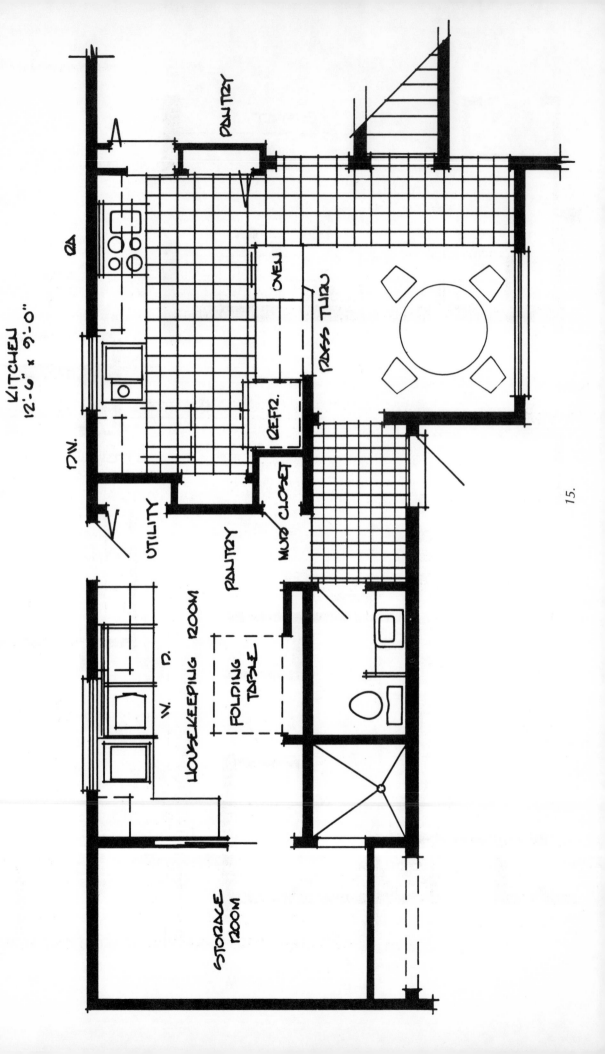

KITCHEN
12'-6" x 9'-0"

DW.

PANTRY

OVEN

PASS THRU

REFR.

MUD CLOSET

UTILITY

PANTRY

HOUSEKEEPING ROOM

W. D.

FOLDING TABLE

STORAGE ROOM

94

15.

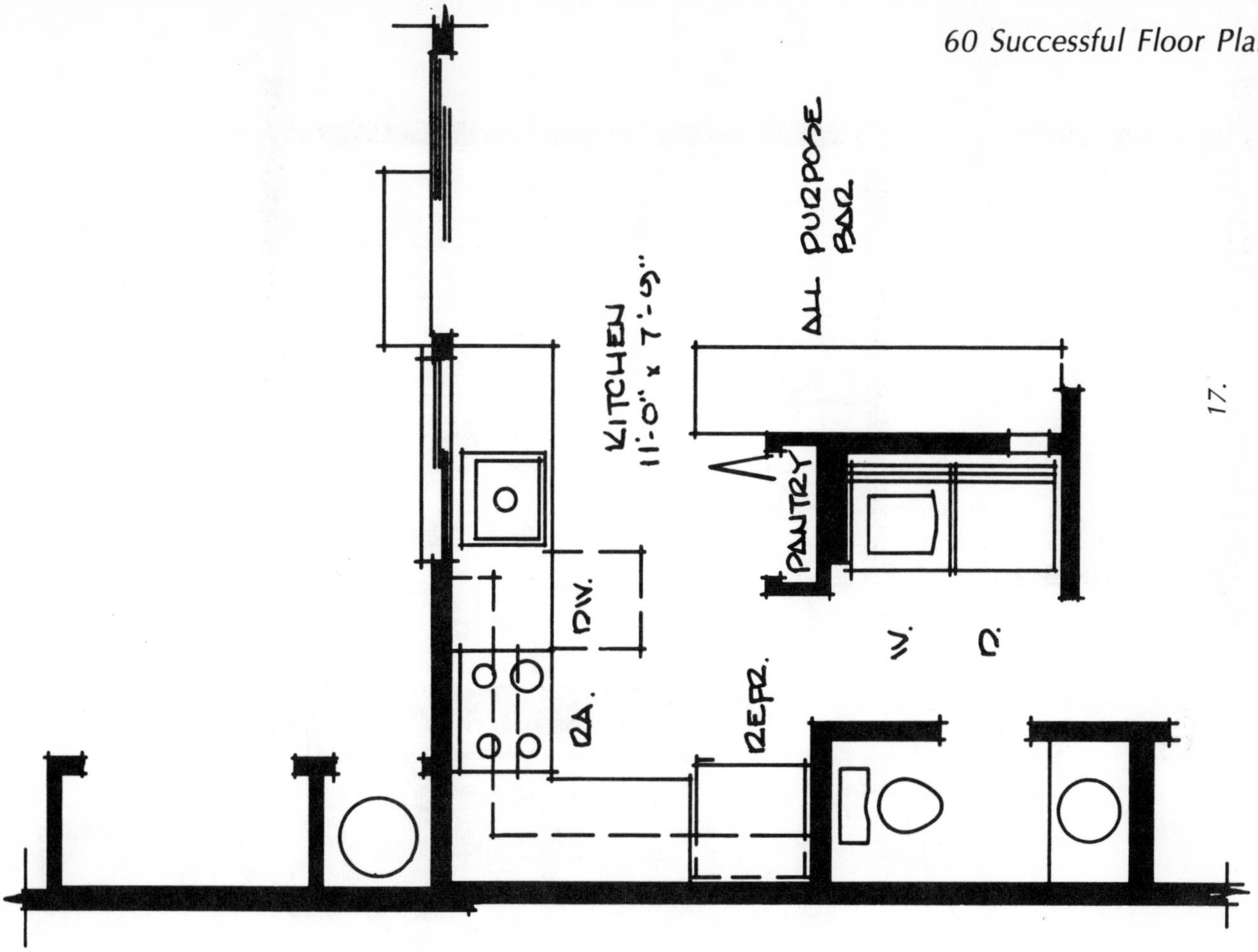

KITCHEN
11'-0" x 7'-9"

ALL PURPOSE
ROOM

PANTRY

D.W.

RA.

REFR.

17.

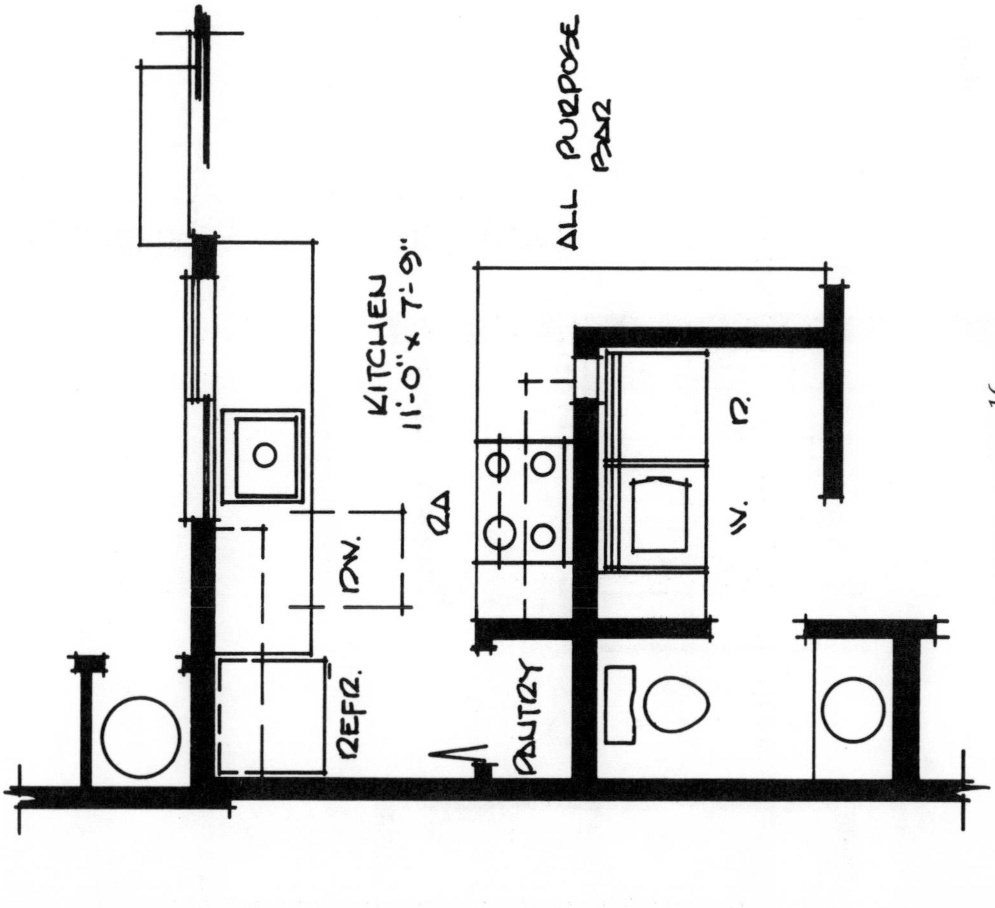

KITCHEN
11'-0" x 7'-9"

ALL PURPOSE
ROOM

DN.

RA.

REFR.

PANTRY

16.

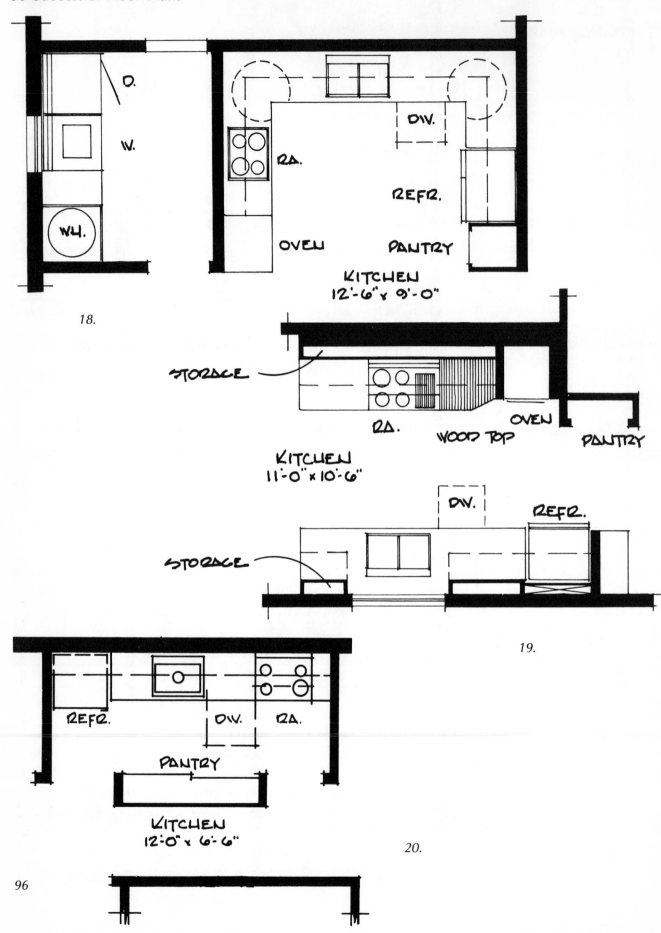

D.

W.

WH.

RA.

DW.

REFR.

OVEN

PANTRY

KITCHEN
12'-6" x 9'-0"

18.

STORAGE

RA.

WOOD TOP

OVEN

PANTRY

KITCHEN
11'-0" x 10'-6"

DW.

REFR.

STORAGE

19.

REFR.

DW.

RA.

PANTRY

KITCHEN
12'-0" x 6'-6"

20.

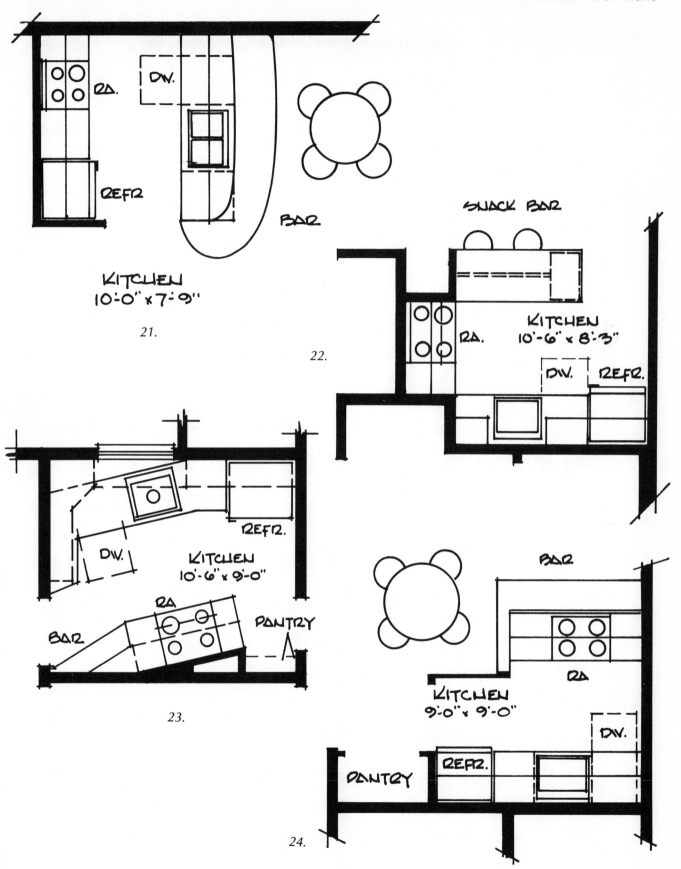

KITCHEN
10'-0" x 7'-9"

21.

22.

SNACK BAR

KITCHEN
10'-6" x 8'-3"

RA.

DW.

REFR.

REFR.

DW.

KITCHEN
10'-6" x 9'-0"

RA

BAR

PANTRY

23.

BAR

RA

KITCHEN
9'-0" x 9'-0"

DW.

PANTRY

REFR.

24.

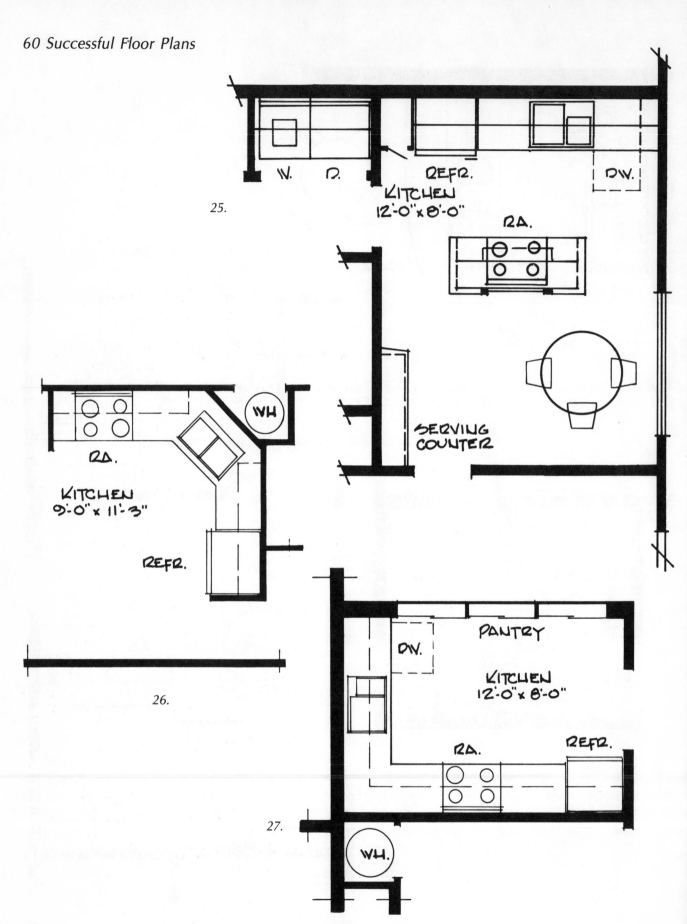

W.   D.   REFR.   DW.

25.

KITCHEN
12'-0" x 8'-0"

RA.

SERVING
COUNTER

RA.

WH

KITCHEN
9'-0" x 11'-3"

REFR.

26.

PANTRY

DW.

KITCHEN
12'-0" x 8'-0"

RA.   REFR.

27.

WH.

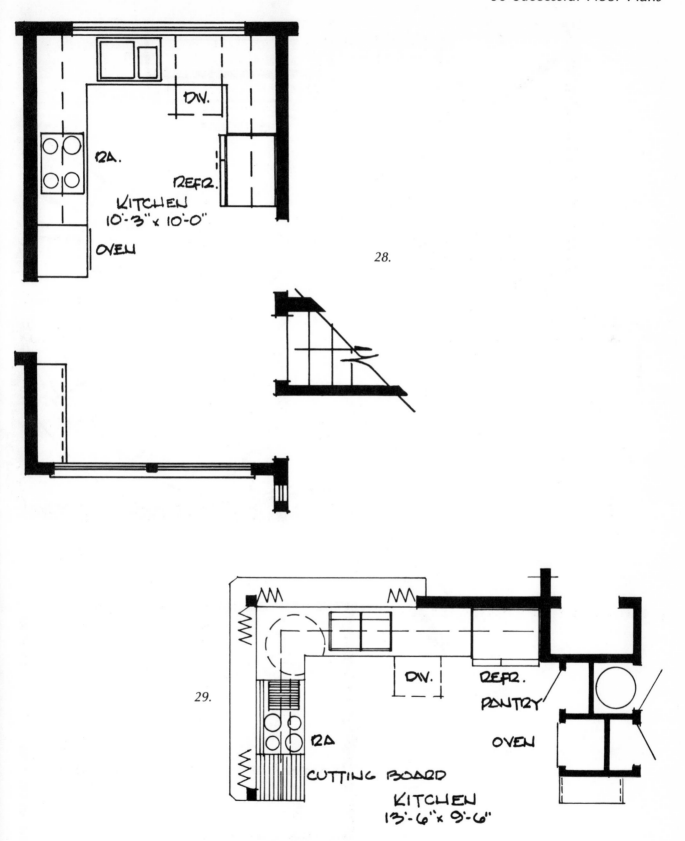

RA.

DW.

REFR.

KITCHEN
10'-3" x 10'-0"

OVEN

28.

29.

DW.

REFR.

PANTRY

OVEN

RA

CUTTING BOARD

KITCHEN
13'-6" x 9'-6"

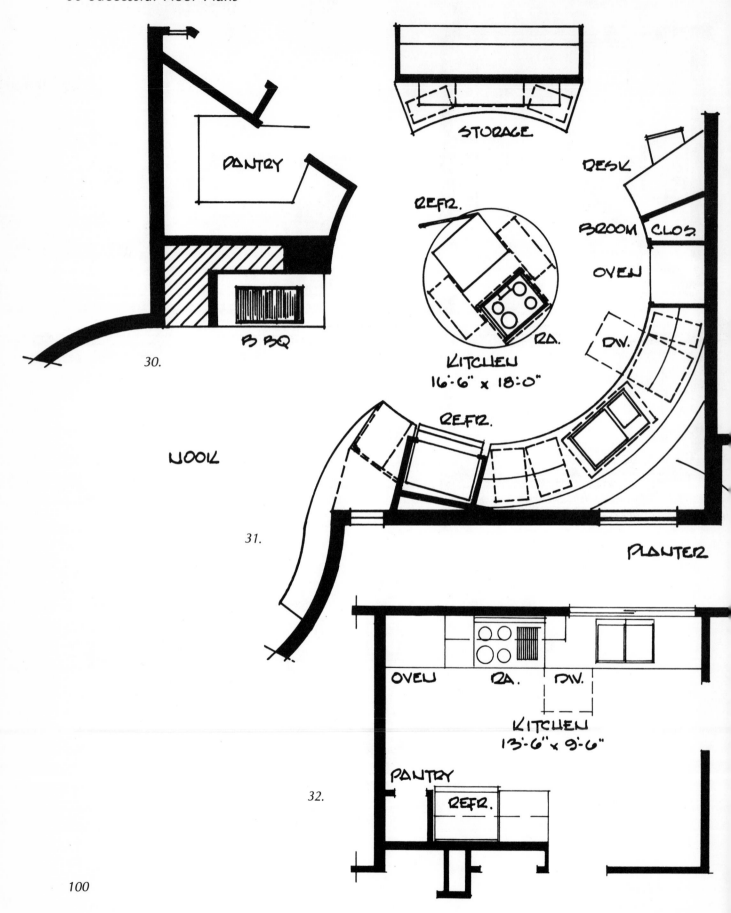

STORAGE

PANTRY

DESK

REFR.

BROOM CLOS.

OVEN

D.V.

RA.

KITCHEN
16'-6" x 18'-0"

30.

B BQ

REFR.

NOOK

31.

PLANTER

OVEN   RA.   DV.

KITCHEN
13'-6" x 9'-6"

PANTRY

32.

REFR.

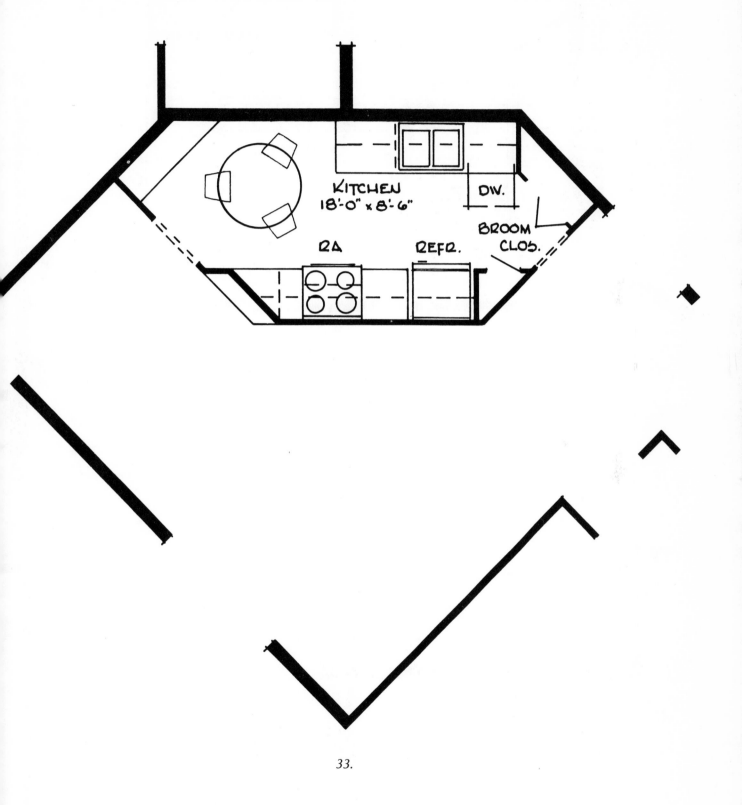

KITCHEN
18'-0" x 8'-6"

DW.

RA

REFR.

BROOM
CLOS.

33.

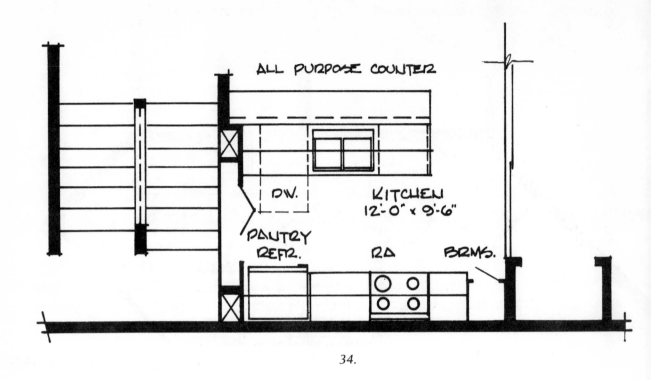

ALL PURPOSE COUNTER

DW.

KITCHEN
12'-0" x 9'-6"

PANTRY
REFR.

RA

BRMS.

34.

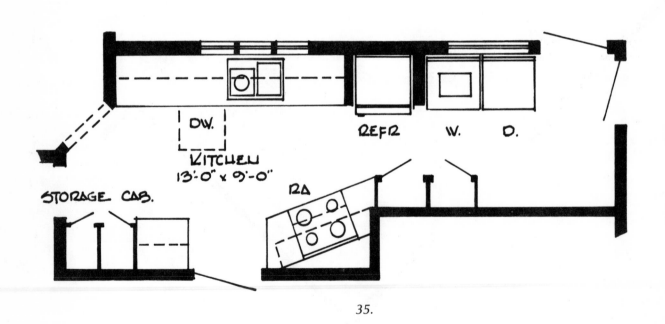

DW.

REFR

W.

D.

KITCHEN
13'-0" x 9'-0"

STORAGE CAB.

RA

35.

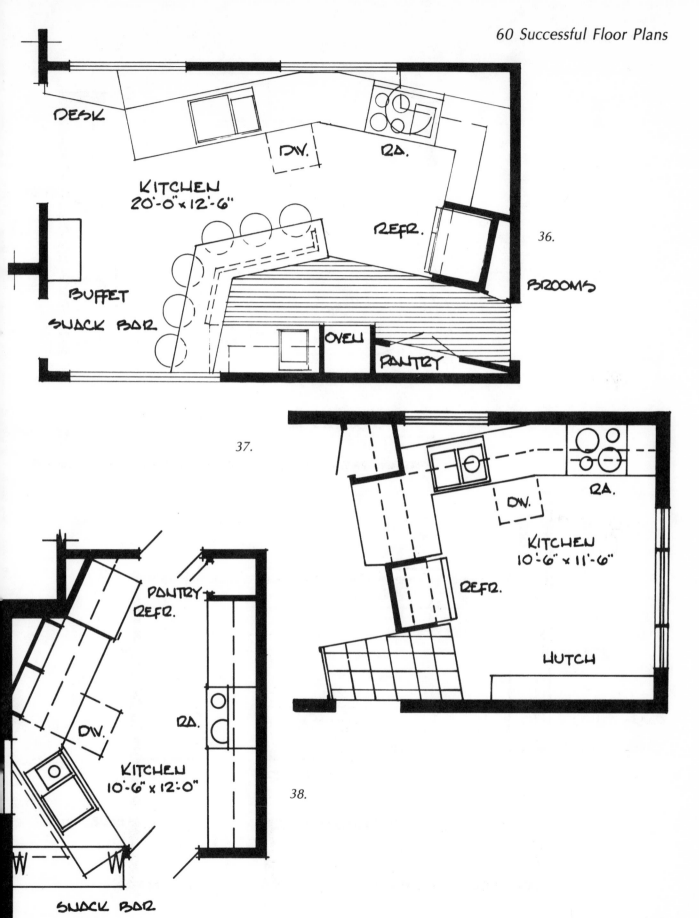

DESK

KITCHEN
20'-0" x 12'-6"

DW.

RA.

REFR.

36.

BUFFET
SNACK BAR

BROOMS

OVEN

PANTRY

37.

KITCHEN
10'-6" x 11'-6"

DW.

RA.

REFR.

HUTCH

PANTRY
REFR.

DW.

RA.

KITCHEN
10'-6" x 12'-0"

38.

SNACK BAR

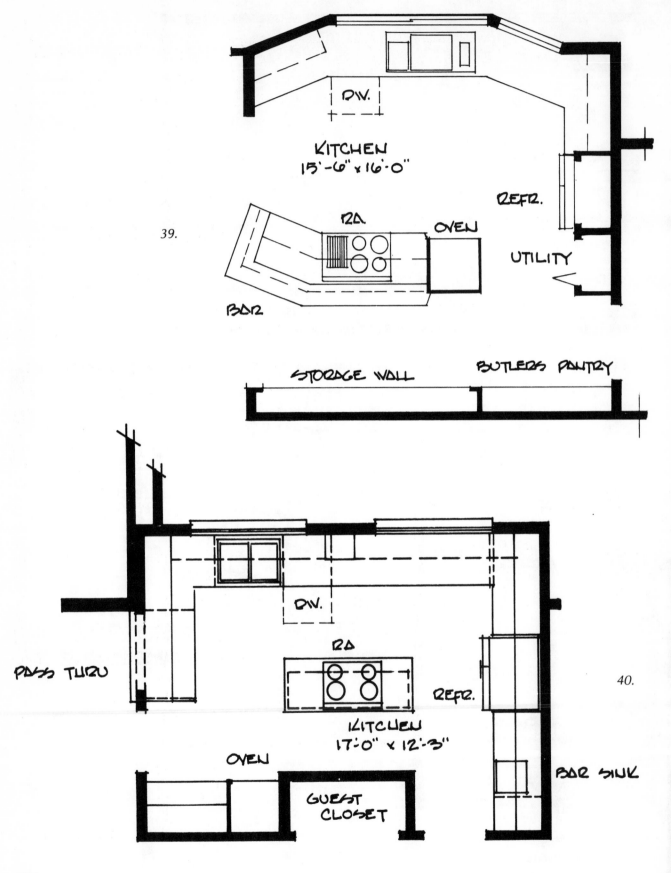

KITCHEN
15'-6" x 16'-0"

39.

DW.

REFR.

UTILITY

RA

OVEN

BAR

STORAGE WALL   BUTLERS PANTRY

PASS THRU

DW.

RA

REFR.

40.

KITCHEN
17'-0" x 12'-3"

BAR SINK

OVEN

GUEST
CLOSET

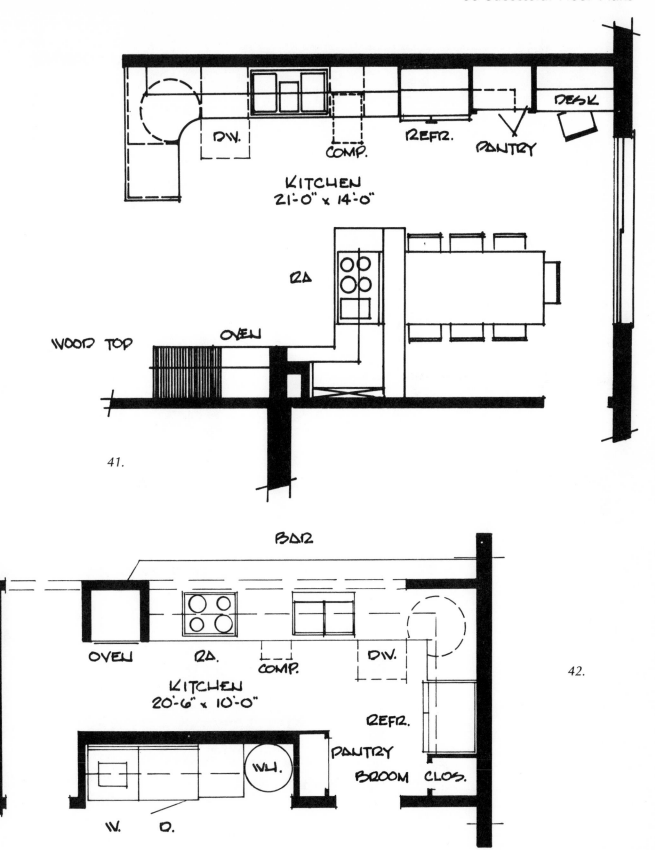

D.W.

COMP.

REFR.

PANTRY

DESK

KITCHEN
21'-0" x 14'-0"

RA

WOOD TOP

OVEN

41.

BAR

OVEN

RA.

COMP.

D.W.

42.

KITCHEN
20'-6" x 10'-0"

REFR.

PANTRY
BROOM CLOS.

W. H.

W.   D.

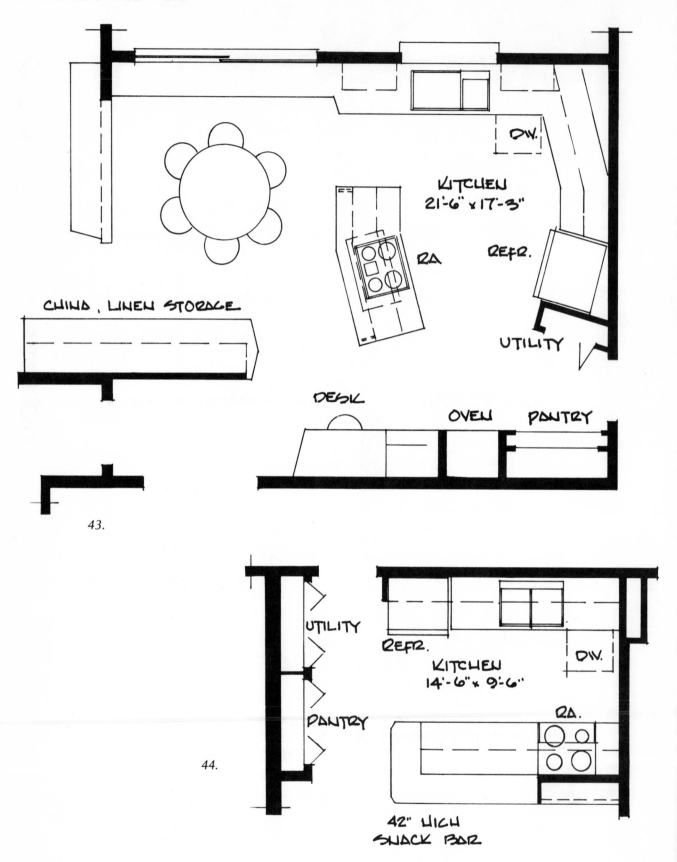

CHINA , LINEN STORAGE

KITCHEN
21'-6" x 17'-3"

RA.

REFR.

DW.

UTILITY

DESK   OVEN   PANTRY

43.

UTILITY

PANTRY

44.

REFR.

KITCHEN
14'-6" x 9'-6"

DW.

RA.

42" HIGH
SNACK BAR

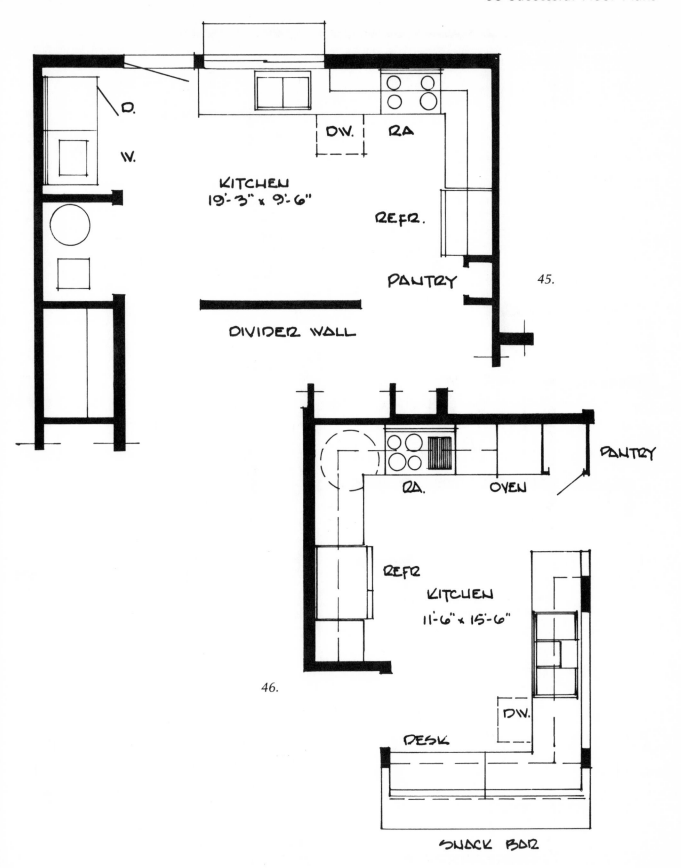

D.

W.

KITCHEN
19'-3" x 9'-6"

DW.

RA

REFR.

PANTRY

45.

DIVIDER WALL

PANTRY

RA.

OVEN

REFR

KITCHEN
11'-6" x 15'-6"

46.

DW.

DESK

SNACK BAR

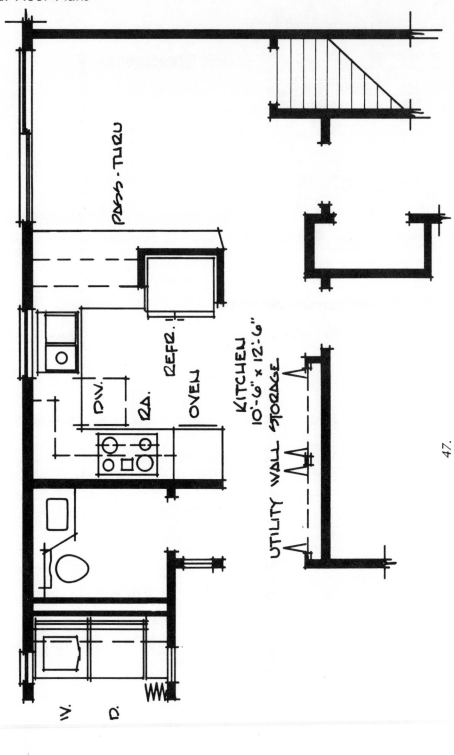

KITCHEN 10'-6" x 12'-6"

PASS-TRU

REFR.

OVEN

D.W.

R.

W.

D.

UTILITY WALL STORAGE

47.

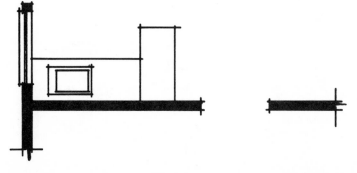

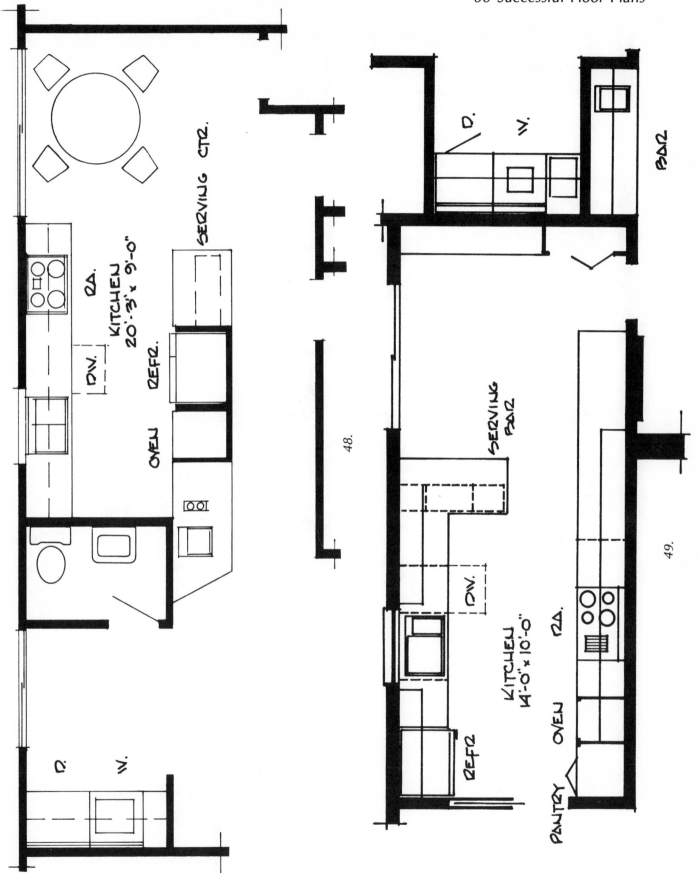

KITCHEN 20'-3" x 9'-0"

SERVING CTR.

OVEN

REFR.

DW.

D.

W.

48.

SERVING BAR

KITCHEN 14'-0" x 10'-0"

DW.

REFR.

D.

W.

BAR

PANTRY

OVEN

R.

49.

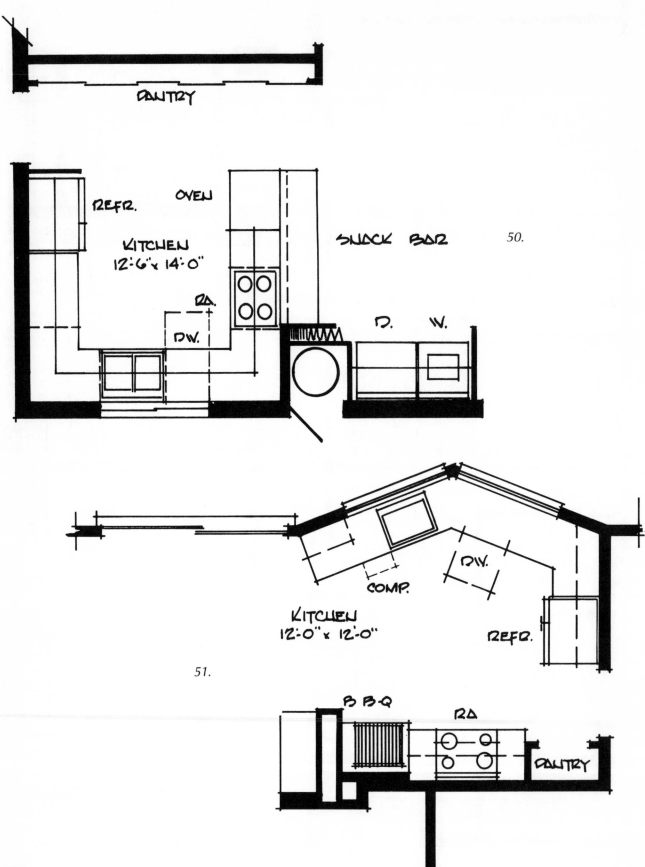

PANTRY

REFR.

OVEN

KITCHEN
12'-6" x 14'-0"

SNACK BAR

50.

RA.

DW.

D.   W.

COMP.

KITCHEN
12'-0" x 12'-0"

REFR.

51.

BBQ

RA

PANTRY

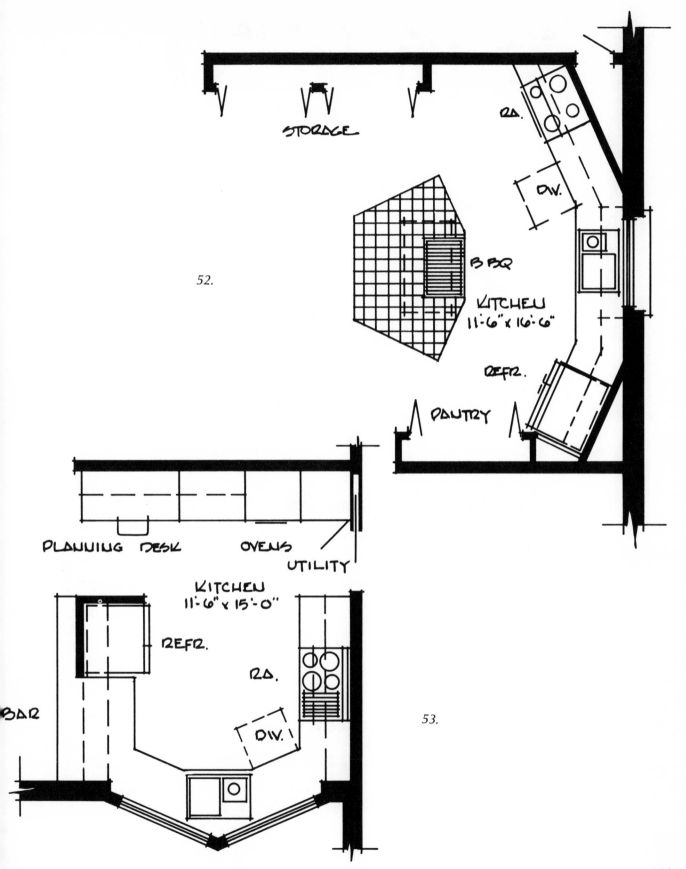

52.

STORAGE

RA.

DW.

BBQ

KITCHEN
11'-6" x 16'-6"

REFR.

PANTRY

PLANNING DESK   OVENS

UTILITY

KITCHEN
11'-6" x 15'-0"

REFR.

RA.

DW.

BAR

53.

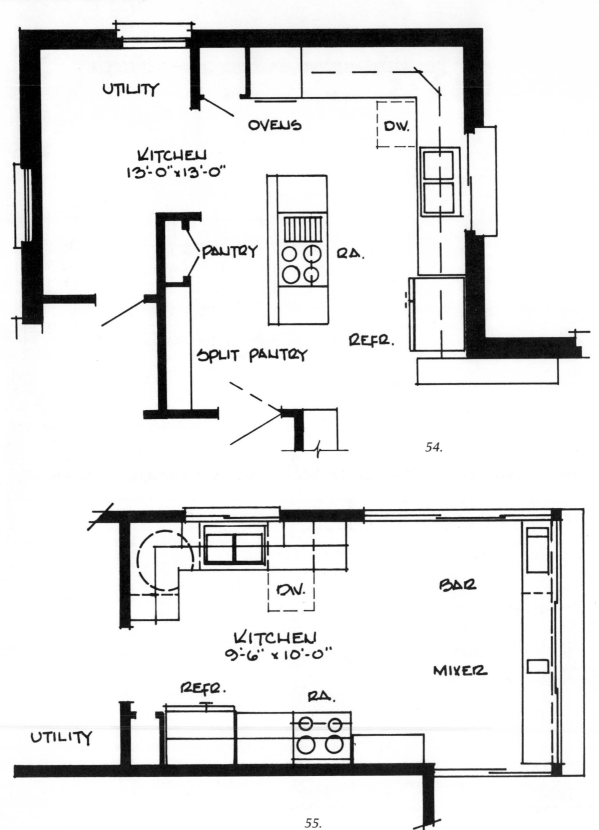

UTILITY

OVENS

KITCHEN
13'-0"x13'-0"

DW.

PANTRY

RA.

SPLIT PANTRY

REFR.

54.

DW.

KITCHEN
9'-6" x 10'-0"

BAR

MIXER

REFR.

RA.

UTILITY

55.

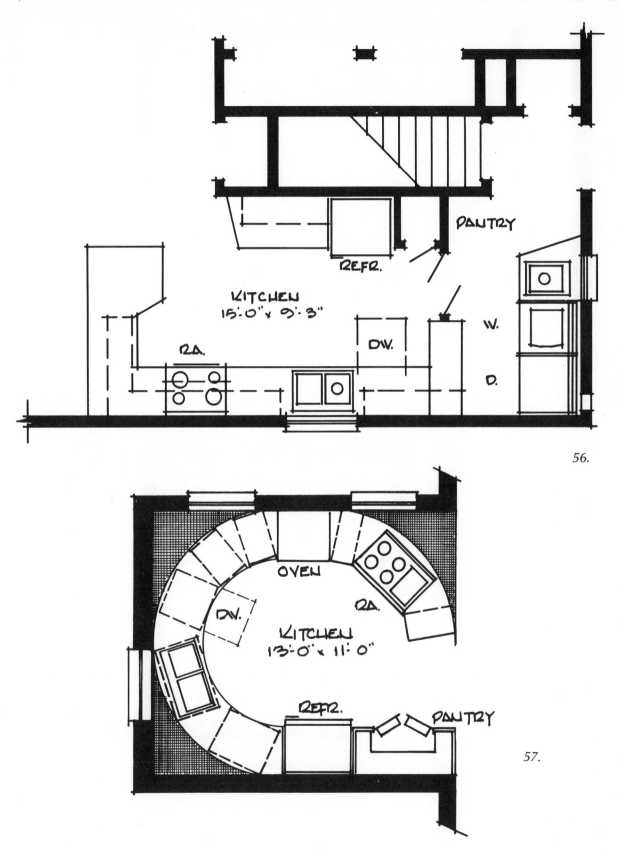

KITCHEN
15'-0" x 9'-3"

PANTRY

REFR.

R.A.

DW.

W.

D.

56.

OVEN

DW.

R.A.

KITCHEN
13'-0" x 11'-0"

REFR.

PANTRY

57.

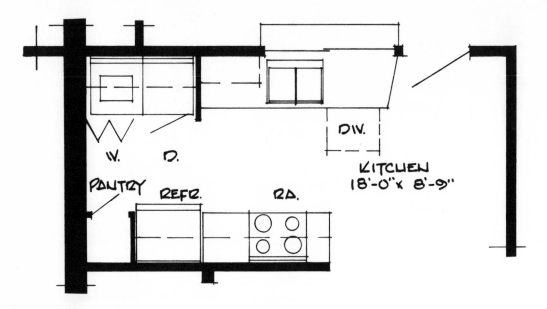

W.   D.

PANTRY   REFR.   RA.

DW.

KITCHEN
18'-0" x 8'-9"

58.

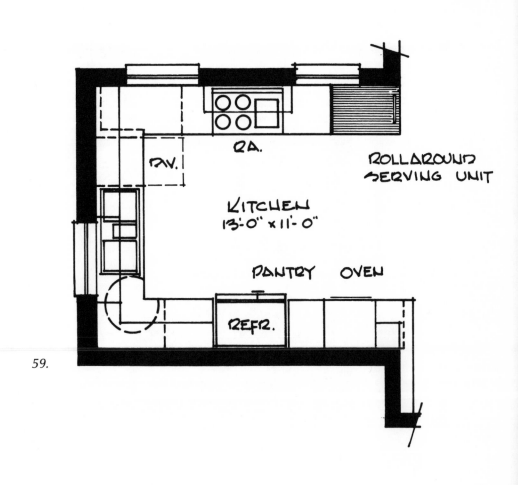

RA.

DW.

ROLLAROUND
SERVING UNIT

KITCHEN
13'-0" x 11'-0"

PANTRY   OVEN

REFR.

59.

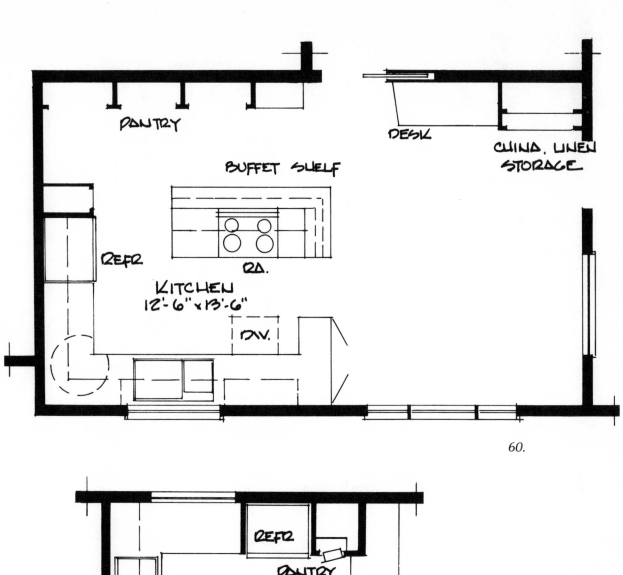

PANTRY

DESK

CHINA, LINEN
STORAGE

BUFFET SHELF

REFR

RA.

KITCHEN
12'-6" x 13'-6"

DV.

60.

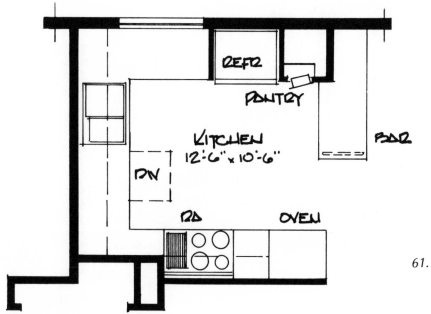

REFR

PANTRY

KITCHEN
12'-6" x 10'-6"

BAR

DW

RA

OVEN

61.

A built-in Sub-Zero refrigerator was used in this kitchen, and decorator panels matching the cabinets were used on both refrigerator and KitchenAid dishwasher to integrate the design.

This kitchen, designed by Imperial Cabinet Co., forms a peninsula to provide both counter space and brunch area, then adds a brick peninsula to that for the Jenn-Air cooktop. Chandelier gives general light, supplemented by recessed down lights.

Quaker Maid's Clarion cabinets are used in this spacious kitchen which includes even a fireplace. Notice the large wood-framed ventilating hood which serves cooking island that has both a cooktop and a barbecue grill.

Simple, roomy kitchen is fully carpeted, gains extra distinction with wood treatment at window to match cabinets. This is Centennial line marking 100th anniversary of Connor Forest Industries.

Southwest-style kitchen, with diagonal corner treatment of drop-in range, is a cross between a U and a one-wall. Dishwasher has wheels so it can be rolled over to the sink. Ceramic tile is used for backsplash and door framing. GE photo.

Kemper's Manor Oak cabinets form a cooking island in this kitchen, giving a work triangle not interrupted by passing traffic.

U-shaped kitchen designed by Howard Sersen of Reynolds Enterprises, River Grove, Ill., has wood beams to frame the chandelier. Countertop is angled at corner to avoid constricting the entrance, and corners are radiused to prevent hip bruises.

House & Garden magazine's 1972 "Super Family Room Kitchen" has a complete wall of equipment that disappears behind folding doors. The wall includes double wall oven, dishwasher, sink and refrigerator (all showing) plus incinerator, heater and laundry.

Textures and contrasts are the story in this kitchen, small but complete. Cabinets are wood, painted white to contrast with black decorative hinges and pulls.

Lattice work in window throws interesting lighting effect. Outside window is around corner, and a duplicate window has been created over sink to adjacent living area. Wood framing and crisscross members match cabinetry. Floor covering is Congoleum.

Yes, there are round kitchens. This unusual one has solid maple countertops and a space-saving drop-in range. Open shelving demands extra neatness from the housewife. Floor covering here is Armstrong's Carriage Park cushioned vinyl.

You might notice first the bold stripes on the walls, or the massive monogram or the wood cutouts beside the brunch table in foreground. But a very valuable feature of this Hotpoint kitchen is the lowered counter behind the model. It's a pass-through area.

This is a real wrap-around kitchen, but the island cooking center keeps the work triangle tight and the eating counter in the foreground is great for entertaining. Cabinets are Kemper's Cortina, an oak line.

Super kitchen by Modern Kitchens of Syracuse (N.Y.) has built-in refrigerator at far end, double wall ovens in brick wall, barbecue under brick arch.

Another by Kitchens Unlimited features ceramic tile again on countertop, backsplash and floor, but appearance is quite different with free-standing range and white dishwasher. Appliances are Westinghouse. Base cabinet in corner is a pie-cut lazy susan.

Spacious cooking island by Kennedy Kitchens, Horseheads, N.Y., has a properly-raised section behind Thermador cooktop to form protective backsplash. It also has food warming drawer at bottom left. But the brightest idea shows in background—

—This opening in the cabinet wall, beside the built-in refrigerator, has AM-FM radio-intercom at top, infra-red warming light recessed along with a matching white flood (because you can't really see by infra-red) and even a convenience outlet at back.

Another bright idea in the same Kennedy kitchen is this lowered work surface with maple block top. Kennedy studied some kitchen research at Cornell University, found that most work surfaces were too high for most women. That's a Trade-Wind built-in can opener in wall.

124

Bisulk Kitchens, Garden City, N.Y. used Dacor artificial brick for this cooking wall with Waste-King double wall oven. Designer put the wood beam across cooking alcove to hide vent equipment and lighting, made the crisscrosses on base cabinets himself to add to ambience.

Swiss theme was followed in every detail in this by Modern Kitchens of Syracuse, N.Y. It has flowered Swiss wallcovering on ceiling, wood beams, wrought iron hanging light fixture, artificial brick, big maple chop-block table. Note diagonal corner wall cabinet to fit over Radarange, skylight in ceiling. Cabinets are Wood-Mode, drop-in range is Thermador.

Wood-beamed ceiling complements the Quaker Maid cabinets in this kitchen by Kitchens, Inc., Narrowsburg, N.Y. Plastic-laminate-covered window box pushes sink out from wall, so countertop was made to protrude to compensate.

St. Charles kitchen has interesting serpentine layout, with steel cabinets relieved by wood beams in ceiling and massive wood vent hood. Wall cabinets also have wood doors, and walls are wood.

Another Betterhouse kitchen has candlelight fixtures mounted on two blank wall cabinets flanking sink, recessed shelf over sink, spice box recessed into wall over Corning cooktop.

Swiss Chalet kitchen by Betterhouse, Wyoming, Pa., combines with family entertainment center at other side of same large room. Woodlike beams are Williams polyurethane. Curved doors in mixing center island are exclusive with MarVell.

Betterhouse specializes in innovative cover-ups for peninsulas that face other rooms. Here carpet is run up the front of the peninsula and glued. In other picture, artificial leather was stretched across front, punched and buttons tied to plywood behind.

↓ Kitchens by Krengel, St. Paul, Minn., was designed first and then the home was built to fit it. Kitchen sink is at far wall. Center island has two Corning cooktops. Near island has a bar sink plus eating bar. Circular soffit defines kitchen area. Cabinets are solid cherry by Keystone.

Totally different Mediterranean effect by Ray Swearingen Co. of Chevy Chase, Md., uses Keystone white glacial ash cabinets with colorful bullfighters on front of island.

A complete food and beverage service center for office suites or home entertainment centers, in the Crane Chef line of unit kitchens, has the appearance of a fine piece of contemporary furniture when closed.

7
Lighting in the Kitchen

As a last resort, one can go to the statistics of the National Safety Council to underscore the need for good lighting in the kitchen. According to the NSC the kitchen is the most dangerous room in the home, accounting for 1,150,000 accidents per year, 26 percent of all falls and burns in the home, and 12 percent of all home fatalities.

All of these accidents are chiefly the results of poor illumination, according to the council.

But who needs last resorts? Lighting has a lot more going for it than the threat of accident.

It's useful, enabling us to see quickly and easily.

It can contribute to the beauty and individuality of the kitchen and the entire home. It even can be the salient feature of overall decor, if one wants to use it that creatively.

Unfortunately, the single ceiling fixture in the kitchen still is too much with us. It dates back to past decades when putting more light in the kitchen could be accomplished only by putting in a bigger bulb and hoping the fuse wouldn't blow.

It still probably is the most common way to light a kitchen, although modified now by a somewhat more modern fixture with three or four smaller bulbs and a much more efficient diffusing shield, or shade.

This is adequate, if bright enough, but adequacy does not add the charm that sells homes or makes an efficient kitchen.

This chapter will tell specifically how much light to use and where to put it, but first, the elementary facts of light.

In the planning stage and in choosing products, there are three basic terms that need definition.

The *candela* is the unit of luminous intensity of a light source in a specific direction. While its precise definition may be more than anyone really wants to know, for those interested it is 1/60 of the intensity of a square centimeter of a black body radiator operated at the freezing point of platinum, which is 2047 degrees Kelvin.

A *lumen* is the unit for measuring the light-producing power of a light source, and lamps are usually rated by their total lumen output. A lumen is the rate at which light falls on a one-square-foot area surface from a source which has an intensity of one candela. The number of lumens per watt indicates the efficiency of the light source.

A *footlambert* is a unit for measuring the brightness of light emitted or reflected from a surface directly into the eye at the rate of one lumen per square foot of area as viewed from any direction.

Light in the kitchen, as in other rooms of the house, usually is expressed in terms of watts. This is sufficient only when related to distance from light source to use area, transmittance through whatever shades are used, reflectance from all kitchen surfaces (which can make a tremendous difference in lighting efficiency) and absorptance, which is the amount of light lost by being absorbed by dark surfaces.

All of those factors can be calculated but, practically speaking, common sense can be relied on to make sure there is enough light—if it is educated common sense. The common sense of an architect will be much more reliable than the common sense of a home owner who seldom appreciates such technicalities as absorption or reflection factors.

The ultimate proof of lighting efficiency is measurement of the lumens in the various areas of the kitchen. They can be measured by using a General Electric light meter available from any photographic store or from the GE Large Lamp Department, Nela Park, Cleveland. (There are many brands of light meters, but many of them do not read in lumens, hence cannot be used for this purpose.)

Nela Park, incidentally, is a virtual university of lighting knowledge and techniques. Short courses are available there and many booklets are available, notably *Residential Structural Lighting* and *Light Measurement and Control.*

There are three sources of light to be considered in kitchen design:

1. *Natural daylight,* available through
   a. Windows, bright and cheerful in the morning with east exposure, miserable in late afternoon if exposure is west. No factor at night.
   b. Skylights, available in transparent or translucent plastics and a great sales point.
2. *Incandescent light,* from bulbs available in various shapes and sizes ranging from small night lights up to 300 watts. This light is produced by heating any material, usually metal, to a temperature at which it glows. Usually bulbs have a tungsten filament in a vacuum or mixture of argon and nitrogen.
   a. Bulbs can be clear or frosted, or colored to give a warmer light.
   b. Special types have reflector surfaces so they can be directed upward for indirect lighting, or downward for spot or floodlighting, broad or narrow beam.
3. *Fluorescent light,* glass tubes coated on the inside with fluorescent powder, filled with vaporized mercury and argon and sealed with two cathodes. Electric current activates the gas which produces invisible ultraviolet rays which causes the powder coating to fluoresce, producing visible light.
   a. All bulbs are tubular, but they might be straight or circular.
   b. Straight tubes vary generally from 9 to 60 inches and 6 to 100 watts. Length of the tube is a factor in the wattage.
   c. Color choices are all shades of white including Daylight, which emphasizes blues and greens; White, emphasizing yellows and yellow greens; Standard Cool White and Standard Warm White, lacking in reds; Deluxe Cool White and Deluxe Warm White, with some reds; Soft White, good for pinks and tans.

   d. Deluxe Warm White is generally most satisfactory.

Incandescent and fluorescent bulbs both have their advantages, and that means it is a good idea to use a mixture of both in the kitchen.

Advantages of incandescence are:

1) Fixtures and bulbs are less costly.
2) Light is warmer and generally more acceptable because we are accustomed to it.
3) Textures and forms usually are more attractive because the light comes from a relatively small source.
4) The light is instant-on.
5) There is no flicker or hum, as is often the case with fluorescence, and less chance of interference with radio or television.

Advantages for fluorescent tubes include:

1) Much more efficient light production, about 250 percent more than incandescence for the current used.
2) Bulbs last about seven times longer than incandescent bulbs.
3) Large light source produces much less glare and spreads the light more.
4) Almost no heat is produced, whereas incandescent bulbs are a definite heat factor.

In planning for lighting, bulbs and tubes can be mixed. For example, the heat and glare factors are insignificant if an incandescent ceiling fixture is used for general lighting, and here the instant-on factor would be valuable. So the planner might want this pleasant general illumination.

But the planner also must have sufficient glareless light where it is needed for close work, and good illumination at danger points, and there must be an esthetic consideration—the lighting should add to the beauty of the kitchen.

If the cabinets in the kitchen are dark the quantity of light must be increased, since dark surfaces absorb a lot of light. Dark flooring also calls for more light.

A dim light level tends to be relaxing and restful.

A bright light level tends to be stimulating and makes people feel more energetic.

Lights at eye-level are not desirable, usually, and must be well shielded so they do not shine directly

Well-lighted kitchen has general lighting, as provided by this cornice installation that shines light both above and below, plus task lighting as is gained here from fixtures below wall cabinets.

The standard in too many homes still is the single ceiling fixture, as shown here. This was modernized with addition of cornice lighting plus a pull-down fixture which puts light directly onto table.

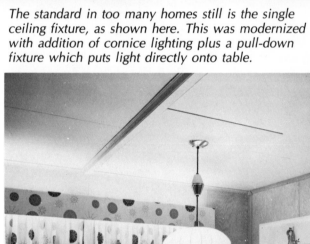

Here a full luminous ceiling is the best of all, affording generous general light, supplemented by task lighting under wall cabinets. (AIKD photo).

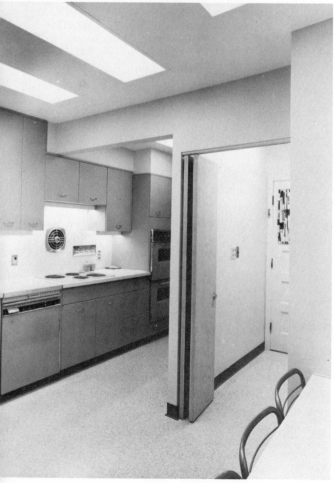

Another well-lighted kitchen has luminous ceiling panels for general light, fixtures under all wall cabinets.

133

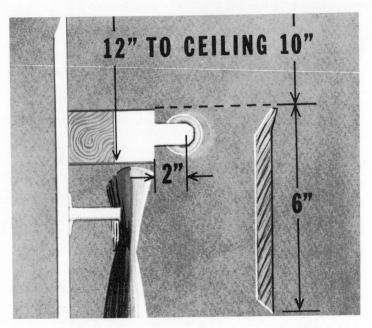

Structural lighting offers good solutions for the kitchen as well as for other rooms in the house. This drawing shows recommendations for a valance lighting installation. Faceboards should be not less than 6", not more than 10". Inside should always be painted flat white.

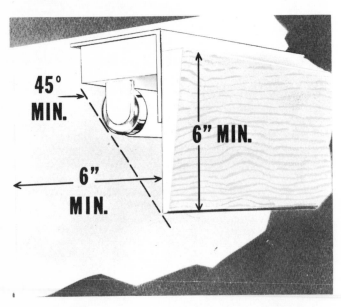

In cornice construction, there should be 2" to 3" between center of fluorescent tube and surface to be lighted. Faceboard should be painted flat white on inside, and channel should be as close to faceboard as possible.

into the eyes. Lights at levels high in the room tend to seem formal, and lights below eye-level seem friendly and attractive. But here again, they should not shine directly into the eyes.

Warm light is flattering to people and good for warm color schemes in the kitchen, but it deadens the blue end of the spectrum. Cool light is unflattering to people, but it adds to a sense of spaciousness. A favorable combination of these qualities would use warm light for general illumination and cool light for more specific lighting, but probably the best over-all solution, in the absence of an expert to develop special lighting effects, is to combine warm incandescence with warm fluorescent tubes.

All lighting experts and all kitchen experts and all home economists (and all lighting salesmen) will recommend two types of lighting in any kitchen:

1) General illumination, such as might be provided by the single ceiling fixture, an illuminated ceiling or perimeter soffit fixtures.
2) Task lighting, which puts light from separate sources directly onto specific work areas.

For general lighting, the American Home Lighting Institute recommends one fixture for every 50 square feet of area.

Each fixture should contain from 175 to 200 watts if incandescent, with a minimum 14-inch diameter for the fixture, or 60 to 80 watts if fluorescent; or, if the floor area of the kitchen is no more than 50 square feet, one suspended luminous-ceiling fixture measuring 24 square feet and with at least 360 watts incandescence.

For a fluorescent luminous ceiling in this application, the minimum depth from louvers to tube centers is 8 inches. A 40-watt tube is needed for every 12 square feet of room area. With incandescent bulbs, a 60-watt bulb is needed for every square feet of panel.

This applies, of course, for a normal, 8-foot ceiling. Light loses its effectiveness inversely with the square of the distance, and a 10-foot ceiling would call for more light. The visual criterion is that the general illumination should give adequate vision into drawers and cabinets, and there should be no difficulty reading labels.

Task lighting is needed in all food preparation areas along the countertop, over the range, over the sink, and at any other place where specific tasks are performed.

For countertop work surfaces, a fluorescent tube mounted at the bottom front of the overhanging wall cabinet will be about 15 inches above the counter, normally, and this calls for one 20-watt tube for every three feet of counter.

To break this down to a practical situation, this means a 20-watt tube for from 24 to 36 inches of counter; a 30-watt tube for from 36 to 48 inches of counter, and a 40-watt tube for from 48 to 60 inches of counter.

This wattage is good for up to 22 inches above the counter, a height that is unfortunately high for wall cabinets, but it is not uncommon in cost-cutting kitchens.

A 2-socket incandescent bracket with 60 watts in each socket is the equivalent for each three feet of counter, but the fluorescent tube adapts so easily to this application that there is little reason to make the job harder with incandescence. Overhang of the wall cabinet's face frame often provides all the shielding necessary for a fluorescent tube.

If there is no wall cabinet, the tube will have to be shielded fully so it does not shine in the eyes. In this case it will be wall-mounted with the tube toward the front. When a standard channel fixture is mounted at the bottom front of a wall cabinet, the tube goes toward the rear. In this case shielding will not be needed even if there is no face frame overhang, as long as the wall cabinet is at standard height—51 inches from the floor.

Task lighting over the sink may come from the ceiling or the soffit, or it may be wall-mounted.

From ceiling or soffit, a situation where normally there is a window flanked by cabinets, there can be:

1) One recessed fixture with three 75-watt incandescent bulbs in a box at least 24 inches long, or two 40-watt or three 30-watt fluorescent tubes, or

2) Two recessed fixtures with inner reflectors with a 100-watt incandescent bulb in each, centered 18 inches apart, or

3) Two, or preferably three, bullets which might be recessed, pendant or surface-mounted, each with a 75-watt flood bulb.

All of these might or might not be shielded by a face frame connecting the flanking wall cabinets.

The same requirements apply to a cooktop or range in this location. But a range is usually mounted under

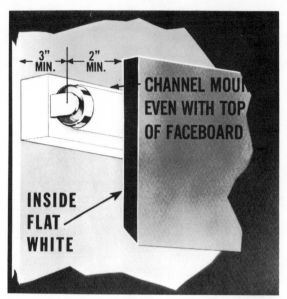

Wall brackets are most useful in structural lighting. The high wall bracket is really a valance without a window. Bracket must be high so light will spread over ceiling.

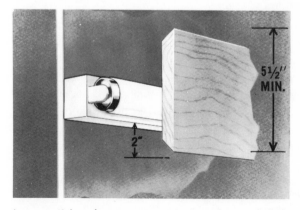

Low wall brackets are good for local or task lighting. Lamp should not be lower than 2" above bottom of shield. These are not used at more than 65" from floor.

135

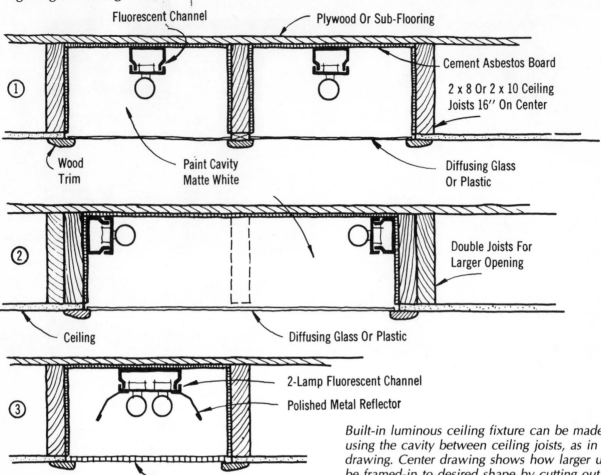

① Fluorescent Channel — Plywood Or Sub-Flooring — Cement Asbestos Board — 2 x 8 Or 2 x 10 Ceiling Joists 16'' On Center — Wood Trim — Paint Cavity Matte White — Diffusing Glass Or Plastic

② Ceiling — Diffusing Glass Or Plastic — Double Joists For Larger Opening

③ Louvers — 2-Lamp Fluorescent Channel — Polished Metal Reflector

Built-in luminous ceiling fixture can be made by using the cavity between ceiling joists, as in top drawing. Center drawing shows how larger units may be framed-in to desired shape by cutting out center joist and using double framing. Lamp arrangement shown is for decorative, non-uniform effect. Where more light is desired, two lamps with reflectors can be used, using louver as bottom shield instead of diffusing plastic.

a plain wall, with a hood 24 inches above and a cabinet above the hood. The hood should have one or two incandescent sockets or tubes.

If there is no hood there should be a wall bracket mounted from 14 to 22 inches above the range (or sink) allowing some upward light. Minimum is one 30-watt fluorescent tube or multiple-socket incandescent in a box at least 18 inches long with 60 or 75 watts in each socket.

A dining area in the kitchen area (not a brunch counter) requires separate illumination, even though it will benefit from the lighting in the kitchen.

Incandescence is favored here. It makes food look better and it is more flattering to the people and the colors of dishes and clothing.

It requires at least 150 watts in a fixture that directs light both upward and downward. A close-to-ceiling pendant fixture, or other suspended fixture, should be at least 17 inches in diameter, single or multiple sockets.

If fluorescence is used, a wall bracket would require one 36-inch 30-watt Deluxe Warm White tube, and light should be directed both upward and downward.

A brunch area in the kitchen that uses a countertop can use the same task lighting that has been installed for food preparation, but if any light is added, it should be consistent in design with the kitchen lighting. A higher intensity is called for here, as compared with the dining area, because brighter light makes people feel more energetic, as they would want to feel at breakfast or lunch time.

In this chapter there have been various references to the effect of light on color. It should be remembered that light and color are so inter-related that there really is no such thing as a light that shows color ''as it really is.'' Color is a function of light. For more on this, see Chapter 8, which discusses the use of color in the kitchen.

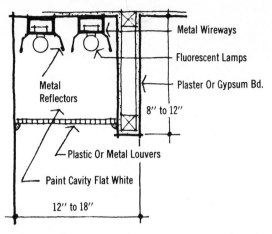

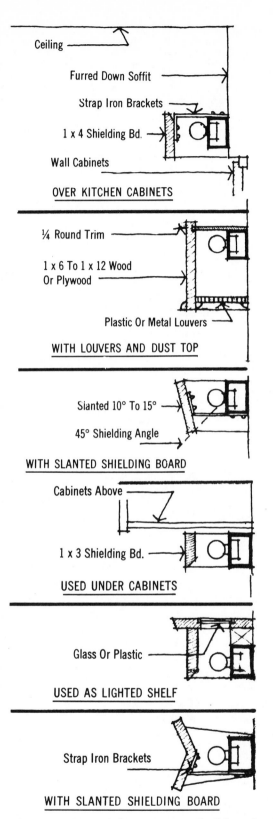

Ceiling

Furred Down Soffit

Strap Iron Brackets

1 x 4 Shielding Bd.

Wall Cabinets

OVER KITCHEN CABINETS

¼ Round Trim

1 x 6 To 1 x 12 Wood Or Plywood

Plastic Or Metal Louvers

WITH LOUVERS AND DUST TOP

Sianted 10° To 15°

45° Shielding Angle

WITH SLANTED SHIELDING BOARD

Cabinets Above

1 x 3 Shielding Bd.

USED UNDER CABINETS

Glass Or Plastic

USED AS LIGHTED SHELF

Strap Iron Brackets

WITH SLANTED SHIELDING BOARD

Here are some of the options in building the light on the job in the kitchen, for over the cabinets, shelving or under the wall cabinets.

Metal Wireways

Fluorescent Lamps

Plaster Or Gypsum Bd.

Metal Reflectors

8″ to 12″

Plastic Or Metal Louvers

Paint Cavity Flat White

12″ to 18″

When soffit over work area must provide a high level of light directly below, polished reflectors can double light output when used with open louvers. Only two rows of lamps are needed when polished metal reflectors are used.

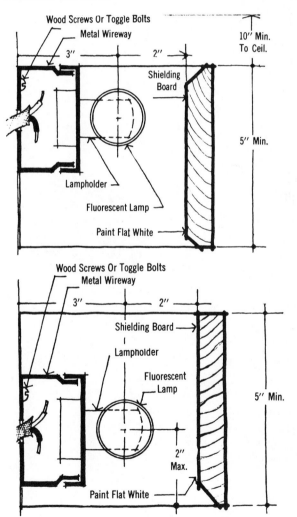

Wood Screws Or Toggle Bolts

Metal Wireway

3″   2″

10″ Min. To Ceil.

Shielding Board

Lampholder

Fluorescent Lamp

5″ Min.

Paint Flat White

Wood Screws Or Toggle Bolts

Metal Wireway

3″   2″

Shielding Board

Lampholder

Fluorescent Lamp

5″ Min.

2″ Max.

Paint Flat White

Detail of high and low type wall brackets.

137

Soffit Data; Lighting Photos

Location	Use	Cavity Dimensions				Deluxe Warm White Lamps	Parabolic Aluminum Reflectors	Material for Bottom Closure
		Depth	Width	Length	Finish			
Kitchen	Over sink or work center	8 to 12 in.	12 in.	38 in. min	Flat white	Two rows to fill length. Two 30-watt minimum.	Yes	Louvers
Bath or Dressing Room	Over large mirror	8 in.	14 to 18 in.	Length of mirror	Flat white	Two rows to fill length. Two 40-watt minimum.	No	White diffusing glass or plastic
		8 in.	18 to 24 in.	Length of mirror	Flat white	Three rows to fill length. Three 40-w. minimum.	No	White diffusing glass or plastic
								Lightly etched material acceptable
Living Area	Over piano, desk, sofa, or other seeing area	10 in.	Fit space Available 12 in. min	Fit Space Available 50 in. min	Flat white except matte black painted back wall surface	Two rows to fill length. Two 40-watt minimum.	Yes	Lightly figured or etched glass or plastic

Soffit construction data, as recommended by Nela Park.

Lighting fixture manufacturers make "false" luminous panel lights also, as well as fixtures that recess. Recessed squares are by Progress Lighting. Progress, Lightolier and NuTone are among those who make the types that attach below the ceiling.

Everything is plastic laminated in this, by Kennedy Kitchens, Horseheads, N.Y., including walls and ceiling. Horizontal panel over cooktop, just left of built-in oven, actually hides a fluorescent tube (and vent fan) which gives interesting wash of light above and below.

Those are windows under the wall cabinets in this kitchen by Charlotte Clark Kitchens, Detroit, a very unusual design feature. Fluorescent lighting is hidden above, where slope of ceiling meets tops of wall cabinets. Cabinets are plastic laminated, by National Industries.

Fluorescent luminous ceiling panels located over
work areas are supplemented by lights under the
hood and a dramatic pendant fixture.
(Hedrich-Blessing photo)

Well-designed small kitchen lighted by carefully
located ceiling fixtures and a light under the hood.
(Suter, Hedrich-Blessing photo)

"Bullet" fixtures light work areas, supplemented by
borrowed light from the dining area. (Bill Engdahl,
Hedrich-Blessing photo)

Antique lanterns provide accent lighting in colonial
kitchen. (Hedrich-Blessing photo)

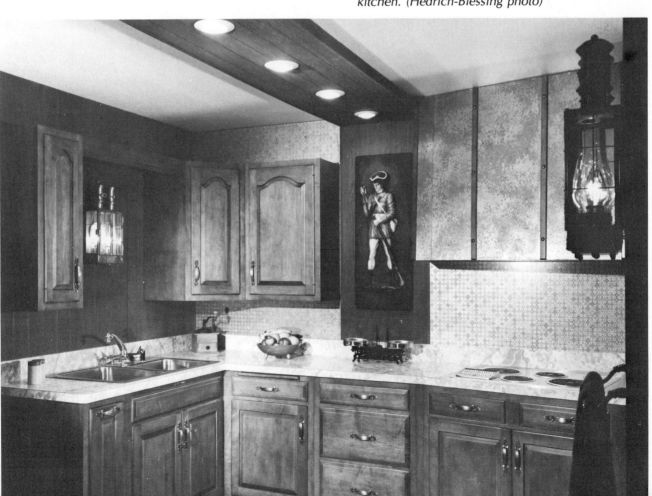

8
Color in the Kitchen

A New York tool manufacturer, bothered by production and quality-control problems, decided to coordinate colors of all machinery and walls. Production jumped 15 percent, rejected parts were reduced by 40 percent and absenteeism was reduced by 60 percent.

Firebrand football coach Knute Rockne had his team's dressing room walls painted bright red so the players would be stimulated through the halftime break. But he had the dressing room of the visiting team painted a restful blue so those players would lose their edge.

You can win a bet with your bartender by betting that a green $5 bill actually is red. Actually, it is every color except green because it absorbs all other colors and reflects, or rejects, green. So it isn't green. But try this only on a bartender who will listen to reason.

Color is possibly the most-used and least-understood phenomenon of both our physical and psychological worlds. It can be defined in terms of pigments and dyes, but the definition will fall short because it ignores both sensation and light. Some theorists insist it really is a sensation relating very personally to the viewer.

Anyone who buys a bright red car, parks it in daytime and then tries to find it later under a mercury street light will attest to the fact that color is very much a function of light source.

The consumer may become confused by the vagaries of light and color. A homeowner may visit a kitchen showroom and select cabinets for their warm, rich, reddish woodtones. When they are installed in his home, however, they may appear flat and gray. But he got the right cabinets. The difference in this case was that the showroom was lit by incandescent bulbs and his kitchen was lit by fluorescence.

Light has its peculiarities. We call it white light,

but when it is directed through an optical prism we find it contains all colors, splitting up into a spectrum ranging from infrared to ultraviolet. This is white light, and with all those colors in it, light itself is invisible. Yet without it, everything else is invisible.

The full spectrum contains more radiant energy both above and below the visible spectrum. Above ultraviolet, progressively, are X-rays, gamma rays, and cosmic rays. Below infrared are microwaves (used for cooking in microwave ovens, and used in radar), television, radio, and electric power.

All of these have repeating wave patterns traveling in straight paths, in all directions from their source. All travel at 186,000 miles per second. All are identified by their particular ranges of frequencies, or number of wave cycles per second. The shortest wavelength known is that of the cosmic ray, one thousand-millionth of a second, or one twenty-five millionth of an inch. An electric power wave, at the other end of the spectrum, has an average wavelength of 3100 miles.

The visible spectrum is but a small part of this broad band, from 15 to 30 millionths of an inch. Wavelengths longer or shorter than this do not stimulate the receptors of the eye and so cannot be seen. Physically, the only difference between ultraviolet and infrared, or between blue and green and yellow and red, is progressively longer wavelengths.

Without light there would be no colors, since colors are simply other ways to describe different mixtures of wavelengths of light.

How then can colors be physical properties of objects?

An apple is always red or a head of lettuce is always green because of "color constancy," which means they always reflect or transmit light waves only in a particular narrow color range while absorbing all others. They are selective in the waves they reflect and this selectivity remains the same.

When we look at a red apple, however, we look at it and can see it only because light is present from whatever light source. That light might be white light, which contains all colors. The apple absorbs all the blues and greens and reflects only red and it looks as we think it should look. If we put a green filter over the white light it will absorb all colors other than its own color, transmitting only green. The apple then will appear much darker and virtually colorless because there is very little red energy to be reflected in the green light.

That is, what happened to the consumer we mentioned earlier, whose red car turned brown and whose kitchen cabinets turned gray.

It becomes obvious, then, that all this talk of wavelengths is not quite enough. There also is the matter of the human eye—plus the element of human interpretation.

A person who is totally color blind cannot distinguish between the various wavelengths of light. They all look gray to him, but this does not change the facts of those wavelengths. If one person sees a red apple and the other person sees the same apple as gray, it is only the *concept* that is different. Now we are out of the realm of physical laws and in the realm of personal concepts.

From there it is an easy step to *impressions,* or what we think or how we feel.

There are three primary colors, but they are different for light and for pigments.

The primary colors of light are red, green, and blue. They are called additive primaries because they can be added to produce the secondary colors, magenta (red plus blue), cyan (green plus blue), and yellow (red plus green). A secondary color of light, mixed with its opposite primary, will give white light.

Primary colors in pigments are magenta, cyan, and yellow. These are subtractive primaries because in pigments a primary color is defined as one that subtracts, or absorbs a primary color of light and reflects the other two.

To get familiar with all the terms:

1) Hue is the name of the color.
2) The lightness or darkness of a color is its value.
   a. Adding black to a color gives a shade.
   b. Adding white to a color gives a tint.
   c. Adding gray gives a tone.
3) A color's purity or strength is called its intensity.

Complementary hues are those directly *opposite* each other on the color wheel. Analogous hues are those *next* to each other. *(for a typical color wheel, see page 24.)*

To mix complementary hues is to neutralize. If you physically mixed the pigments you would end up with a neutral gray, but putting them next to each other adds contrast—extreme contrast.

Extreme contrast is great, if not overdone. If the entire color scheme of a room is based solely on contrast, the result is disastrous.

There are as many color theories as there are color theorists.

From this point on we will be thoroughly practical and use the terms as they probably will appear on the color wheel that might be picked up from any paint supplier. If a retail paint store does not have one, the retailer can order it from any major manufacturer.

To blend colors properly in a kitchen, a color wheel should be used.

The color wheel will show three primary colors, red, blue and yellow. Secondary colors will show as the blending of any two primary colors. Between red and blue there will be purple. Between blue and yellow will be green. Between yellow and red will be orange. All of these are secondary colors.

If any chosen color is mixed in with its complementary color (the color directly across from it in the color wheel) the mixture results in a neutral gray. The sum of all colors, remember, is gray. If red is the chosen color the complement must be the sum of the other colors to make up a gray so, going directly across the color wheel, that would be the point directly between yellow and blue, which would be green. So green, containing both yellow and blue, is the complement of red.

The human eye always strives for natural balance. The eyes like colors which, if mixed, would add up to a gray.

A kitchen that is all red might look exciting at first to a homeowner, but it will wear on the nerves and, sooner or later, need to be changed. One that contains all elements of all three primaries, with one

Color as Wave Length

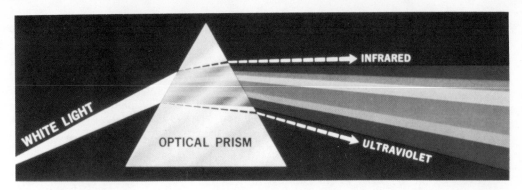

We call it white light, but it contains all colors. We discover that by bending a ray of light through a prism. This is the visible spectrum.

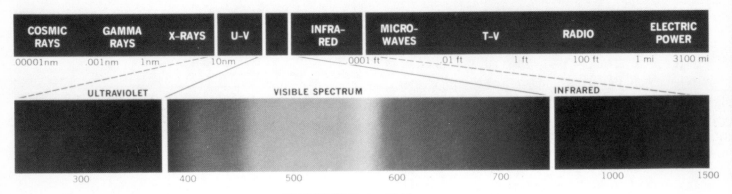

COSMIC RAYS	GAMMA RAYS	X-RAYS	U-V		INFRA-RED	MICRO-WAVES	T-V	RADIO	ELECTRIC POWER
.00001nm	.001nm	1nm	10nm		.0001 ft	.01 ft	1 ft	100 ft	1 mi 3100 mi

ULTRAVIOLET   VISIBLE SPECTRUM   INFRARED

300   400   500   600   700   1000   1500

WAVELENGTH (Nanometers)

The visible spectrum is only a small part of the total spectrum of radiant energy, as indicated here. It ranges from a cosmic ray, one 25 millionth of an inch, to electric rays with wave lengths 3100 miles long.

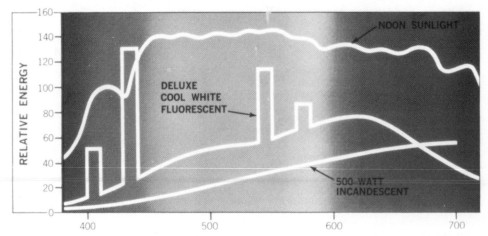

WAVELENGTH (Nanometers)

(From "Light and Color," publication of the Large Lamp Dept., General Electric)

This drawing shows the relative color rendering of different light sources. Incandescent lamps, the bottom line, have higher relative energy in the red end of the spectrum, which is to the right. Fluorescent lamps drop off in the red end, but are high in the blue area of the spectrum to the left.

dominating and the others highlighting, will be pleasing for a long time.

In a kitchen the elements to consider for color are the cabinets, the appliances, the countertops, the ceiling, the walls, and the floor. Beyond that, accessories can be color highlights.

The procedure is:

1) Establish the dominating color.
2) Decide where it will go.
3) Using the color wheel, establish the complementary colors.
4) Decide where they will go.

For the dominating color—and by dominating, here, we mean the one that will be most generally used in the kitchen—you might decide on the popular avocado, which is a green. The color wheel shows red directly across, so some red will have to be used in the kitchen. There might be avocado cabinets, and the green could be picked up in a lighter tint in the soffit and on the ceiling. There could be a dramatic red countertop, or even red appliances, or the red might be only a curtain at the window. Red would have to be there somewhere.

You might choose a blend of greens and yellows for cabinets, countertop, appliances, walls, and ceiling. Directly across the wheel from green and yellow is red-purple, and even a simple dish display on a wall in this tertiary color would suffice. But it must be there, however small.

Here are some other points to remember:

1) You cannot get appliance and cabinet colors to match exactly. So use complementary colors, or contrasting shades of the same color.
2) Usually, the fewer colors used the better, and keep window and door trim the same color as the walls.
3) Color intensifies in a north room or in a small room, so use tints except for accents.
4) North light is cold. If the room has a north

window it is best to use colors from the warm side of the wheel with the cold colors for accents.
5) A strong color on the ceiling tends to make the ceiling "come down" oppressively. Use very light colors on the ceiling or keep it neutral gray or white.
6) It usually is better to keep darker colors lower in the kitchen than the countertop.
7) Remember the lighting. Incandescence can brighten warm colors, such as yellow. Blue shaded toward green can appear green when the lights are on.
8) An *expensive* dish or drape can furnish a ready-made color scheme. Such expensive items are not color-keyed by cheap labor. They are designed by the best color brains in the business.
9) Warm hues are conspicuous, cheerful, stimulating. They appear to come toward you, to pull things together, to make objects look larger.
10) Cool hues are more restful, separate things, and make objects look smaller. They can be cold and depressing.
(There is a physiological explanation for some of that. Red rays register behind the eye's retina, and the eye pulls them forward simply by pulling them into focus. Cool rays register in front of the retina and are pushed back in focusing.)
11) While warm hues *increase* the apparent size of things within a room, when these hues are used as wall colors they *decrease* the apparent size of the room. The same is true of high intensities. Sharp contrast brings objects forward.
12) Be sure colors are selected under the same lighting conditions as will exist in the kitchen. All colors, even white and black, will look different under fluorescence and under incandescence.
13) If there is a lot of natural light in the kitchen, dark colors can be used more effectively. If the kitchen must depend on artificial light, lighter colors are usually more satisfactory.

9

Floors, Walls and Ceilings

Floorcovering is one of the most important parts of the kitchen because it is one of the most readily noticeable design elements. It affects color scheme. It affects lighting. It can help make the room seem larger or smaller, warmer or colder.

The first choice that must be made is between carpeting and resilient floorcovering.

The resilients dominate by far. As a category there are no bad ones, although some are better than others. They range from cheap to expensive, and the really good ones incorporate softness without sacrificing durability.

Carpeting is used more in remodeled kitchens, although still far outdistanced by resilients. It puts a real luxury look and feel into a kitchen and, despite its critics, it is very practical. It does, however, arouse considerable sales resistance among people who have never tried it.

Here are the flooring choices, with their good and bad points.

1. *Asphalt Tile*—low in cost and resistant to alkali stains. This material is fairly easy to maintain and it can be installed directly over a concrete base below or above grade.

   However, it is only fair in resiliency and, being harder, is not as quiet as other materials. Lighter colors are much higher in price.

2. *Asbestos Vinyl Tile*—an improvement over asbestos tile, blending asbestos and vinyl for clearer, cleaner colors and more resiliency. It can be laid on, above or below grade. It is somewhat more expensive than asphalt tile. It is durable and stain resistant.

3. *Vinyl*—in tiles or sheets, plain or cushioned. In tiles, this is luxury material with excellent colors and patterns. In sheet form it is moderately priced. It is very durable and has superior resistance to stains and can be laid on, above or below grade. Tiles are fairly expensive, and any vinyl must be laid over very smooth base. It scratches fairly easily.

4. *Linoleum*—the well-known material is moderately priced, fairly durable, easy to maintain, but does not resist alkali stains very well. Very wide choices of colors and patterns, including sculptured and inlaid effects. It is somewhat porous and so needs good home maintenance to guard against ground-in dirt. Overall, a best buy, despite its deficiencies. Lay only on suspended floors.

5. *Others* include rubber tile, very quiet and very resilient with good resistance to grease and alkalis; vinyl cork tile, very expensive, but worth it; vinyl bonded ceramic tile, a new, very expensive product which overcomes many objections of ceramic tile because the little 1-inch tiles are embedded in vinyl, making it softer, quieter and more acceptable to the home buyer.

For an ultra-luxury look, a builder might want to use ceramic tile or experiment with the genuine wood veneers embedded in clear plastic, offered only by Parkwood Laminates.

And then there is carpeting. The advent of man-made fibers such as nylon made it a suitable material for kitchen installation, and residential kitchen installations are known that date back to 1955.

Now there are several such chemical fibers, and

Carpeting made with synthetic fibers is the growing thing in the kitchen, although it may never approach resilient flooring. This chart shows some of the comparative qualities of the various synthetic fibers.

Comparison chart of carpet fiber characteristics

Performance characteristics	Acrylic	Polyester	Nylon	Poly-propylene	Wool
Wear life	high	high	extra high	extra high	high
texture retention	good	good to medium	exceptional	good	good
abrasion resistance	good	very good	exceptional	exceptional	good
soil resistance	high	medium	medium	high	high
stain resistance	high	medium	medium	exceptional	medium
wet cleanability	good	good	high	high	good
static buildup	little	only in low humidity	very much	very little	only in low humidity
moisture absorbency	little	little	some	lowest	highest
mildew	resists	resists	resists	resists	subject to mildew
moth protection	no effect	no effect	no effect	no effect	needs treatment
non-allergenic	completely	completely	completely	completely	minor
Appearance characteristics					
Appearance	warm, soft, luxurious	soft, luxurious	dull to lustrous	subdued luster	soft, warm, luxurious
Dyeability	good	good, but brilliance limits	good	medium	good
Crush resistance	medium	medium	good	low	medium
Resilience	high	medium	high	medium	high
Fade resistance	good	good	medium	good	medium
Economy characteristics					
Price range	medium	medium	low-medium	low-medium	high
Carpet yield per lb. fiber	medium	medium	high	highest	lowest

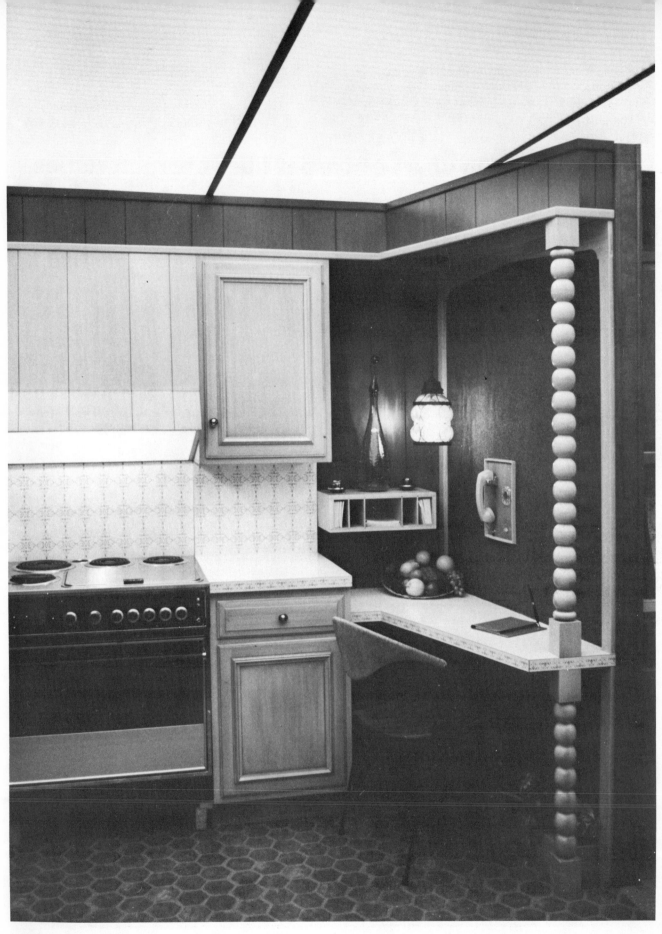

Cabinets and appliances cover most of the kitchen walls, and what's left usually is painted or covered with wall panels of wood or simulated wood. Here genuine wood is used at the desk wall, plastic laminate is run up the backsplash. Ceiling is fully luminous. The desk, incidentally, is a great addition in what would have been dead space. By Kitchens by Wieland, Allentown, Pa.

their comparative characteristics can be seen in the accompanying chart.

The important point to recognize is that kitchen carpet is not the same as indoor-outdoor carpet, although salesmen often tend to confuse this issue.

Indoor-outdoor carpet is a good, practical material for its application because water passes through it. It can be washed with a hose. This is great for a patio, but hardly practical in a kitchen.

Kitchen carpet, on the other hand, consists of a carpet surface separated from its sponge or foam backing by a water-proof bonding membrane. Water can not pass through it to the floor underlayment below. This means any spill—milk, eggs, or grease—can be washed up almost as easily as from resilient floorcovering. In the event of more serious damage, it can be patched easily. One brand, at least, even comes with a patching kit. It is a great kitchen flooring material.

Manufacturers recommend that a mastic be used to hold it tight to the floor. This author laid it loose, wall to wall and coved up into the kick-space of the cabinets, with 2-sided Scotch tape to hold it down at the two doorways, where it served for six years in a New York City apartment. It was then lifted and moved to a new suburban home, cut and patched to fit the new kitchen, with 2-sided tape used again to hold down all cut edges. The patchwork is absolutely undetectable, and it has served in the new home for three years and still looks like new. This is a good material.

Few things are more luxurious on a lazy Sunday morning.

Any flooring material must be chosen with design and color in mind. A small kitchen demands small patterns. A large kitchen can take bold motifs and large patterns. Stripes can add length or width to a room, adding the dimension in the direction of their axis.

Light colors are nearly always preferred for kitchen floors, unless a skilled decorator specifies otherwise for dramatic effect.

Walls

In the common concept, the walls of any kitchen are nearly covered with the cabinets and appliances, so what is there to do with them except paint them?

That is one easy solution, but visit any good kitchen showroom for some surprising answers to what is possible and much more commendable.

A kitchen is a special place. Things happen there that don't happen anywhere else in the home, things such as food preparation and cooking and cleanup. There are differences in heat, humidity, and in the characteristics of the air. In addition, it is a separate enclave with its own design that usually is quite independent of the design characteristics of the rest of the house.

Here are some of the options.

1) Plastic brick or stone, a lifetime material that simulates the original very precisely, but is light-weight and easily cleaned. It can be used on a wall or a section of one wall, but if more than that is used it tends to dominate the room. It is good for the sides of islands or peninsulas.

2) Plastic laminate, the same as on the countertop, often is extended all the way from the countertop to the bottoms of the wall cabinets. This is an excellent treatment and is unbeatable for clean-ability and neat appearance. It is not advisable behind a cooktop, however, because it can be darkened by the heat. It can be used on other walls and above the wall cabinets.

3) Panels of copper, stainless steel, porcelain enam-eled steel, or aluminum can be used behind a cooktop, in either sheet or tile form, for good protection and a very decorative effect.

4) Ordinary wall coverings can be decorative and effective, but they must not be of poor quality. A vinyl-coated wallpaper must be high quality to hold up under the necessary washing. A vinyl-coated fabric would be much better. When any of these are used, use large patterns only for large areas and small patterns for small areas. Light colors go best in small areas, and darker colors should be used only in large areas with good natural lighting.

5) Paint is the most common material for kitchen walls. A semigloss is best because enamels with their high gloss characteristics result in too much glare, and flat finishes are difficult to wash.

6) Vinyl-surfaced wall paneling can be very effective, especially in the light woodgrains. Darker wood-grains often are used to achieve separation of

In this kitchen (by Kitchen Concepts, Ft. Lauderdale, Fla.), desk area is covered by cabinetry, drape and shingled soffit above. Imitation brick is used for oven wall. Built-in Sub-Zero refrigerator occupies other wall.

Stucco and plaster also are favorites among kitchen specialists, especially for cooking walls. This is a Tappan design.

a dining area in or adjacent to the kitchen.

7) Ceramic tile is a beautiful and luxurious material for backsplash areas or for entire walls, although high first-cost and high installation costs usually have ruled it out among builders of speculative homes.

In Mexico, where both tile and labor are inexpensive, this bright and colorful material is used often for entire walls, floors and even ceilings. The effect is love at first sight, although the color combinations that we applaud in Mexico are usually too uninhibited for our homes in the United States.

It is well worth considering, though, for a spectacular model home or a distinctive option.

8) Kitchen carpeting is used effectively as a wall material by many kitchen specialists. They seldom use it all the way to the ceiling (although they might if it is a large room), but they often will cove it up to the window line or up the walls of an island or peninsula. This can be done easily and inexpensively with simple flooring adhesives.

Ceilings

Kitchen ceilings, like kitchen walls, usually are painted. Paint always is adequate. It should be light colored semigloss.

The best surfacing for a kitchen ceiling is acoustical tile or sheet. It can absorb up to 70 percent of the noise striking it, according to research by Armstrong Cork, and it also helps prevent kitchen noise from invading quiet areas above the kitchen.

Acoustical ceiling systems have matching lighting fixtures for clean-looking recessed installation.

The problem with acoustical tile is to get the border tiles on opposite sides of the room the same size, and as large as possible. The easy (cheap) way is simply to start at one end with full tiles and then to cut them off to the required size when the other end of the room is reached.

Armstrong Cork's formula for finding the right size for border tile is a simple one:

To find the size of the border tile for the *long* wall, using 12"×12" tile:

1) Measure one of the *short* walls of the room.
2) If this is not an exact number of feet, add 12

Armstrong's vinyl-coated Lyria Cushiontone acoustic panels have abstract pattern that conceals the acoustical perforations. This is a suspended ceiling.

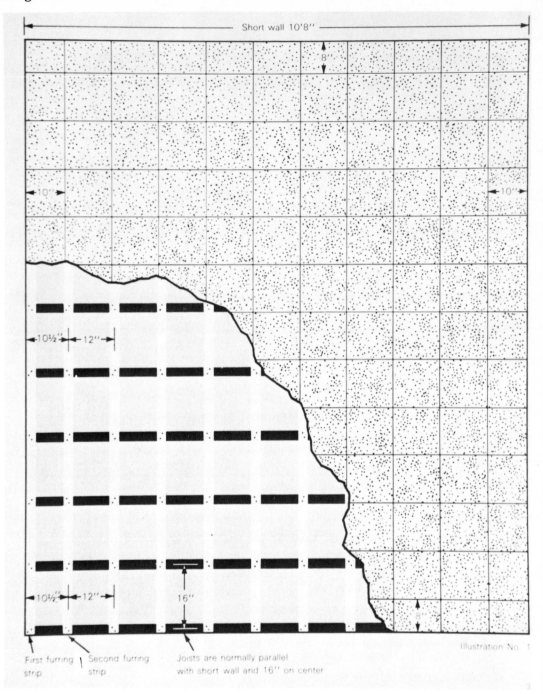

Short wall 10'8"

8"

10"

10"

10½" 12"

10½" 12"

16"

8"

Illustration No. 1

First furring strip | Second furring strip

Joists are normally parallel with short wall and 16" on center

Acoustical tile is the best material for a kitchen ceiling because of noise in the kitchen, and this material can deaden 70 to 75 percent of the noise striking it. These two illustrations show how to make it work out right, as described in text.

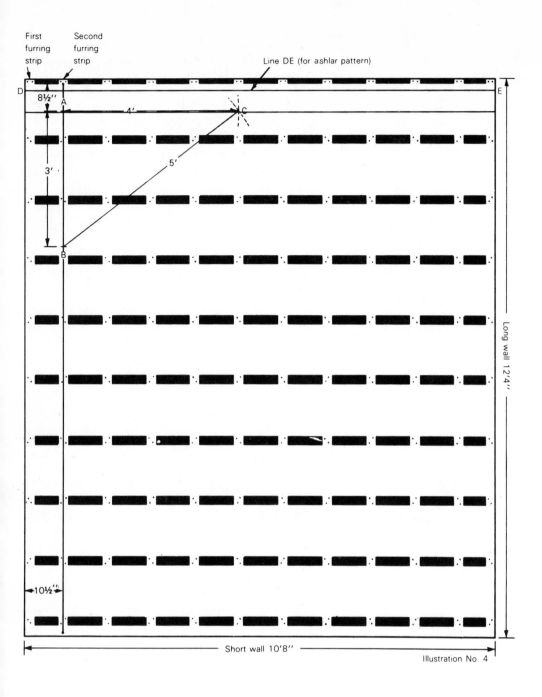

First furring strip

Second furring strip

Line DE (for ashlar pattern)

D

E

8½''

A

4'

C

3'

5'

B

Long wall 12'4''

10½''

Short wall 10'8''

Illustration No. 4

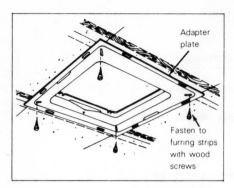

Ceiling systems using acoustical tile have lighting fixtures engineered to work with them. As an example, here is Armstrong system using its fixture, called Tilemate. In consecutive steps: (1) Adapter plate is installed; (2) Junction box is installed, according to directions; (3) Reflector pan comes next, fitting into tabs; (4) Glass lens then is installed in frame; (5) Frame/lens assembly then is attached to adapter plate; (6) For changing bulbs, assembly slides down and stops, allowing room for 100-watt bulb.

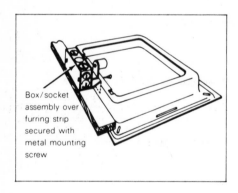

Box/socket assembly over furring strip secured with metal mounting screw

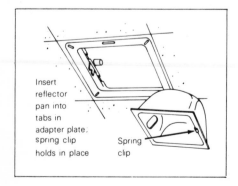

Insert reflector pan into tabs in adapter plate; spring clip holds in place

Spring clip

inches to the inches left over.

3) Divide the total number of inches (ignoring the feet) by two.

For example, if the short wall measures 10'8", there are 8" left over. Following step 2, add 12 inches to the leftover 8" which gives you 20". Divide this by two and you get 10", the size of the border tile along the two long walls of the room.

Border tiles for the short walls can be figured with the same procedure, this time measuring the long walls.

When using 16"×16" tile, convert the room measurement into inches. Divide this measurement by 16. Treat the extra inches the same way as with 12" tile, except that in step 3 add 16" instead of 12" and then divide by two.

Before installing acoustical tile, steps must be taken to be sure it goes up straight. Here is how to do it.

First, snap a chalk line the length of the second furring strip, down the center, along the long wall. Using our previous example, this will be 10-1/2 inches from the wall because that is the width of our border tile (10" plus 1/2" for the stapling flange). The first furring strip, of course, went flush against the wall.

Second, establish a second reference line at right angles to the first chalk line. To do this we follow the same formula we used to determine how much walls were out of square. Referring to the accompanying drawing:

1) Locate point A on the reference line, using short border tile measurement.
2) From Point A measure in exactly 3 feet along the reference line and mark that point as Point B.
3) Starting with Point A, measure exactly 4 feet and mark a small arc on the sixth furring strip.
4) From Point B measure exactly 5 feet toward the first arc, marking the point of intersection as Point C.
5) Snap a chalk line through Points A and C across all furring strips. This second reference line will be precisely perpendicular to the first.

In all cases, the first furring strips should be placed flush against the wall, the second strips at the widths of the border tiles, and the remainder on centers corresponding with tile size.

There are other things that can be done with ceilings.

154

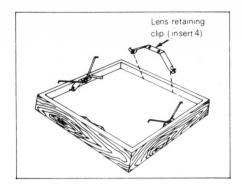

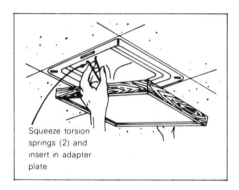

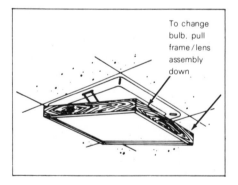

But there are other interesting methods. This effect is gained with Armstrong's Marquee vaulted lighting system.

Kitchen carpeting can be used creatively, as can be seen in the "Successful Kitchens" illustrations elsewhere in this book.

Solid wood (or apparent solid wood) beams are often used in large kitchens, but the heir apparent to the wood beam is the polyurethane beam. It is totally realistic, looking exactly like wood, but it is so light that a housewife can lift it with one hand and apply it to the ceiling with adhesive.

There is the modern version of the familiar skylight, made now of clear plastic that lets in lots of daylight but eliminates some of the old leakage problems.

10

Noise Control: The Growing Need

A University of Wisconsin psychiatrist, Dr. J. C. Westman, has reported that "the average kitchen is like a boiler room." He blames the growing cacophony for deterioration in marriage and family life.

The effects of noise, both in the home and at work, are being studied increasingly by government, industry, and consumer groups. Not too long ago a U.S. Department of Commerce panel on noise abatement produced a preponderance of evidence that noise—independent of loudness—can degrade the quality of our lives.

The problem is real enough for anyone to test in his own home, although most of us have become so accustomed to the various noises that we can ignore most of them.

Try this test. Adjust the television sound level for comfortable hearing, then relax in an easy chair and wait for the dishwasher, disposer, vent hood, any small appliance to start up in the nearby kitchen. Notice the bang of the solenoid as the dishwasher cycles, the hum of the refrigerator, and even the noise of a stream of water hitting the stainless steel sink. What about the squeak of an oven door, and the banging of cabinet doors and drawers, and the noise of drawer slides. We are only talking about the kitchen. There is also the flushing of toilets, the loud hum of the furnace blower or the air conditioner, etc.

Manufacturers are really doing something about it. Some disposers come with rubber mounts and rubber hose sections, and therefore, are much more quiet than others. Members of the Home Ventilating Institute have not only quieted their products but put stickers on them with their sone ratings.

The builder or remodeler can do much more, and he should, not only for the good of his customers but also for his own protection. With the growing awareness of environmental noise, standards will come. That's for sure.

Here are some of the minimums.

1) Mount the dishwasher, garbage disposer, and other appliances on pads or springs to prevent vibrations from being transmitted through the floor and countertops.
2) Wrap the sides of the dishwasher with glass fiber insulating material to prevent transmission of sound to cabinets and counter tops.
3) Use sponge rubber isolation gaskets at the mouth of the disposer to prevent the sink bowl from amplifying the grinding noise.
4) Balance the refrigerator by adjusting the set screws on the front of the unit to eliminate annoying vibration. It is balanced properly when the door closes automatically from a half-open position.
5) Place sound-absorbing mountings on the exhaust fan, and make sure the fan is large enough to operate efficiently at low speeds.
6) Install a flexible pipe, similar to an automobile radiator hose, between the drain and the trap to keep vibrations from being transmitted to other plumbing and into the walls.
7) Install pneumatic anti-hammer devices in the water lines.
8) Place rubber bushings behind cabinet doors to eliminate banging.
9) Check the drawer slides, and if they are noisy demand something better. Quiet ones are available.
10) Install an acoustical ceiling to help stifle reflected noises.

The accompanying drawings are by courtesy of Owens-Corning Fiberglas Corp.

TABLE I
Home Task Area Product Generated Noise Levels*

Column descriptions (left to right):
- maintains auditory attention and stimulates eye movement for localization
- threshold of annoyance environment – (50 to 90dB)
- airplane noises relatively unnoticed with background mus.
- activates automatic nervous system***
- increase in peristalsis, saliva & gastric juice flow
- annoyance threshold**
- work efficiency reduced
- eyes close, pupils dilate, skin pales, adrenalin increases
- increased response and error averages over lower pressure levels
- perceptible ear discomfort human pain threshold
- "feeling" sensation noticeable in ear
- painful sensations

AREA																						
Kitchen	30	35	40	45	50	55	60	65	70	75	80	85	90	95	100	105	110	115	120	125	130	135	140

PRODUCTS*
- Range vent fan
- Garbage disposal
- Dishwasher
- Electric mixer
- Blender
- Refrigerator
- Wall exhaust fan
- 12" portable fan
- Knife sharpener

*Recorded at operator's or housewife's normal ear distance (dBA scale)
**Intermittent sounds
***Also occurs with loud or unexpected noises

Koss Electronics asked the Environmental Design department of the University of Wisconsin for deep research into "The Auditory Environment in the Home" and found the kitchen is a rough equivalent of a boiler factory. Tables I and II show everything except the refrigerator is above the annoyance threshold.

TABLE II
Home Task Area Product Generated Noise Levels*

Column descriptions (left to right):
- maintains auditory attention and stimulates eye movement for localization
- threshold of annoyance environment – (50 to 90dB)
- airplane noises relatively unnoticed with background mus.
- activates automatic nervous system***
- increase in peristalsis, saliva & gastric juice flow
- annoyance threshold**
- work efficiency reduced
- eyes close, pupils dilate, skin pales, adrenalin increases
- increased response and error averages over lower pressure levels
- perceptible ear discomfort human pain threshold
- "feeling" sensation noticeable in ear
- painful sensations

AREA																						
Kitchen	30	35	40	45	50	55	60	65	70	75	80	85	90	95	100	105	110	115	120	125	130	135	140

PRODUCTS*
- Coffee grinder
- Elec. can opener
- Pots and pans
- Faucet
- Drain (sink)
- Range vent fan and dishwasher
- Range vent fan and disposal

*Recorded at operator's or housewife's normal ear distance (dBA scale)
**Intermittent sounds
***Also occurs with loud or unexpected noises

WHAT TO DO ABOUT IT:

Ventilating systems can be improved greatly by following these recommendations.

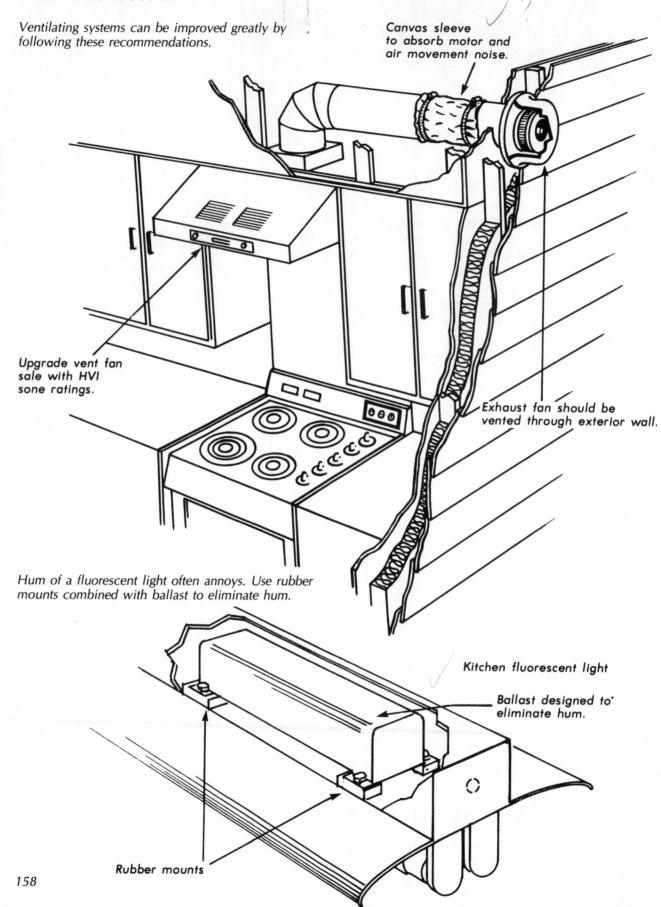

Canvas sleeve to absorb motor and air movement noise.

Upgrade vent fan sale with HVI sone ratings.

Exhaust fan should be vented through exterior wall.

Hum of a fluorescent light often annoys. Use rubber mounts combined with ballast to eliminate hum.

Kitchen fluorescent light

Ballast designed to eliminate hum.

Rubber mounts

Suspended ceilings with acoustical panels absorb up to 75% of the noise striking the surface.

Acoustical panels in ceiling, either suspended or applied direct, deaden all reflected noise.

Holes cut through common walls for plumbing and heating may leak noise. Seal them with a resilient material.

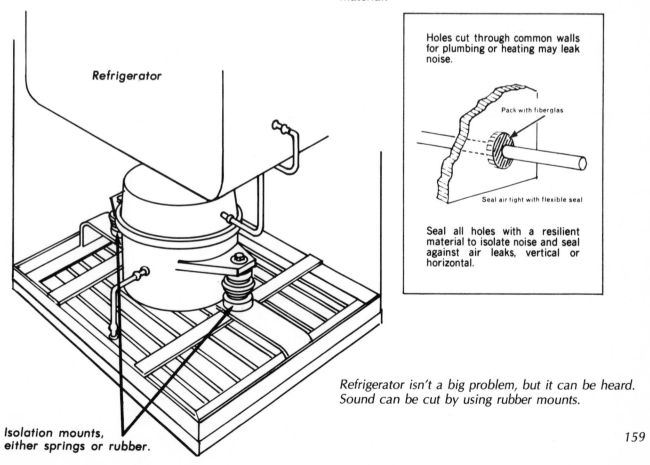

Refrigerator

Holes cut through common walls for plumbing or heating may leak noise.

Pack with fiberglas

Seal air tight with flexible seal

Seal all holes with a resilient material to isolate noise and seal against air leaks, vertical or horizontal.

Refrigerator isn't a big problem, but it can be heard. Sound can be cut by using rubber mounts.

Isolation mounts, either springs or rubber.

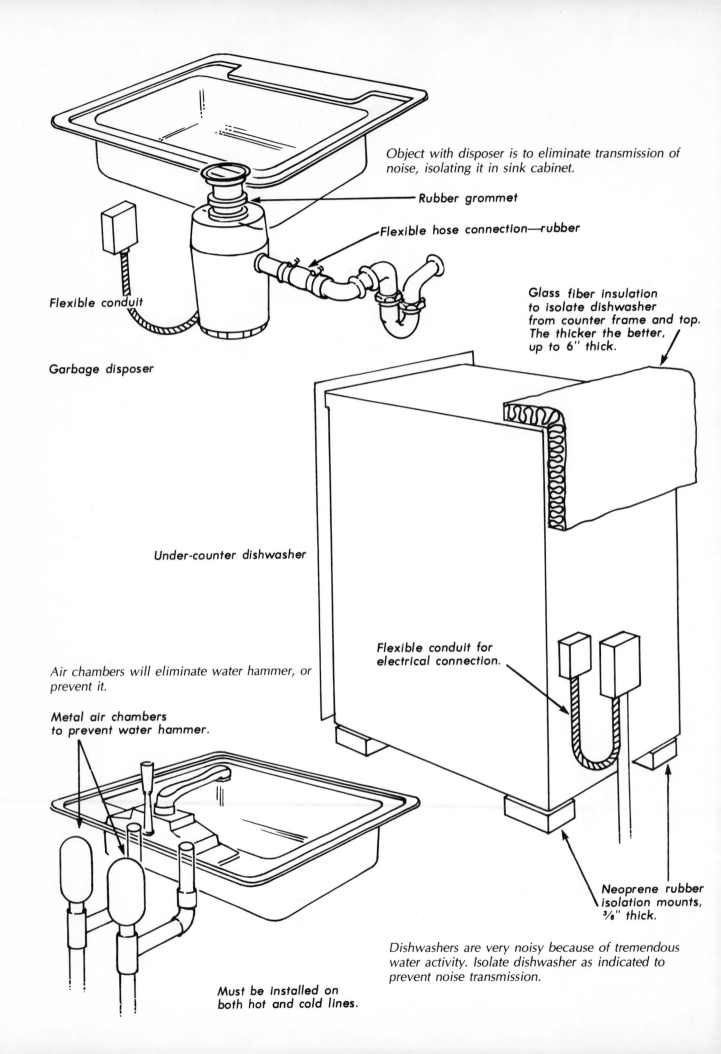

Object with disposer is to eliminate transmission of noise, isolating it in sink cabinet.

Rubber grommet

Flexible hose connection—rubber

Flexible conduit

Garbage disposer

Glass fiber insulation to isolate dishwasher from counter frame and top. The thicker the better, up to 6" thick.

Under-counter dishwasher

Flexible conduit for electrical connection.

Air chambers will eliminate water hammer, or prevent it.

Metal air chambers to prevent water hammer.

Neoprene rubber isolation mounts, 3/8" thick.

Must be installed on both hot and cold lines.

Dishwashers are very noisy because of tremendous water activity. Isolate dishwasher as indicated to prevent noise transmission.

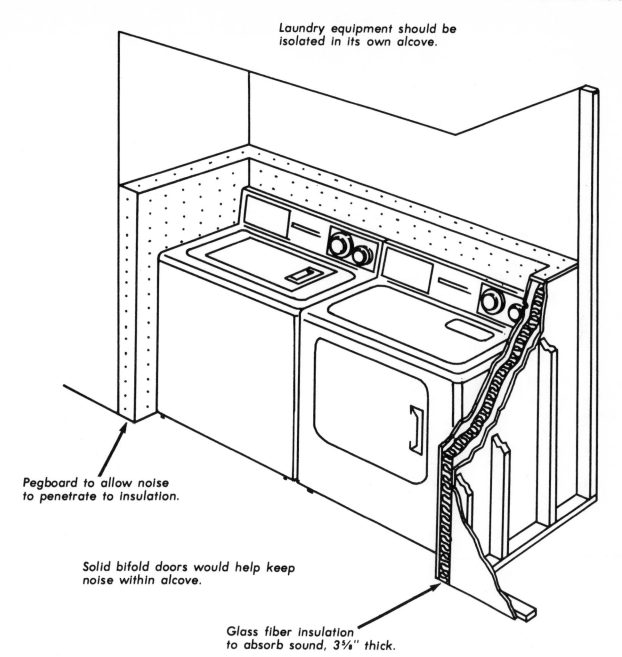

Laundry equipment should be isolated in its own alcove.

Pegboard to allow noise to penetrate to insulation.

Solid bifold doors would help keep noise within alcove.

Glass fiber insulation to absorb sound, 3⅝" thick.

Laundry equipment often is near kitchen. It should be isolated in an alcove. There's no other way to keep out the noise.

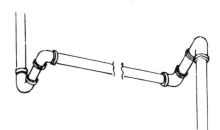

Long runs of hot water supply creak or snap as they expand or contract. Differences up to 100 degrees can exist in piping, can cause expansion up to 1/8 inch in 10 feet. To eliminate, use a swing arm to allow movement and use collars of Fiberglas insulation in straps.

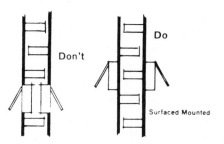

Noise travels through walls when medicine cabinets are mounted back to back. Put cabinets in separate stud spaces, or surface-mount.

11

Kitchen Trends and Future Concepts

All things change.

And in the changing, will the kitchen of tomorrow become another part of the future shock of modern man?

We think not. There is a need for the kitchen as it exists today. And if it didn't exist, we would have to invent it.

There are many who predict home electronic computers for the housewife. We have looked at some of them, and no doubt they are useful. There is serious doubt, however, as to who *needs* them.

To go to the moon? Absolutely essential. To control inventory and production in a large cabinet factory? Great. But to tell your wife how many sirloins and how many cans of beans she will need next week? Ridiculous!

There are changing trends. There are new and exciting products and materials that are fast becoming parts of the kitchen of the future. Here are some of the ones to watch for.

Cabinetry

More and more, they are spreading throughout the house. Nearly all cabinet manufacturers now are promoting built-in cabinet installations for every room in the home.

Polyurethane will be popular for doors and drawer fronts. It has greater dimensional stability than wood, greater design capability, and has a greater production capability for better products at far less labor cost. Still, wood will always be in demand.

All-plastic cabinets are a possibility, built of reinforced glass fiber or polystyrene, not one by one but

in assemblies which include the countertop and a molded-in sink. On this basis you might buy a 6-ft. kitchen assembly, or an 8-ft. assembly, or combinations to form L or U kitchens.

Ranges

The newest item right now is the magnetic induction system by Westinghouse. This is truly cool, safe cooking, with absolutely no heat generated in the cooktop. When a pan is placed over an induction heating coil, intercepting an oscillating magnetic field, heat results in the pan and it cooks the contents. Lift the pan and the range is off. Of course, it is a smoothtop, with not a single hole, not even for the controls, which are magnets on the top. At $2,500 it is not a mass-market item, but the price will go down fast.

Smooth, glass-top cooking surfaces are definitely the in thing for the mid-70's. They were exclusively Corning's for several years while other glass companies tried to figure out how to do it. Now the others have solved the problems and the material is available to other range manufacturers. These are very popular with consumers.

Refrigeration

The big box is neat, efficient and pretty near failsafe, but it does not fit in with modern kitchen design. It can be great when built-in, but many kitchens are budgeted too low for built-in installation, and always will be.

A better system, known for years to technologists, is a central refrigeration plant with refrigeration piped or ducted to points of use. Thus there could be cool drawers and cool cabinets in different parts of the kitchen, den, bedrooms, or where desired. If the technology is known, can the product be far behind?

Microwave

The microwave oven, first marketed by Tappan in 1955, popularized by Amana, and now brought to a peak of sophistication by Thermador really belongs in every home above poverty level.

It has survived the radiation scare (it is about as dangerous as sunlight) and now is within reach of anyone with a credit card. As more wives join the work force, the need for this fast-cooking appliance increases. When both husband and wife get home from work at 5:30 or 6, a regular, conventional family meal is easily possible through the wonders of microwave. This product will become really big through the mid-70s.

Countertops

High-pressure plastic laminates may finally be challenged by the new cast marbles (synthetic, polyester or acrylic) and by a new material being developed by Corning.

The latter is Pyram, a thin surfacing material applied to a substrate but with the characteristics of Pyroceram, which is the material Corning uses for its glass-ceramic cooktops and counter inserts.

This possibly will not be a serious challenge for the plastic laminates, but in the ever-expanding marketplace there is more and more room for new materials, and they do have their points.

Fractional Kitchens

These are the bits of kitchens scattered through the house. There will be more of them. Compact refrigerators already are selling profusely for offices, and that engenders ideas.

At home they are popping up in bedrooms, dens, and recreation rooms. With them frequently goes a

Is there a computer in our future? At $10,600 we doubt if this will show up in any HUD housing, but here it is, by Honeywell. In the price you get a 2-week course in programming for such things as menu-planning, home budgeting and income tax computation. Fiberglas components are made for Honeywell by Wehco Plastics, West Trenton, N.J.

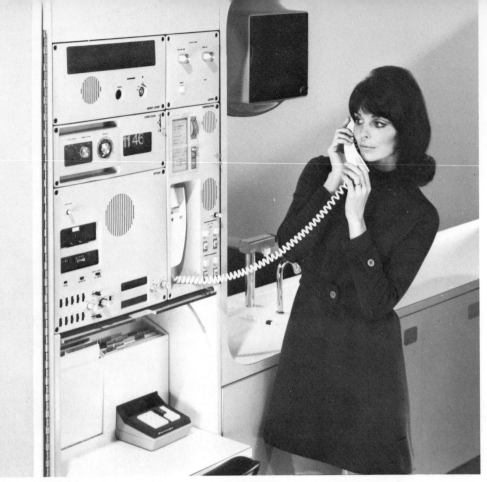

This "Homemaker's Command Post" by
Westinghouse includes closed circuit TV on all of the
house. Telephone has 500 names and numbers stored
in memory bank. She can unlock doors and windows
by touching a button, or lock them, or a button will
call firemen or police. It's in the Electra 71 home
in Coral Springs, Fla.

wet bar, which means bar sink with running water
and cabinets, possibly even a microwave oven.

The industry makes unit kitchens, or compact kitchens, incorporating a small oven, sink, refrigerator,
and one or two burners in as little as 19 inches
of wall space. These usually are constructed of steel
and are too commercial looking for a home. The
fractional kitchens now showing up in homes are
designed and made up for a particular place in the
home.

The Cabinet-Appliance

Back in the early 1950s Remington Rand developed
an automated filing cabinet for its office equipment
division, called the Cardveyor.

Now it has been brought up to date as a kitchen
appliance—automated storage space that brings the

various bins of foods, dishes or pans at the press
of a button.

It costs around $2,000 to a builder or dealer. It
replaces several hundred dollars worth of cabinets and,
although it is bulky, it can gain space if engineered
into the floorplan properly.

This automated cabinet-appliance might be combined with a dumb waiter, bringing selected shelves
from their storage spaces in the basement and thereby
releasing much space in the living area of the home.
It may never happen, but it is not difficult to imagine.

Other Gadgetry

Built in intercom systems are sophisticated and highly
useful. They can be wired to as many rooms in the
house as desired, and the deluxe ones include fire
and burglar alarms and even phonographs.

Closed-circuit television can be a great thing for mother working in the kitchen. Covering the backyard play area it can be much more useful and convenient than the window in the kitchen, and it also can cover upstairs or downstairs play areas. The coming age of home videotaping has ramifications that can only be suggested.

The world is full of super-kitchen visions of the future, but it is not our purpose here to discuss them. We speak here of what exists, what is imminent, or what is both possible and logical. And so it isn't unrealistic to say this is the way it is going to be.

Whirlpool's MOD kitchen has power/water modules in floor that can be picked up and snapped into place elsewhere if woman wants to move her appliances. (Circles in floor). Touch of button raises or lowers appliances to eye level. Drawing shows power module.

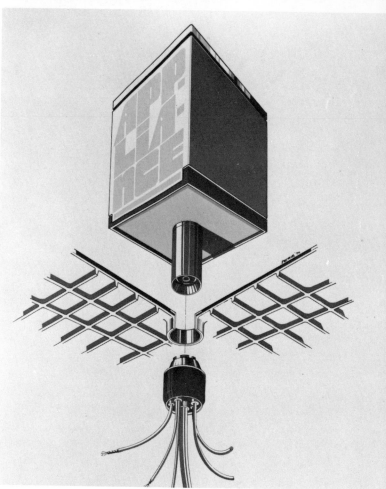

Elkay conceptualizes this visionary sink of the future, its Cuisine 80. It combines all sink functions—food preparation, cooking and cleanup, plus closed-circuit TV, and, of course, a small computer.

166

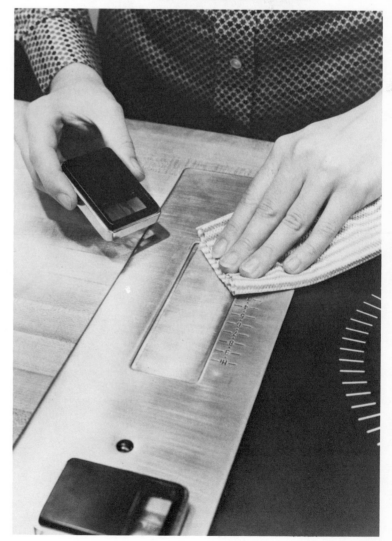

Range of the future may use magnetic induction for really cool cooking. This, by Westinghouse, is available now and boiling water through a kitchen towel proves that cool means cool. Full view shows that it is a glass-top, with absolutely no holes for dirt to get in. Even the controls are magnetic. They slide along in their proper places, and can be picked up for cleaning. Its principle: oscillating magnetic field creates similar field when it encounters resistance of metal cooking vessel. This causes heat in pan, not on cooktop, causing food to cook.

APPENDICES

1. ANSI A161.1/1970, Minimum Construction & Performance Standards for Kitchen Cabinets.

2. Minimum Light for Living Standards of American Home Lighting Institute.

3. Members, National Kitchen Cabinet Assn.

4. Members, National Assn. of Plastic Fabricators

5. Members, Council of Certified Kitchen Designers.

6. Addresses of all Firms Mentioned in Text and Photo Captions

Appendix 1

Minimum Construction & Performance Standards for Kitchen Cabinets.

Construction

General: **1.** All lumber and plywood parts shall be kiln dried to a moisture content of 12 percent or less at time of fabrication.

2. Both wall and base cabinet assemblies shall consist of individual units joined into continuous sections, and with the exception of sink units, vanity units, oven cabinets, refrigerator cabinets and bottoms and backs of all drawer cabinets, all units shall be fully enclosed with backs, bottoms, and panels and tops on wall cabinets.

3. Fastenings shall be accomplished to permit removal and replacement of built in units, such as dishwasher, counter top range, oven, etc., without affecting the remainder of the installation. Cabinets containing water heaters or other equipment shall be provided with access panels for servicing or replacement of equipment.

4. Face frames, if used, shall be of necessary thickness to provide rigid construction. Face frames shall be stapled, dowelled, screwed or nailed to end panels.

5. Corner or lineal bracing shall be provided at points where necessary to insure rigidity and proper joining of various components, i.e., wall backs and bottoms.

6. All fixed shelves shall be recessed into grooves in the ends or in the fronts and backs or supported by cleats, if frame construction is used, and must comply with Test No. S-1 and S-2.

7. Intermediate shelves, both fixed and adjustable, shall be supported on ends and comply with Test No. S-1 and S-2.

8. Base cabinets designed to rest directly on the floor shall provide for a toe space at least 2 inches deep and 3 inches high.

9. Drawers shall be properly con-

structed to comply with Test No. S-1. Drawers of formed plywood, formed plastic, or any new type of construction shall comply with Test No. S-1 and S-2. All drawer guides shall comply with Test No. S-6.

10. All exposed construction joints shall be fitted in a workmanlike manner, nails sets and holes filled as per drawings 1 through 3.

11. Swinging doors will have a device sufficient to hold doors closed.

12. When installed, doors shall be in proper alignment with cabinet and adjacent doors. They shall be balanced or warp resistant constructions and operate freely.

13. Improper application of the various finishing coats, such as runs, orange peel, fatty edges, blushing, etc., shall not be acceptable on exterior of cabinet.

14. Finish shall be clean and touchup colors and/or burn-in repairs shall blend with the surrounding areas of finished surface. The finish will be

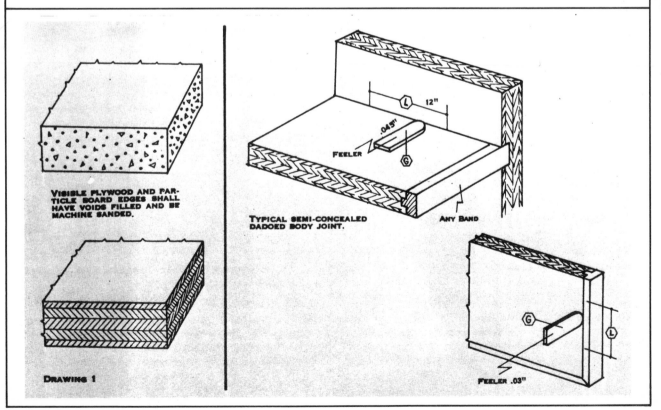

VISIBLE PLYWOOD AND PARTICLE BOARD EDGES SHALL HAVE VOIDS FILLED AND BE MACHINE SANDED.

TYPICAL SEMI-CONCEALED DADOED BODY JOINT.

ANY BAND

FEELER .03"

DRAWING 1

free of any printing and/or pad marks.

15. Miscellaneous hardware such as drawer slider, shelf standards, brackets, rotating shelf hardware, etc., will support the design loads and operational functions described in this standard. It will be free from scratches and other damages. Paint or other cabinet finish not intended as a finish for the hardware will be removed.

16. Cabinet units will be installed level, plumb and true to line. They shall be fastened to suitable grounds as per fabricator's or manufacturer's instructions. When instructions are for other than normal mounting (such as ceiling hung units in island type installations), the cabinets will be tested in this installed position.

17. Use closer, filler strips and finish moldings as necessary for sanitary and appearance purposes.

18. The elastic limit of any material used in the cabinet system will not be exceeded when calculated by sound engineering practice for the anticipated design loads.

Base Cabinet Construction. In addition to general construction specifications, base cabinets shall have bottoms of sufficient thickness to support intended loads. If needed, spreader supports and support blocks adequately nailed and/or glued to frame of cabinet to prevent warping and deflecting shall be installed. These bottoms must comply with Tests No. S-1 and S-2.

Wall Cabinet Construction. In addition to general construction specifications, the front frame shall be of rigid construction. Wall cabinets shall be able to withstand the full weight of loaded cabinet without racking or pulling loose in any joint. See Tests No. S-1 and S-2.

Door Construction. In addition to general construction specifications, doors shall be in alignment with cabinet and adjacent doors when installed. Doors shall latch without excessive binding or looseness and shall comply with Wood Finish Specifications.

Edges of plastic, plywood or veneer faced doors with exposed particle board core shall be capped or filled and painted to provide a finish complying with Wood Finish Specifications.

Doors shall be of balanced or warp resistant construction. Hollow core doors shall have (1) minimum of one piece of filler strip for each six inches of width or length in hollow portion; (2) filled with paper honeycomb or equal.

All doors shall conform to Tests S-3, S-4, S-5.

Oven and Utility Cabinet Construction. In addition to general construction specifications, minimum construction to be the same as for base and wall cabinets.

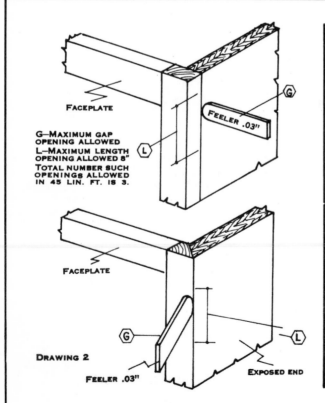

FACEPLATE

G—MAXIMUM GAP OPENING ALLOWED
L—MAXIMUM LENGTH OPENING ALLOWED 8"
TOTAL NUMBER SUCH OPENINGS ALLOWED IN 45 LIN. FT. IS 3.

FACEPLATE

DRAWING 2

FEELER .03"   EXPOSED END

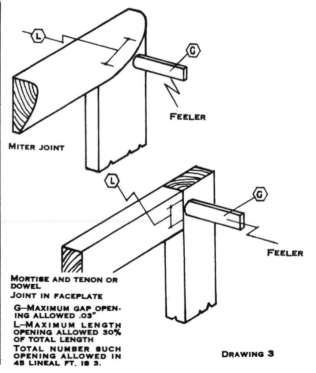

FEELER

MITER JOINT

MORTISE AND TENON OR DOWEL
JOINT IN FACEPLATE

G—MAXIMUM GAP OPENING ALLOWED .03"
L—MAXIMUM LENGTH OPENING ALLOWED 30% OF TOTAL LENGTH
TOTAL NUMBER SUCH OPENING ALLOWED IN 45 LINEAL FT. IS 3.

FEELER

DRAWING 3

Contents of Tests

1. Structural Tests for Cabinets. Structural tests are basically concerned with the structural integrity of the cabinet and its installation. Each of the following structural tests were specialy designed to measure the ability of the cabinet to withstand probable loadings and operational aspects.

S-1 Static Loading Test. This test measures ability of cabinets to withstand above average weight which would normally be kept on cabinet shelves and in drawers.

S-2 Impact on Shelves Under Static Load. This test will indicate the structural integrity of dropping cans and other objects onto cabinet shelves and drawers.

S-3 Impact on Cabinets Fronts (Doors), Base Cabinets. The test is designed to measure the impact received on base cabinet doors from knee closing, children hitting door with tricycles and other toys, and other impacts usually received on base cabinet doors.

S-4 Hinge Permanent Set Test and Door Racking. This test is designed to measure the structural integrity of a door when a four to six year old child attempts to climb on the counter by standing on the base cabinet door, or an adult pulling on the wall cabinet door to elevate himself to the counter.

S-5 Operating Test for Door and Door Holding Device. This test designed to measure results of 10 years or more of normal opening and closing of doors.

S-6 Operating Test for Drawers. This test is designed to measure results of 10 years or more of normal opening and closing of drawers with above normal loads.

II. Exterior Wood Finish Specification. A cabinet door shall be used to evaluate the finishing tests. The door shall be representative of a normal production run. All tests shall be run on new surfaces after cabinet finish has aged 10 to 14 days.

The following tests were created to show the acceleration of kitchen conditions on pre-finished cabinets. Years of evaluation by paint manufacturers and wood fabricators of furniture, kitchen cabinets, TV, and other wood products, have determined through experience that finishes properly applied and performing under the following tests should last a minimum of five years or more.
F-1 Shrinkage and Heat Resistance
F-2 Hot/Cold Check Resistance
F-3 Chemical Resistance
F-4 Detergent and Water Resistance

III. Hardware Specifications and Standards. Cabinet hardware used on products complying with this standard shall comply with the Builders Hardware Manufacturers Association Cabinet Hardware Standard No. 201, October, 1968. (Write Builders Hardware Manufacturers Association, 60 East 42nd Street, New York, N. Y. 10017, for information on this standard.)

Structural Tests for Cabinets

S-1 Static Loading Test. A. Mount upper and lower cabinet as per manufacturer's (fabricator's) instructions. Room temperature (68° to 80°F) and humidity (35% to 70%).

B. Load all shelves — uniform distributed load — 15 pounds per square foot. Load all drawers — uniform distributed load — 10 pounds per square foot. Arrange loads to avoid bridging effect. Metal revolving shelves shall meet the BHMA Cabinet Hardware Standard.

C. Maintain loading for 14 days under room temperature (68° to 80°F) and humidity (35% to 70%).

The following shall be the minimum performance for this test:

1. Examine loaded cabinet at end of 14 day test. There shall be no visible sign of joint separation or failure in any part of cabinet or mounting system.

2. The loaded shelves shall not deflect more than 1/16" per lineal foot between supports, at the completion of the 14 day test. Maximum deflection will be 1/4" between supports.

3. The loaded drawers will be operable. Drawer bottoms will not be deflected to a positon where they interfere with drawer operation.

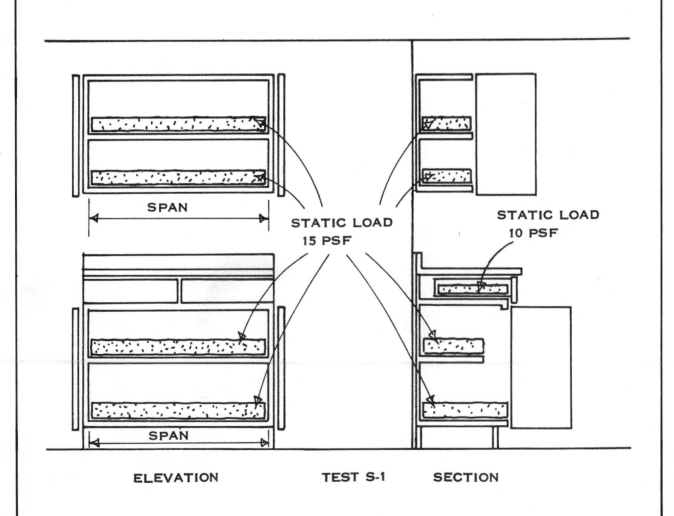

SPAN

SPAN

STATIC LOAD
15 PSF

STATIC LOAD
10 PSF

ELEVATION   **TEST S-1**   **SECTION**

S-2 Impact on Shelves and Drawer Bottoms. **A.** Mount upper and lower cabinet as per manufacturer's (fabricator's) instructions. Room temperature (68°-80°F) and humidity (35% to 70%).

B. Drop a 3 pound weight from 4 inches above the shelf surface — see drawing.

C. Drop a 3 pound weight from 4 inches above the drawer bottom with drawer open ⅔ of the operating distance — see drawing.

The following shall be the minimum performance for this test:

1. The shelf shall not be damaged (except for superficial indentation where ball strikes) and will retain its original position.

2. The drawer shall not be damaged (except for superficial indentation where ball strikes) and will operate as before the test.

3. There shall be no visible sign of joint separation or failure in any part of the cabinet or mounting system.

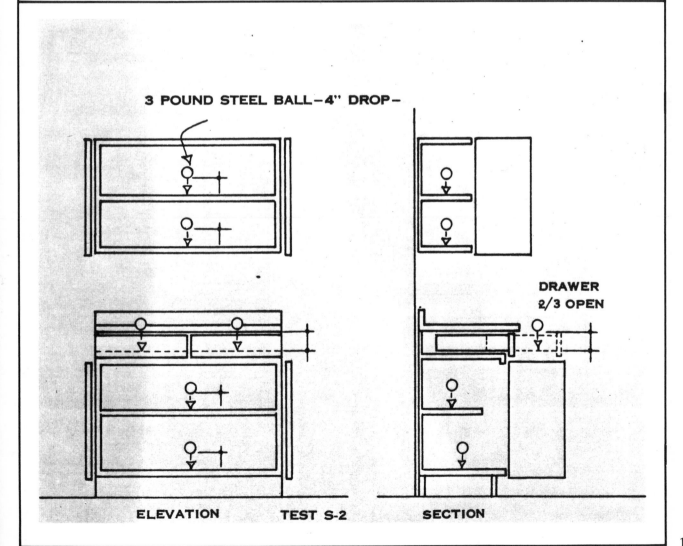

3 POUND STEEL BALL–4" DROP–

DRAWER 2/3 OPEN

ELEVATION **TEST S-2** **SECTION**

S-3 Impact on Cabinet Fronts (Doors) Base Cabinets. A. Mount lower cabinet as per manufacturer's (fabricator's) instructions. Room temperature (68° to 80°F) and humidity (35% to 70%).

B. Apply impact to center of cabinet door in accordance with test principle shown in drawing. Use 10 pound sandbag and 12 inch drop.

C. 45° open, Impact Test. This same test should be repeated with the door open at 45°.

The following shall be the minimum performance for this test:
1. After impact there will be no visible sign of damage to the cabinet door, hardware, or hardware connec-tions, after re-adjustment of hardware. Doors will operate as before the test.

2. There shall be no visible sign of joint separation or failure on any part of the cabinet or mounting system.

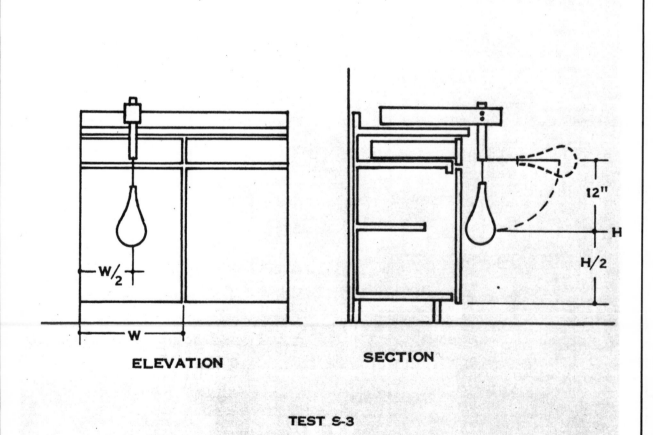

ELEVATION

SECTION

TEST S-3

S-4 Door Racking and Hinge Set Test. A. Mount upper and lower cabinet per manufacturer's (fabricator's) instructions. Room temperature (68° to 80°F) and humidity (35% to 70%).

B. Record the shape of door with adjustable square or other device before application of weight.

C. With door in 90° open position, set measuring device at (M) and slowly apply weight, in accordance with test principle shown in drawing. Slowly operate from 90° open position to 20° open and return to 90°

open position. Remove weight and test each door.

The following shall be the minimum performance for this test:

1. Measure the shape of the door after weight is removed. Door must retain its original shape and show no visible sign of damage. Door shall resist a minimum racking load of 45 pounds.

2. Measure the amount of set at point M. This will be called the hinge set, and shall not exceed .09 inches.

3. Hinges and hinge connections shall show no visible sign of damage.

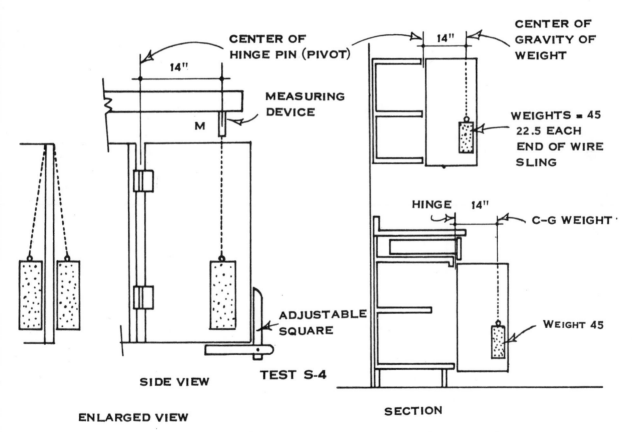

CENTER OF HINGE PIN (PIVOT)

MEASURING DEVICE

14"

CENTER OF GRAVITY OF WEIGHT

WEIGHTS = 45 22.5 EACH END OF WIRE SLING

HINGE 14" C-G WEIGHT

WEIGHT 45

ADJUSTABLE SQUARE

SIDE VIEW

TEST S-4

SECTION

ENLARGED VIEW

NOTE: FOR CABINET DOORS LESS THAN 15 INCHES WIDE. APPLY WEIGHT AT A POINT 1 INCH IN FROM OUTER EDGE.

S-5 Operating Test For Door and Door Holding Device. **A.** Mount upper and lower cabinet as per manufacturer's (fabricator's) instructions. Room temperature (68° to 80°F) and humidity (35% to 70%).

B. The door holding device (spring catch, magnetic catch, self-closing hinges, or other) will be part of this test.

C. Record the shape of the door with adjustable square or other device and record the door elevation (open 90°) at point M, before cycling. See drawing.

D. Attach cycling mechanism to door at normal operating position so that no additional loads are placed on hinges. One cycle shall consist of operation through 90° swing with full engagement and disengagement of holding device. Operate door through 25,000 cycles at a speed where excessive heat through friction is not developed.

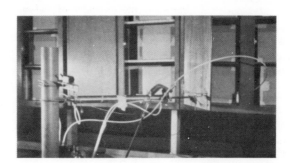

The following shall be the minimum performance for this test:

1. The door will be operable and the door holding device will be adequate to hold door in closed position.

2. The door shape will be the same as before the test recorded in part C.

3. The measurement at point M (sag) will not exceed .09 inches.

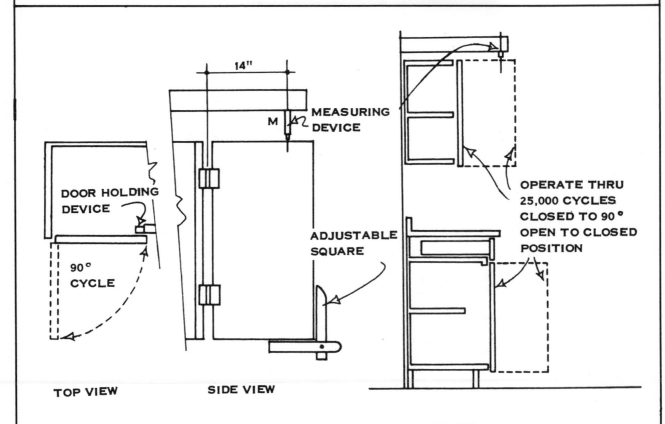

TOP VIEW   SIDE VIEW

ENLARGED VIEWS   TEST S-5   SECTION

NOTE: FOR CABINET DOORS LESS THAN 15 INCHES WIDE, POINT M SHALL BE 1 INCH FROM OUTER EDGE.

S-6 Operating Test For Drawers. A. Mount a lower cabinet unit as per manufacturer's (fabricator's) instructions. Room temperature (68° to 80°F) and humidity (35% to 70%).

B. Load drawer — uniform distributed load — 10 pounds per square foot. See drawing.

C. Operate drawer through 25,000 cycles. One cycle shall consist of opening drawer ⅔ of travel distance and return to closed position. Attach cycling mechanism so that no additional loads are placed on drawer. Operate at a speed where excessive heat through friction is not developed.

The following shall be the minimum performance for this test:

1. Drawer will be operable at completion of test.

2. There shall be no failure in any part of drawer assembly or operating system.

3. Drawer bottoms will not be deflected to a position where they interfere with drawer operation.

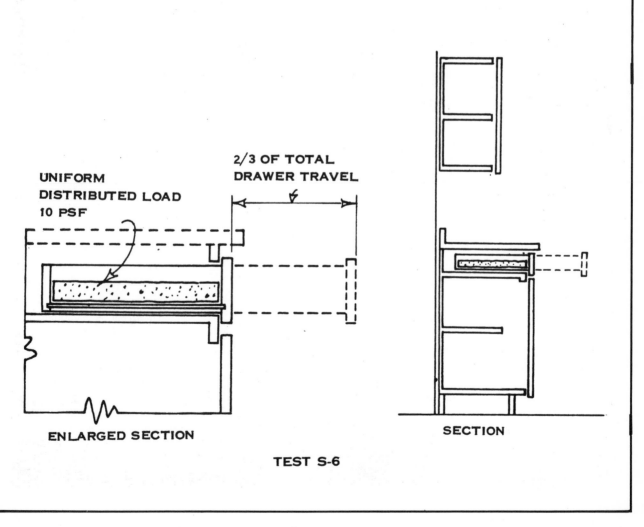

UNIFORM
DISTRIBUTED LOAD
10 PSF

2/3 OF TOTAL
DRAWER TRAVEL

ENLARGED SECTION

SECTION

TEST S-6

Exterior Wood Finish Specifications

General. This specification defines the requirements in respect to appearance and durability of exposed surfaces of finish of completed factory finish wood kitchen and vanity cabinets and total door area. It is not a specification for finishing materials as such, but is intended to allow the cabinet manufacturer maximum freedom in the choice of finishing materials.

Appearance. All exposed construction shall be fitted in a workmanlike manner with nails set and holes filled. All exposed surfaces, interior and exterior, including door and drawer edges, shall be free of saw marks and other inperfections and shall be sanded. Improper application of the various finishing coats on exterior of cabinet, i.e., runs, orange peel, fatty edges, blushing, etc., shall not be acceptable. Finish shall be clean and free of excessive dirt, dust, scratches, mats and residue. Touch-up colors and/or burn-in repairs shall be matched with the surrounding areas of the finished surfaces. The finish shall be free of any printing and/or pad marks which may be caused by padding.

Finish Tests for Cabinet Exteriors

F-1 Shrinkage and Heat Resistance. A. A cabinet door, without screw holes, or with all screw holes covered, shall be used for this test. Stabilize at room temperature (68° to 80°F) and humidity (35% to 70%).

B. Door, by visual examination will be free of finish defects.

C. Place the door in a hot box (120°F ± 5°F and 70% ± 5% humidity) for a 24 hour period.

The following shall be the minimum performance for this test:

1. By visual examination, the door finish will show no appreciable discoloration, evidence of blistering, film rupture, shrinkage checks or other film failure.

F-2 Hot/Cold Check Resistance. A. A cabinet door (as described in Test F-1-A) shall be used for this test.

B. Door, by visual examination, shall be free of finish defects.

C. Cycle as follows: Place door in hot box (110° and humidity 70%) for one hour. Remove and allow to reach original room temperature and humidity conditions. Place in cold box (−5°F) for one hour. Remove and allow door to reach original room temperature and humidity conditions. This will be one cycle.

The following shall be the minimum performance for this test:
1. After five cycles (see C), the door finish will show no appreciable dis-

coloration, evidence of blistering, film rupture, shrinkage checks or other film failures.

F-3 Chemical Resistance. A. Place 3 cc's of each of the following substances on the surface of the cabinet door tilted at an angle of 70 to 80° with the horizontal: Vinegar, Lemon, Orange and Grape juice, tomato catsup, coffee (prepared for drinking at 115° — one teaspoon of coffee per cup), olive oil, 100 proof alcohol.

B. Allow these substances to stand on the surface for a period of 24 hours under room temperature (68° to 80°F) and humidity (35% to 70%).

C. Mustard will be tested under similar conditions for one hour.

D. Sponge wash the surface with clear water and dry with a clean cloth.

E. In the event of any initial failure on F-3 Tests, the test laboratory will allow the door to sit for seven to ten days and re-examine for performance under these tests.

The following shall be the minimum performance for this test:

1. No excessive discoloration, stain or whitening shall result which will not disperse with ordinary polishing.

2. There will be no indication of film rupture or shrinkage.

F-4 Detergent and Water Resistance.
A. See drawing for suggested test equipment. Room temperature (68° to 80°F) and humidity (35% to to 70%).

B. Sponge; 1½" thickness, Dupont cellulose #8A, or equal.

C. Detergent solution; 1% by weight, 1 ounce of Dreft to 1 gallon of water.

D. Level trough and fill with detergent solution to approximately ½ inch below top level of sponge.

E. Place the base cabinet door upright (top edge down) on the sponge as shown in drawing. Examine at 24 hours for delamination and finish failure.

The following shall be the minimum performance for this test:

1. After 24 hours there will be no delamination or finish failure.

2. The finish will show no appreciable discoloration, evidence of blistering, film rupture, shrinkage checks or other film failure.

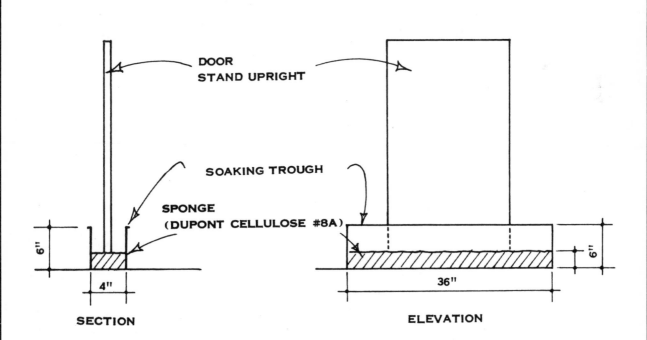

SECTION

ELEVATION

TEST F-4

Appendix 2

Minimum Light for Living Standards of American Home Lighting Institute.

GUIDE to ADVANCED LIGHT for LIVING

Recommendations by the American Home Lighting Institute for fixture lighting installations which go beyond the MINIMUM Light for Living Standards.

Kitchen

1) For Local Work Surface—Counters
   a. Wall or cabinet-mounted (14 to 22 inches above counter) one 20-watt fluorescent or a two socket (60 watts each) incandescent bracket for every 3 ft. of counter. (See following 2 and 3, when no cabinets.)
2) For Local Sink or Range Surface—for ceiling or soffit location
   a. One recessed fixture containing three 75-watt incandescent in box at least 24 inches long, or two 40-watt or three 30-watt fluorescent tubes, OR . . .
   b. Two recessed fixtures with inner reflectors for 100-watt incandescent bulb each, centered 18 inches apart, OR . . .
   c. Minimum 2, preferably 3, "bullets" (recessed, surface or pendant) for 75-watt R-30 flood-lamps.
3) For Local Sink or Range Surface—wall mounting
   a. Wall bracket 14 to 22 inches above range, allowing some upward light; Minimum one 30-watt fluorescent, or multiple socket incandescent bracket (60 to 75 watts) approx. 18 inches long.
   b. When range hood is used, select one with one or two incandescent sockets.
4) For General Lighting—(in addition to local) use one fixture for approx. every 50 sq. ft. of area. May be surface mounted, recessed or pendant, depending on ceiling height, slope, construction, placed for harmony with room shape, and contain each:
   a. 175 to 200 watts, incandescent (fixture minimum 14 inch diameter), 60 to 80 watts fluorescent, OR . . .
   b. One 24 sq. ft. suspended luminous ceiling-type fixture (minimum 360-watt incandescent) for rooms with finished floor area no greater than 50 sq. ft.

NOTE: When a luminous ceiling, or ceiling panels are desired, a minimum depth of 8 inches above plastic or louvers to tube centers is required. Use minimum of one 40-watt fluorescent tube for every 12 sq. ft. of room area, or 60-watt incandescent for every 4 sq. ft. of panel. In bathroom, add appropriate lighting at mirror.

MINIMUM LIGHT for LIVING STANDARDS

Recommended by AMERICAN HOME LIGHTING INSTITUTE

Kitchen Area

General Lighting: A minimum of one 12" diameter fixture to accommodate one 150-watt, two 75-watt, or three 60-watt bulbs

. . . OR a minimum of two 40-watt, four 20-watt, or two circline fluorescent tubes

. . . OR at least two 150-watt recessed fixtures,

Local Lighting: Above a sink, use recessed or surface-mounted fixture with 150 watts of incandescent or 80 watts of fluorescent.

Sink under cabinets, range, and work counter, use a minimum of one 20-watt fluorescent tube or two 40-watt incandescent bulbs for each 4' of counter.

Appendix 3

Members, National Kitchen Cabinet Assn.

There are about 6,000 manufacturers of kitchen cabinets in the United States, not counting the "garage operators" that could add many thousands to the total.

However, less than 150 cabinet manufacturers account for $500 million in cabinet shipments, or one-third of all U.S. production.

Purpose of this appendix is to provide a representative nationwide list of manufacturers, and the membership of the National Kitchen Cabinet Assn. includes most major manufacturers and provides such a list. A few non-members have been added at the end of the list because they are of such stature that it would be a disservice to exclude them.

Members

AAA-Lapco, Inc., 11223 Plano Rd., P.O. Box 38269, Dallas, Texas 75238

Acme Cabinet Corp., 909 Hwy. 37, Toms River, N.J. 08753

Adler Kay Co., Inc., 3737 Venoy Road, Wayne, Mich. 48184

Alderman Interior Systems, Inc., 4511 W. Buffalo Ave., P.O. Box 15557, Tampa, Fla. 33614

American Cabinet Corp., 301 N. Seventh Ave., Scranton, Pa. 18503

American Evans, Inc., W. Main St., Evans City, Pa. 16027

Arnold Mfg. Co., 4180 E. Raines Rd., Memphis, Tenn. 38118

Artcraft Cabinets, Inc., 1861 E. Bergman, Springfield, Mo. 65802

Belwood Industries, Inc., P.O. Box A, Ackerman, Miss. 39735

Bilt-In Wood Products Co., 808 Low St., Baltimore, Md. 21202

Boise Cascade/Raygold Div., P.O. Box 1028, Winchester, Va. 22601

Boro Industries, 2901 Stanley, P.O. Box 11558, Ft. Worth, Texas 76110

Boro Wood Products Co., Inc., Box 636, Bennettsville, S.C. 29512

Brammer Mfg. Co., 1441 Rockingham Rd., Box 3547, Davenport, Iowa 52808

Brandom Mfg. Corp. of Texas, P.O. Box 437, Keene, Texas 76059

Brennan Western, Inc., 11803 N.W. 116 St., Kirkland, Wash. 98033

Cabinet Group, The Tappan Co., Kemper/Tappan/Quaker Maid Cabinets, 701 South N St., Richmond, Ind. 47374

Cabinet N Counter, P.O. Box 304, Waldorf, Md. 20601

Carr, Henry M., Inc., 1150 Vermont St., Frankfort, Ind. 46041

Carroll Industries, Inc., Box 510, Conway, N.H. 03818

Colonial Products Co., Redco Ave., P.O. Box 231, Red Lion, Pa. 17356

Connor Forest Industries, Inc., 131 Thomas St., Wausau, Wis. 54401

Conwed Cabinetry, Ladysmith, Wis. 54848

Coppes, Inc., 401 E. Market St., Nappanee, Ind. 46550

Crestwood Kitchens Ltd., 225 No. 5 Rd., Richmond, B.C., Canada

Del Mar Div., U.S. Plywood-Champion Papers, 2865 Gordon Rd., N.W., Atlanta, Ga. 30311

Dixie Cabinet Co., Inc., 1007 Trade St., P.O. Box 457, Morristown, Tenn. 37814

Dura Supreme, Inc., 10710 County Rd. #15, Minneapolis, Minn. 55441

E. & E. Mfg. Co., 912 W. Cedar, Box 447 Cedar Hill, Texas 75104

Excel Wood Products Co., Inc., P.O. Box 819, Lakewood, N.J. 08701

Francisco Cabinet Corp., 1525 Illinois St., Des Moines, Iowa 50314

Gregg Cabinets, Ltd., 200 Bedard Ave., Chambly, Quebec, Canada

Haas Cabinet Co., 613 Utica St., Sellersburg, Ind. 47172

Hager Mfg. Co., 1512-32 N. Front St., Mankato, Minn. 56001

Cabinet Manufacturers

Hogan-Scarboro Corp., P.O. Box 60, Dudley, Ga. 31022

Home Crest Corp., Goshen Industrial Park, Eisenhower Dr. E., P.O. Box 595, Goshen, Ind. 46526

Imperial Cabinet Co., Inc., P.O. Box 427, Gaston, Ind. 47342

International Paper Co., Long-Bell Div., Box 579, Longview, Wash. 98632

IXL Furniture Co., Inc., R.R. #1, Elizabeth City, N.C. 27909

Kabinart Corp., 2515 Bransford Ave., Nashville, Tenn. 37210

Keller Kitchen Cabinets Southern, Inc., State Road #44 W., Box 1089, Leland, Fla. 32720

Kemper Bros., Div. of The Tappan Co., 701 So. N St., Richmond, Ind. 47374

Kinzzee Products, Inc., 259 2nd St., Saddle Brook, N.J. 07662

Kitchen Kompact, Inc., KK Plaza, Jeffersonville, Ind. 47130

Kitchen Mart, Inc., 7815 National Tpke., Space Center, Louisville, Ky. 40214

Lady Fair Kitchens, Inc., 3447 S. Main St., Salt Lake City, Utah 84115

L-Co Cabinet Corp., S. Fifth St., Shamokin, Pa. 17872

J. P. Long Cabinets, 2500 Citrus Rd., P.O. Box 97, Rancho Cordova, Cal. 95670

N. J. MacDonald & Sons, Inc., 45 Johnson Lane, Braintree, Mass. 02185

Major-Line Products Co., Inc., P.O. Box 478, Hoquiam, Wash. 98550

Mastercraft, Inc., 6175 E. 39 Ave., Denver, Col. 80207

Medallion Kitchens, Inc., 8609 Lyndale Ave., S., Minneapolis, Minn. 55420

Merillat Industries, 2075 West Beecher Rd., Adrian, Mich. 49221

Mutschler Brothers Co., Nappanee, Ind. 46550

National Homes Corp., 1657 Grant Line Rd., New Albany, Ind. 47150

Noblecraft Industries, Inc., P.O. Box 88, Hillsboro, Ore. 97123

Olympia Sales Co., 1537 S. Sixth West, Salt Lake City, Utah 84115

Oxford Mfg. Co., U.S. Rte. 1, So., P.O. Drawer L, Oxford, Pa. 19363

Prestige Wood Products, Inc., P.O. Box 2329 Metropolitan, Kansas City, Kan. 66106

Raywal, Ltd., 68 Green Ln., Thornhill, Ontario, Canada

Riviera Products, Inc., 1960 Seneca Rd., St. Paul, Minn. 55122

Rutt-Williams Div. of Leigh Products, Inc., P.O. Box 42, Goodville, Pa. 17528

The Sanderson Harold Co., 1 Railway St., Paris, Ontario, Canada

Sawyer Cabinet, Inc., 12744 San Fernando Rd., P.O. Box 4157, Sylmar, Cal. 91342

H. J. Scheirich Co., P.O. Box 21037, 250 Ottawa Ave., Louisville, Ky. 40221

Schrock Bros. Mfg. Co., P.O. Box 247, Arthur, Ill. 61911

Texas Cabinet Mfg. Co., Div. of Ben Griffin Enterprises, Inc., 3000 W. Pafford, Fort Worth, Texas 76110

Thiokol Texas, Inc., 3215 N. Pan Am Expressway, San Antonio, Texas

Triangle Pacific Cabinets, Inc., 9 Park Pl., Great Neck, N.Y. 11201

United Cabinet Corp., 14th & Aristocraft, P.O. Box 420, Jasper, Ind. 47546

Valley Cabinet Mfg. Inc., 4339 Jetway Ct., North Highlands, Cal. 95660

Valley Kitchens, Inc., State Rd. 42, Mason, Ohio 45040

Geo. C. Vaughan & Sons, Box 7367, San Antonio, Texas 78207

Villa Mfg., 1 Curlew St., Rochester, N.Y. 14606

Weather-Seal Div., Georgia-Pacific Corp., 324 Wooster Rd. N., Barberton, Ohio 44203

Welsh Kitchens, 1312 W. Washington St., Orlando, Fla.

Westwood Products, Inc., 560 21st S.E., P.O. Box 506, Salem, Ore. 97038

White-Meyer Wood Products, Inc., 141st & Rte. 45, Orland Park, Ill. 60462

Whitehall Cabinets, Inc., Whitehall Bldg., East Rockaway, N.Y. 11518

Wilson Cabinet Co., Inc., Box 489, Port Clinton, Ohio 43452

Major Non-Member Manufacturers

Jeffrey Steel Products, 1345 Halsey St., Brooklyn, N.Y. 11227.

St. Charles Mfg. Co., 1611 E. Main St., St. Charles, Ill.

Wood-Mode Kitchens, Kreamer, Snyder County, Pa. 17833.

Excel Wood Products, Lakewood, N.J. 08701.

Acrite Industries, 1120 Leggett Av., Bronx, N.Y.

Geneva Industries, Geneva, Ill.

Appendix 4

Members, National Association of Plastic Fabricators

There is no way to list all of the thousands of large and small manufacturers of residential counter-tops.

But most of the major ones are members of the National Association of Plastic Fabricators, many of whom also make plastic-laminated cabinets. This list of fabricator members is to provide a representative list of sources for countertops made with high-pressure decorative plastic laminate.

Fabricator Members

AAA-Lapco, Inc., 11223 Plano Rd., Dallas, Texas 75238

Aabco, Inc., 808 W. Cedar St., San Diego, Cal. 92109

ABC Kitchen Center, 10906 Wayzata Blvd., Minnetonka, Minn. 55343

Acme Cabinet Corp., 909 Highway 37 W., Toms River, N.J. 08753

Allcraft, Inc., 1047 W. 115 St., Chicago, Ill. 60643

Altmann Kitchen & Supply Co., Inc., 450 E. Clinton Pl., Kirkwood, Mo. 63122

American Sink Top Co., 10811 Russet St., Oakland, Cal. 94603

Ampco Products, Inc., P.O. Box 4190, Hialeah, Fla. 33014

Architectural Cabinets, Inc., Somervell Rd., Greater Wilmington Airport, New Castle, Del. 19720

Artcraft Industries, 548 N. First St., Turlock, Cal. 95380

Baldwin Sales Corp., 795 Merrick Rd., Baldwin, N.Y. 11510

Bay View Plastics, Inc., 7821 South 10 St., Oak Creek, Wis. 53154

Becker Specialties & Mfg. Inc., 3238 E. 45 St., Tucson, Ariz. 85713

Billco Products, 1671 South Shore Dr., Holland, Mich. 49423

Blount Lumber Co., Lacona, N.Y. 13083

Bob-Leon Plastics, Inc., 5151 Franklin Blvd., Sacramento, Cal. 95820

Byco Plastics, Inc., Box 1105, Decatur, Ala. 35601

Cabinet Craft, Inc., 1310 Valley High Dr. N.W., Rochester, Minn. 55901

Caldwell Furniture Shop, Inc., 6215 Clarksville Hwy., P.O. Box 35, Joelton, Tenn. 37080

Chandler's Plywood Products, Inc., 3716 Waverly Rd., Huntington, W. Va. 25722

Commercial Cabinet Installations, Inc., 8924 Perrin Dr., Livonia, Mich. 48150

Crest Mfg., 2628 The Alameda, Santa Clara, Cal. 95050

Crown Plastics, 745 Industrial Rd., San Carlos, Cal. 94070

Custom Counters, 1920 Packard, Ann Arbor, Mich. 48104

Custom Fabricators, Inc., Box 2171, 310-1/2 N.P. Ave., Fargo, N.D. 58102

Tops of America, Inc., d/ba Custom Hall, Inc., 105 Meadow St., Fairfield, Conn. 06611

C & W Precision Products, Inc., 80-39th St., Bldg. 22, Brooklyn, N.Y. 11203

Customline Products, Inc., 564-25 Rd., P.O. Box 1512, Grand Junction, Col. 81501

Custom Wood Products, Inc., P.O. Box 4072, 3304 Aerial Way Dr., Roanoke, Va. 24015

Design Vanity Co., 808 Low St., Baltimore, Md. 21202

Economy Suppliers & Fabricators, Inc., 6400 East Columbus Dr., Tampa, Fla. 33169

Edge Rite, Inc., 200 N. Harrison St., North Prairie, Wis. 53153

Erlanson Lumber Co., 310 Belknap St., Superior, Wis. 54880

Farina Brothers, Inc., 145 Union St., Holbrook, Mass. 02343

Fashion Form, Inc., 2602 N. 43 St., Tampa, Fla. 33605

Foote Woodworking Inc., 417 S. Main St., Stewartville, Minn. 55976

Formco, Inc., 7745 School Rd., Cincinnati, Ohio 45242

Formitex Plastic Fabricators, 870 North 22 St., Columbus, Ohio 43219

Grandview Products, P.O. Box 874, Parsons, Kan. 67357

Great River Industries, Wabasha Industrial Park, P.O. Box 31, Wabasha, Minn. 55981

Hain Wolf Associates, Inc., 1816 Paxton St., P.O. Box 2043, Harrisburg, Pa. 17105

F. A. Highley Co., Inc., 2405 Northwest 10th St., Oklahoma City, Okla. 73107

Hoffmeister Cabinets of Nevada, Inc., 3069 Sheridan St., Las Vegas, Nev. 89102

Homewood Industries, 17641 S. Ashland Ave., Homewood, Ill. 60430

Independent Plastics Co., 22001 Meekland Ave., Hayward, Cal. 94541

Inland Laminates, Inc., 12 N.E. 28th, Oklahoma City, Okla. 73105

Irving Countertop, Inc., 1810 E. Pioneer Dr., Irving, Texas 75060

Jacknob Corp., 11 Sarah Dr., East Farmingdale, L.I., N.Y. 11735

Keel Mfg. Co., Inc., 235 Cumerland St., Memphis, Tenn. 38112

Klein's Tri-Cove Co., 1030 S. Sixth West, Salt Lake City, Utah 84104

Kopfmann Co., The, Inc., 4911 W. Good Hope Rd., Milwaukee, Wis. 53223

Chris J. Krogh, Inc., 164 Milton Ave., Alpharetta, Ga. 30201

Kruger's Plastic Fabricators, 1002 Second St., N.E., Rochester, Minn. 55901

Lachecki Cabinet & Millwork, Inc., 23-1/2 E. 4th St., Duluth, Minn. 55805

Laidlaw-Goodwood Ind., Ltd., 50 Oak St., Weston, Ontario, Canada

Lake Street Industries, Inc., 3325 Republic Ave., Minneapolis, Minn. 55426

Laminated Plastics, Inc., 1008 Hanley Industrial Ct., St. Louis, Mo. 63144

Laminated Plastics of Dallas, 2340 Valdina St., Dallas, Texas 75207

Laminated Products, Inc., 12100 Riverwood Dr., Burnsville, Minn. 55378

Lemons Millwork, Inc., 224 E. 13 Ave., Albany, Ore. 97321

Lifetime Plastics Co., 1011 Knox Ave., Bldg. 8, San Jose, Cal.

Lincoln Laminating, Inc., 5601 S. 50th, Lincoln, Neb. 68516

Mar-Van Industries, 117 Middle Rd., Dublin, Pa. 18917

Miami-Carey Co., Div. of Panacon Corp., 203 Garver Rd., Monroe, Ohio 45050

Michigan Kitchen Distributors, 428 S. Linden, Marshall, Mich. 49068

Modern Plastic Laminating Co., Inc., Div. Evans Products Co., 2750 S. Raritan, Englewood, Colo. 80110

Modern Plastics Corp., 268 E. Market St., Wilkes-Barre, Pa. 18702

Morr-Craft Products, Inc., 1414 Spring Garden Ave., Pittsburgh, N.Y. 15212

Modular Laminated Products, 6426 126 Ave. N., Largo, Fla. 33540

M. & W. Products Co., Inc., 1667 Penfield Rd., Rochester, N.Y. 14625

Northwest Industries, 39550 Grand River, Novi, Mich. 48050

H. C. Osvold Co., 2828 University Ave., S.E., Minneapolis, Minn. 55414

Peer Cabinet, Inc., 1001 E. Summit St., Crown Point, Ind. 46307

Peoria Kitchen Tops, Inc., 7726 N. Pioneer Lane, Peoria, Ill. 61614

Pierce Custom Top Co., Inc., 2430 N. Court St., Rockford, Ill. 61103

Pioneer Wood Products, 2679 E. Grand Blvd., Detroit, Mich. 48211

Plastic Clad. Corp., 3900 Second Ave., So., Birmingham, Ala. 35202

Plastic Engineering Co., 2989 Orange Grove Ave., North Highlands, Cal. 95660

Plastic Fabricators, 701 Van Buren St., Amarillo, Texas 79101

Plastic Fabricators, Inc., 511 N. Weingach, Evansville, Ind. 47711

Plastico, Inc., 435 Morehead Ave., Greensboro, N.C. 74401

Plastic Top Co., P.O. Box 3509, Albuquerque, New Mexico 87110

Plastic Top Fabricators, Inc., 1302 W. Troy Ave., Indianapolis, Ind. 46203

Plasticraft Co., 940-944 Eastern Ave., Malden, Mass. 02148

Plastwood Mfg. Co., The Ltd., 1820 Midland Ave., Scarboro, Ontario, Canada

Poncraft Door Co., 2005 Pontiac Rd., Pontiac, Mich. 48057

Quality Tops, Inc., 245 W. Crossroad Sq., 2255 South Salt Lake City, Utah 84115

J. W. Rice Co., 952 Third Ave., Napa, Cal. 94558

Rosebud Mfg. Co., Inc., Box 742, Mission, S.D. 57555

Sager Industries, 325 Rte. 45, Frankfort, Ill. 60423

Sani-Top, Inc., Box 130, Gardena, Cal. 90247

Sanymetals Products Co., Inc. 1705 Urbana Rd., Cleveland, Ohio 44112

Selectile Co., Inc., 3323 Mortor Ave., Los Angeles, Cal. 90034

Soo Empire Plywood, 209 S. Kiwanis Ave., Sioux Falls, S.D. 57104

Suba Mfg., Inc., P.O. Box 605—Bldg. 116 Benicia Industrial Park, Benicia, Cal. 94510

Suburban Cabinet & Fixture Co., P.O. Box 146, Maple Plain, Minn. 55359

Topco Laminates, 1027 N. Monroe, Kansas City, Mo. 64120

Topcraft, Inc., 4207 Menlo Dr., Baltimore, Md. 21215

Tops Unlimited, Inc., 1245 Wazee St., Denver, Col. 80204

Troxel's Inc., 817 S.E. Moores St., P.O. Box 324, Portland, Ore. 97207

Ute Fabricating Co., Box 128, Fort Duchesne, Utah 84026

V-T Industries, Inc., 1000 Industrial Park, Holstein, Iowa 51025

Valley Kitchens, Inc., P.O. Box 167, Mason, Ohio 45040

Vanguard Counter Tops, Inc., Cedar Cross Rd., Dubuque, Iowa 52003

Villa Mfg. Inc., 1 Curlew St., Rochester, N.Y. 14606

Western Laminates, Inc., 3827 Lake St., Omaha, Neb. 68111

Western Plastics Co., 1530 Galvez Ave., San Francisco, Cal. 94124

White-Meyer Wood Products, Inc., 141 & Rte. 45, Orland Park, Ill. 60462

Wilson Hardware Mfg. Co., South Feazel St., Harrisburg, Ill. 62946

Appendix 5

Members, Council of Certified Kitchen Designers

The only measure of true professionalism in kitchen design and planning is recognition of an individual as a Certified Kitchen Designer by the certifying arm of the American Institute of Kitchen Dealers. Certification is awarded only after a minimum number of years in the field, with extensive testing and affidavits from customers.

There are many other good kitchen designers and planners who cannot win CKD recognition because they do not have the required years of experience. Others choose not to be certified.

The following list of Certified Kitchen Designers provides a nationwide list of design and planning sources. In any local area, an alternative would be to look for a kitchen firm that is a member of AIKD. In many cities these are listed in the yellow pages with the AIKD logotype.

Arizona

A. M. Buck, CKD, Crowe Lumber & Construction Co., 1445 E. Indian School Road, Phoenix, 85014

California

J. B. Galloway, CKD, C. A. Olson, CKD, Downey Plumbing & Heating Co., 11829 So. Downey Avenue, Downey, 90241

S. M. Macey, CKD, Quesco Cabinets, Inc., 829 So. Claremont Street, San Mateo, 94402

W. E. Peterson, CKD, Snyder Diamond Co., 1399 Olympic Boulevard, Santa Monico, 90404

Colorado

W. B. Jordan, CKD, Jordan's, Inc., 121 E. Bijou, Colorado Springs, 80902

E. Hanley, CKD, Edward Hanley & Company, 1448 Oneida Street, Denver, 80220

P. G. Hartman, CKD, Kitchen Distributors, Inc., 1235 South Broadway, Denver, 80210

C. W. Kline, CKD, Bill Kline Kitchens, 2640 E. 3rd Avenue, Denver, 80206

B. H. Smith, CKD, Vent-A-Hood of Denver, Inc., 20 East Ninth Avenue, Denver, 80203

Connecticut

G. H. Mann, CKD, Ralph Mann & Sons, 505 Main Street, Ansonia, 06401

A. Kasper, CKD, K. L. & P. Kitchens, 4173 Main Street, Bridgeport, 06606

I. B. Plotkin, CKD, Crown Cabinet Corp., 307 Stratford Avenue, Bridgeport, 06608

A. S. Audibert, CKD, Audibert's, 781 King Street, Bristol, 06010

J. K. Metzo, CKD, Metzo Bros., Inc., 334 Main Street, East Haven, 06512

G. D. Crane, CKD, Paul Dolan Co., Inc., Essex, 06426

L. J. Kowalski, CKD, W. R. Penney, CKD, Kowalski's, Inc., 202 Field Point Road, Greenwich, 06830

R. L. Gelormino, CKD, F. P. Palmer, CKD, Kustom Kitchens of Litchfield, Inc., Torrington Road, Litchfield, 06759

K. L. Bell, CKD, Bell Kitchen Distributors, Inc., 363 Mulberry Street, P.O. Box 12, Plantsville, 06479

E. C. Brady, CKD, Kitchens of Distinction by Brady, 90 Center Street, Southington, 06489

E. L. Chadwick, CKD, Living Kitchens, Inc., 896 Washington Boulevard, Stamford, 06901

G. L. Giguere, CKD, Kitchens by Nefco, 1443 East Main Street, Torrington, 06790

D. L. Davis, CKD, Bradley Kitchens, Inc., 214 Park Road, West Hartford, 06119

B. O. Peterson, CKD, R. C. Aldridge, CKD, M. A.

Peterson, CKD, M. A. Peterson, Inc., 607 New Park Avenue, West Hartford, 06110

S. M. Lefler, CKD, Kitchens by Lefler, 431 East State Street, Westport, 06880

Delaware

W. G. Magan, CKD, R. Walls, CKD, Craft-Way Kitchens, Inc., Evelyn Drive at Kirkwood Highway, Wilmington, 19808

District of Columbia

J. S. Bendheim, CKD, Builder Kitchens, Inc., 1215 Kenilworth Avenue, N.E., Washington, 20019

M. L. Coll-Pardo, CKD, Hechinger Co., 1525 Maryland Avenue, N.E., Washington, 20002

A. R. Dresner, CKD, Douglas Distributing Corporation, 3521 "V" Street N.E., Washington, 20018

R. W. Bauer, CKD, R. D. Schafer, CKD, The Kitchen Guide, 5002 Connecticut Avenue N.W., Washington, 20008

L. E. Schucker, Jr., CKD, L. E. Schucker, III, CKD, Kitchens, Inc., 5027 Connecticut Avenue N.W., Washington, 20008

R. M. Tunis, CKD, Richard M. Tunis, Kitchen Specialist, 4914 Wisconsin Avenue N.W., Washington, 20016

Florida

R. L. Welky, CKD, Mutschler Kitchens of Fort Lauderdale, 233 Southeast Second Avenue, Fort Lauderdale, 33301

W. T. Langohr, CKD, Mutschler Kitchens of Jacksonville, 1919 Beachway Road, Jacksonville, 32207

L. E. Miller, CKD, R.R.1 Box 448A, Lutz, 33549

R. F. Braithwaite, CKD, House of Wares, Inc., 2975 N.W. 77 Avenue, Miami, 33122

R. V. Kucera, CKD, Kitchen Center, Inc., 5124 Biscayne Boulevard, Miami, 33137

Georgia

G. C. Mays, CKD, A. H. Snelling, Jr., CKD, Custom Kitchens Co., 808 W. Oglethorpe Avenue, Albany, 31701

P. B. Gunter, CKD, Marblecast, Inc., 1415 Chattahoochee Avenue, Atlanta, 30318

Hawaii

M. L. Smith, CKD, Ramsay Contractors, 630 Piikoi Street, Honolulu, 96814

Illinois

E. J. Keegan, CKD, Key Kitchens, 1628 W. Northwest Highway, Arlington Heights, 60004

J. E. Lindstrom, Jr., CKD, The Lindstrom Co., 237 W. Illinois Avenue, Aurora, 60506

R. W. Loerop, CKD, Cooper Rite, Inc., 9311 Ogden Avenue, Brookfield, 60513

L. S. Colbert, CKD, M. R. Stalter, CKD, Colberts, 1602 South Neil Street, Champaign, 61820

C. L. Anderson, CKD, Kitchen Shoppe Inc., 5001-03 W. Irving Park Road, Chicago, 60641

B. G. Greenwald, CKD, Suburban Designers, Inc., 2412 West 111th Street, Chicago, 60655

G. A. Reilly, CKD, People's Gas Co., 122 S. Michigan Avenue, Chicago, 60603

G. E. Coutant, CKD, Kitchen Distributors, 1449 East Eldorado, Decatur, 62521

D. B. Cole, CKD, Edwardsville Lumber Co., 201 W. High Street, Edwardsville, 62025

C. H. Seeds, CKD, Design Associates, 115 E. Stephenson, Freeport, 61032

B. G. Stidman, CKD, Galatia Building Center, Box 127, Galatia, 62935

R. P. Gerth, CKD, Geneva Industries, Inc., 201 S. 8th Street, Geneva, 60134

J. P. Descour, CKD, Town & Country Kitchens, Inc., 712 Glencoe Road, Glencoe, 60022

D. Johnson, CKD, Kitchens by Don Johnson, 17930 Dixie Highway, Homewood, 60430

K. Miller, CKD, Kitchens & Baths by Kenneth Miller, 18 West 664 Roosevelt Road, Lombard, 60148

E. L. Zielinski, CKD, Better Kitchens, Inc., 7640 Milwaukee Avenue, Niles, 60648

R. P. Junghans, CKD, The Building Specialties Co., Tucker Beach Road, Paris, 61944

A. G. Ackerberg Jr., CKD, Ideal Millwork Co., Rt. 1, Box 103, Plainfield, 60544

W. A. Reynolds Jr., CKD, Reynolds Enterprises, Inc.,

Certified Kitchen Designers

2938 River Road, River Grove, 60171

F. W. Eber, CKD, Eber's of Rochelle, 426 N. 11th Street, Rochelle, 61068

M. A. Dummler, CKD, J. A. Kathrein, CKD, Totem Lumber Co., 4421 Ruby Street, Schiller Park, 60176

M. H. Braun, CKD, Mark Braun Kitchens, 1805 S. MacArthur, Springfield, 62707

H. R. Buckhold, CKD, McDermand Kitchens, 1831 So. 11th Street, Springfield, 62703

K. G. Knobel, CKD, K. P. Knobel, CKD, Karl G. Knobel, Inc., 1218 Washington Avenue, Wilmette, 60091

Indiana

R. S. Penrod, CKD, Penn Kitchens, 313 East Third Street, Bloomington, 47401

L. G. Routen, CKD, The Kitchen Center, Corner Eleventh & Rogers, Bloomington, 47401

L. W. Alexander, CKD, Dunlap's, 422 Washington Street, Columbus, 47201

A. L. Skomp, CKD, C. E. Skomp, CKD, Cliff's Napanee Kitchens, 1415 E. Division Street, Evansville, 47714

J. M. Boarman, CKD, Boarman Cabinet Co., 1627 Oliver Avenue, Indianapolis, 46221

C. L. Gray, Jr., CKD, Gray-Breese Co., 3750 W. 16th Street, Indianapolis, 46222

C. P. Pippen, CKD, Pippens Kitchens, Inc., 428 N. Washington Street, Muncie, 47305

D. P. Guckenberger, CKD, E. L. Johnson, CKD, R. S. Ringenberg, CKD, Mutschler Bros. Co., 302 S. Madison Street, Nappanee, 46550

J. D. Mitchell, CKD, Kitchen Interiors, R. R. 3 Box 6, Newburg, 47630

J. L. Risley, CKD, Risley's Kitchen Specialists, 212 East Broadway, Shelbyville, 46176

D. E. Carpenter, CKD, Carpenter Enterprises, 3710 Surrey Lane, South Bend, 46628

W. M. Beemer, CKD, Beemer Enterprises, Inc., R.R. #1, Syracuse, 46567

D. A. Rohrberg, CKD, R.R. #1, Syracuse, 46567

W. F. Frazier, CKD, Frazier Distr. Co., Inc., Kitchens & Interior Designs, 1318 Ohio Street, Terre Haute, 47807

C. A. Berg, CKD, Spesco, Inc., 52 Marks Road, Valparaiso, 46383

Iowa

W. C. Fox, CKD, Fox Appliance & Kitchen Center, Inc., 705-11 Jefferson Street, Burlington, 52601

W. T. Gerdes, CKD, Benson Lumber Co., 1207 Lucas Avenue, Burlington, 52601

W. M. Hoffman, CKD, Keystone Products Co., 2880 Mt. Pleasant Street, Burlington, 52601

H. R. Ek, CKD, F. B. Friedl, CKD, St. Charles Kitchens by Friedl, Inc., 1013 Mt. Vernon Road, S.E., Cedar Rapids, 52403

O. F. Maxwell, CKD, Brammer Mfg. Co., 1701 Rockingham Road, Davenport, 52808

G. E. Nordeen, CKD, Nordeen's Home Supply Co., 314 E. 2nd Street, Davenport, 52801

A. A. Johnson, CKD, Kitchen Center, Inc., 5055 Second Avenue, Des Moines, 50333

C. Swanson, CKD, Swanson's Kitchens, 1505 Fremont Street, Marshalltown, 50158

S. C. Gilfoyle, CKD, 1500 Oak Street, Muscatine, 52761

F. H. Thompson, CKD, Thompson & Associates, Inc., 1st & Ashworth Road, West Des Moines, 50265

Kentucky

D. M. Butcher, CKD, Creative Kitchens, Inc., 1269 Eastland Drive, Lexington, 40505

F. R. Smith, CKD, Kitchen Planning Center, 316 N. Ashland Avenue, Lexington, 40502

J. U. Forst, CKD, W. J. Ketcham, CKD, G. T. Warren, CKD, C. J. Mattingly, CKD, General Electric Co., Appliance Park, Louisville, 40225

P. M. Pittenger, CKD, The House of Kitchens, Inc., 106 Bauer Avenue, Louisville, 40207

J. W. Riley, Jr., CKD, Jefferson Kitchens, Inc., 1034 Rogers Street, Louisville, 40204

Louisiana

C. B. Gamble, CKD, Kitchens by Cameron, Inc., 8019 Palm Street, New Orleans, 70125

Maine

C. Bellegarde, Jr., CKD, P. Clifford, CKD, R. O. Dion, CKD, Bellegarde Custom Kitchens, 516 Sabattus Street, Lewiston, 04240

Maryland

R. F. Cox, CKD, R. L. Gibbs, CKD, Cox Kitchens & Baths Inc., 5011 York Road, Baltimore, 21212

C. G. Neubauer Jr., CKD, AAA Remodeling Co., 2907 Taylor Avenue, Baltimore, 21234

A. V. Taylor, CKD, Taylor's Kitchens, 2214 E. Monument Street, Baltimore, 21205

D. S. Wheelhouse, CKD, Murray Saunders Custom Kitchens, Inc., 4918 Bethesda Avenue, Bethesda, 20014

P. V. Chadik, CKD, Mutschler-Division of American Standard, 2920 Greenvale Road, Chevy Chase, 20015

A. W. Neumann Jr., CKD, Ann Dor Kitchens, Route 140 & Sandymount Road, Finksburg, 21048

R. L. Alexander, CKD, Gaithersburg Lumber & Supply Co., Inc., 11 S. Frederick Avenue, Gaithersburg, 20760

J. Dobbs, CKD, N. Granat, CKD, Creative Kitchens, Inc., 8480 Fenton Place, Silver Spring, 20910

H. E. Fowler, CKD, Waldorf Supply, Inc., Md. Route #5, Waldorf, 20601

Massachusetts

R. T. Arnold Jr., CKD, Arnold's 1788 Yards Inc., 44 Spring Street, Adams, 01220

J. Herzenberg, CKD, Kitchens by Herzenberg, Inc., South End Bridge Circle, Agawam, 01001

L. K. Johnson, CKD, Lee Kimball Kitchens, 119 Canal Street, Boston, 02114

T. J. Pitkanen, CKD, Boyd Craft, Inc., 62 Walnut Street, Dedham, 02026

F. R. Angel, CKD, The Angel Co., Inc., 340 Broad Street, Fitchburg, 01420

R. W. Burke, CKD, Kitchen Center of Framingham, Inc., 697 Waverly Street, Framingham, 01701

V. M. Gallivan, CKD, Colonial Floors, Inc., Kitchen Division, 117 Waverly Street, Framingham, 01701

R. L. Norberg, CKD, Suburban Kitchens, 1242 Hyde Park Avenue, Hyde Park, 02136

N. E. Robitaille, CKD, Tailored Kitchens Supply Co., 100 Tarkiln Hill Road, New Bedford, 02745

L. S. Gagliardi, CKD, Gagliardi's, Inc., 9-13 Union Street, North Adams, 01247

H. W. Watkins, CKD, Nickerson Lumber Co., 51 Main Street, Orleans, 02653

W. H. Gustafson, CKD, The Kitchen Center, Route 146, Sutton, 01527

P. J. Garrity, CKD, Newton Sash & Door Co., Inc., 37 River Street, Waltham, 02154

H. C. Hjelm, CKD, Architectural Woodworking Co., Inc., 241 West Boylston Street, West Boylston, 01583

B. F. Rice, CKD, W. E. Rice, CKD, Kitchens by Rice Bros., Inc., 3 R Church Street, Wilmington, 01887

J. F. Boyer, CKD, Sawyer's, Gold Star Blvd., Worcester, 01606

R. A. Cuccaro, CKD, Robert A. Cuccaro Associates, 6 Alvarado Avenue, Worcester, 01604

Michigan

D. J. Thibodeau, CKD, Home Appliance Mart, Inc., 2019 W. Stadium Blvd., Ann Arbor, 48103

W. M. Weinlander Jr., CKD, Weinlander Wood Products & Home Supply, Inc., 8593 E. U.S. 223, Blissfield, 49228

D. N. Streets, CKD, White Supply Co., 639 E. Chicago Road, Coldwater, 49036

J. R. Allcorn, CKD, Artistan Plastic, Inc., 12001 Greenfield, Detroit, 48227

C. E. Clark, CKD, Charlotte Clark Kitchens, 18932 W. McNichols Road, Detroit, 48219

J. M. Damstra, CKD, Gallery of Kitchens, 5243 Plainfield N.E., Grand Rapids, 49505

F. J. Kozak, CKD, The Kitchen Center, Inc., 1219 Burton St. S.E., Grand Rapids, 49407

R. S. Pleune, CKD, Croswell Kitchens, Jordan Sheperd, Inc., 660 Croswell Avenue, S.E., Grand Rapids, 49506

C. A. Kosmalski, CKD, Mutschler Kitchens, Inc., 20227 Mack Avenue, Grosse Pointe Woods, 48236

R. A. Ferle, CKD, D. C. Nicholson, CKD, The Kitchen Shop, Inc., 407 1st Street, Jackson, 49201

M. E. Blake, CKD, The Kitchen Shop, Inc., 5320 S. Pennsylvania, Lansing, 48910

R. B. Vandervoort, CKD, Hager-Fox Co., 1115 S. Pennsylvania Ave., Lansing, 48902

R. E. Hill, CKD, Style Trend Kitchens, 792 W. Laketon Avenue, Muskegon, 49441

L. E. Trevarrow Jr., CKD, Trevarrow, Inc., 23712 Woodward Avenue, Pleasant Ridge, 48069

C. Pajares, CKD, Pajares Construction Products, Inc., 2680 S. Rochester Rd., Rochester, 48063

F. B. Terpstra, CKD, Southfield Kitchens, 22050 W. Ten Mile Road, Southfield, 48075

L. G. Fogelsong, CKD, R. L. Fogelsong, CKD, Tecumseh Building Supply Co., 214 E. Chicago Blvd., Tecumseh, 49286

Minnesota

H. M. Eberhart, CKD, Dura Supreme, Inc., 10710 County Road 15, Minneapolis, 55427

Mississippi

J. P. Campbell, CKD, Campbell Co., Inc., 2022 25 Avenue, Gulfport, 39501

Missouri

A. Baum, CKD, The Kitchen Shop, Inc., 1063 S. Brentwood Blvd., St. Louis, 63117

C. J. Polley, CKD, Coppes, Inc., 5040 A Devonshire, St. Louis, 63109

Montana

J. W. Bergeson, CKD, W. A. Shaffer, CKD, Modern Kitchens, Inc., P.O. Box 1881, 2710 Montana Avenue, Billings, 59103

New Hampshire

J. L. Brown, CKD, R. C. Elliott, CKD, Home Improvement Co., Inc., Meriden Road, Lebanon, 03766

J. R. Higgins, CKD, J. R. Higgins, Inc., 449 Hayward Street, Manchester, 03103

J. Mitrook, CKD, Mitrook's Custom Kitchen Center, 100 Albany Street P.O. Box 1152, Portsmouth, 03801

New Jersey

W. H. Bryce, CKD, Ulrich, Allendale

W. J. Kelly, CKD, Kitchen Creations by Kelly, Div. of Smith & Richards Lumber Co., 110 South Laurel Street, Bridgeton, 08302

A. E. Rosner, CKD, M. Rosner, CKD, Rosner's Custom Kitchens, 1700 W. Marlton Pike, Cherry Hill, 08034

A. J. Giannaula, CKD, Allied Woodcraft, 421 Allwood Road, Clifton, 07012

C. A. Schneider, CKD, C. Schneider & Co., Inc., 158-166 Highland Avenue, Clifton, 07011

W. Begbie, CKD, Begbie's Kitchens, Inc., Route 46, Dover, 07801

J. P. Castronova, CKD, Paramount Kitchens, 211 Central Avenue, East Newark, 07029

L. Lemchen, CKD, M. A. Waimon, CKD, Barmark, Inc., 198 Central Avenue, East Orange, 07018

R. W. Afflerbach, CKD, A.I.K.D., 114 Main Street, Hackettstown, 07840

J. Van Beuzekom, CKD, Van Beuzekom, Inc., 301 Lafayette Avenue, Hawthorne, 07506

C. J. Curtis, CKD, H. M. Forvour, CKD, Curtis Styled Kitchens, Rt. 38 & Rudderow Avenue, Maple Shade, 08052

A. Kessler, CKD, Paterson Stove & Kitchen Center, 88 Broadway, Paterson, 07505

E. M. Peresett, CKD, Peresett Appliance Sales & Service, 875 State Rd., Princeton, 08540

H. Aulert Jr., CKD, Kitchen Planning & Design Center, 29 E. Milton Avenue, Rahway, 07065

G. E. Fross, CKD, Kitchen Planning & Design Center, 29 E. Milton Avenue, Rahway, 07065

W. H. Bryce, CKD, J. D. Ulrich, CKD, P. W. Fluhr, CKD, Ulrich, Inc., 100 Chestnut Street, Ridgewood, 07450

P. E. Horvath, CKD, G. C. Horvath, CKD, Proven Design, Inc., 111 E. Westfield Avenue, Roselle Park, 07204

C. A. Bothers, CKD, A. R. Bothers Woodworking, Inc., 236 Dukes Pky. P.O. Box 127, Somerville, 08876

L. Shur, CKD, H. B. Sobel, CKD, Builders Fair, Inc., 22 Rt. 22, Springfield, 07081

V. R. Loretto, CKD, Allied Craftsmen, Inc., 1543 Teaneck Road, Teaneck, 07666

T. Davis, CKD, Quaker Maid Kitchens by Davis, Inc., 53 Route 33, Trenton, 08619

M. Salinard, CKD, B. R. Tunbridge, CKD, Du-Craft, Inc., 1919 Rt. 71, West Belmar, 07719

G. G. Hurwitz, CKD, A. J. Terragrossa, CKD, Quaker Maid Kitchens of Haddon Twp., Inc., 108 Haddon Avenue, Westmont, 08108

J. L. Whittaker, CKD, Jay L. Whittaker Co., Inc., 15 Bergenline Avenue, Westwood, 07675

New York

F. J. Schneider, CKD, Cox Kitchens, Inc., 1163 Willis Avenue, Albertson, 11507

H. R. Myers, CKD, H. R. Myers Lumber Co., Inc., Box 147 Route 12, Boonville, 13309

L. A. Izzo, CKD, Dream Kitchens, 722 Coney Island Avenue, Brooklyn, 11218

J. L. Clouser, CKD, Clouser Sales, Inc., Rt. 32, Cornwall, 12518

A. Cohen, CKD, Alamode Kitchen Center, 110-29 Horace Harding Blvd., Corona, 11368

A. J. Scott, CKD, Whitehall Cabinets, Inc., 21 Ryder Place, East Rockaway, 11518

L. J. Ryder, CKD, Ryder's Kitchen & Appliances, Inc., 2026 Lake Street, Elmira, 14903

F. M. Frank, CKD, T. L. Frank, CKD, Alamode Kitchen Center, Inc., 2272 Jericho Tpke., Garden City Park, 11530

M. Berkoff, CKD, Herbert P. Bisulk, Inc., 295 Nassau Blvd., Garden City South, 11530

B. Bisulk, CKD, H. P. Bisulk, CKD, Herbert P. Bisulk, Inc., 295 Nassau Blvd., Garden City South, 11530

F. P. Frederick, CKD, Frederick Construction Co., 79-49 Myrtle Avenue, Glendale, 11227

H. Jacoby, CKD, Frederick Construction Co., 79-49 Myrtle Avenue, Glendale, 11227

R. J. Dorey, CKD, Finch Pruyn Sales, Inc., Quaker & Glenwood Ave., Glens Falls, 12801

D. C. Tait, CKD, Dan Tait, Inc., Grand Gorge, 12434

C. Mustello Jr., CKD, D & M Kitchens, Inc., 400 Great Neck Road, Great Neck, 11021

E. E. Berger, CKD, Berger Appliances, 441 Commerce Street, Hawthorne, 10532

C. T. Passaro, CKD, Whitehall Kitchen Center, 1231 Station Plaza, Hewlett, 11557

J. M. Kennedy, Jr., CKD, R. F. Kennedy, CKD, Kennedy Kitchens, Inc., 727 Fox Street, Horseheads, 14845

R. M. Baker, Jr., CKD, Bob Baker's Kitchens, 401 E. State Street, Ithaca, 14850

S. Y. Adams, CKD, R. F. Carbrey, CKD, Valley Crafts, Inc., Valley Plaza, Johnson City, 13790

S. J. Klementowski, CKD, Custom Kitchen Design Center, 501 Kenmore Avenue, Kenmore, 14217

E. M. Soper, CKD, Soper Cabinet & Fixture Co., Inc., 26–28 Downs Street, Kingston, 12401

C. R. Spetts, CKD, Charm Kitchens by Spetts, Commercial Drive, Route 5A, New Hartford, 13413

F. Berg, CKD, Berg & Brown, Inc., 1390 Lexington Avenue, New York City, 10028

R. J. Brady, CKD, General Electric Co., 205 East 42nd Street, New York City, 10017

F. E. Drucker, CKD, Fred E. Drucker & Associates, Inc., 853 Lexington Avenue, New York City, 10021

I. Schwartz, CKD, Bakit Industries, Inc., 32 East 30th Street, New York City, 10016

J. F. Werner, CKD, Werner Associates, Inc., 136 East 74th Street, New York City, 10021

R. A. Ribble, CKD, Ribble Lumber, Inc., 249-1/2 Lake Street, Penn Yan, 100290

D. L. Thomas, CKD, D. L. Thomas Heating & Plumbing, Outer Market Street, Potsdam, 13676

W. A. Locus, CKD, Smart Living Kitchens, 1507 Monroe Avenue, Rochester, 14618

F. Thayer, Jr., CKD, St. Charles of Western New York, Inc., 1400 E. Henrietta Road, Rochester, 14623

I. Taras, CKD, Art-Craft Kitchens, Inc., 144 Sunrise Highway, Rockville Centre, 11570

J. D. Opper, CKD, Opper's Custom Kitchens, 186 W. Dominick, Rome, 13440

C. J. Arzonetti, CKD, Garth Custom Kitchens, Inc., 24 Garth Road, Scarsdale, 10583

C. Van Name, CKD, Staten Island Woodworking Co., Inc., 1475 Hylan Boulevard, Staten Island, 10305

R. F. Martino, CKD, Modern Kitchens of Syracuse, Inc., 2380 Erie Blvd. East, Syracuse, 13224

A. Gulbis, CKD, E. Gulbis, CKD, Lifetime Kitchens, Inc., 269 Columbus Avenue, Tuckahoe, 10707

W. H. Algier, CKD, Empire Kitchen & Woodworking, Inc., 862 South Road, Wappingers Falls, 12590

J. A. Barth, CKD, 306 Ayer Road, Williamsville, 14221

F. A. Tommasini, CKD, Tommasini Bldg. Corp., 485 Willis Ave., Williston Park, 11596

Certified Kitchen Designers

North Carolina

R. D. Finlayson, CKD, Kitchen Creations of Charlotte, 130 West Boulevard, Charlotte, 28203

P. L. Heath, CKD, IXL Furniture Co., Route One, Elizabeth City, 27909

North Dakota

D. W. Smith, CKD, Cabinets, Inc., 2600 Main Avenue, P. O. Box 626, Fargo, 58102

Ohio

H. S. Hembury, CKD, Tailormade Kitchen Co., 1063 S. Arlington Street, Akron, 44306

C. G. Schweikert, CKD, Schweikert Bros. Kitchens, 361 W. North Street, Akron, 44303

F. A. Valentine, CKD, Williams Kitchens, 5308 Fulton Drive N.W., Canton, 44718

R. E. Bolte, CKD, Bolte Home Improvement Co., 9526 Winton Road, Cincinnati, 45231

R. P. Halpin, CKD, Kitchens by Nickoson, 3511 Harrison Avenue, Cincinnati, 45211

R. E. Klein, CKD, Kustom Kitchens by Klein, 4342 Harrison Avenue, Cincinnati, 45211

J. F. Rugh, CKD, Valley Floor Covering Co., 417 Wyoming Avenue, Cincinnati, 45215

R. O. Click, CKD, Cleveland Tile & Cabinet Co., 131 Terminal Tower Arcade, Cleveland, 44113

J. H. Foster Jr., CKD, Higbee's Design Center, 100 Public Square, Cleveland, 44113

A. G. Luzius, CKD, Mutschler Kitchens of Cleveland, Inc., 10523 Carnegie Avenue, Cleveland, 44106

G. Shiekh, CKD, D. Wallace, CKD, Cleveland Tile & Cabinet Co., 131 Terminal Tower Arcade, Cleveland, 44113

P. J. Orobello, CKD, A. C. Zigerelli, CKD, National Heating & Plumbing, 3962 Mayfield Road, Cleveland Heights, 44121

J. F. Fehn, CKD, Scioto Kitchen Sales, Inc., 3232 Allegheny Avenue, Columbus, 43209

W. A. Hagedorn, CKD, H & C Kitchens & Bathrooms, Inc., 1290 West Broad Street, Columbus, 43222

J. A. Jacobs, CKD, T. W. Salt, CKD, JAE Company 955 W. Fifth Avenue, Columbus, 43212

F. A. Lasorella, CKD, Lakeland Building & Construction Co., 36600 Lakeland Blvd., Eastlake, 44094

R. P. Campbell, CKD, A. R. Lingler, CKD, Roth U. Bertsch & Co., Inc., 118 Main Street, Hamilton, 45013

A. R. Driskell, CKD, Mansfield

O. H. Hoge, CKD, Hoge Lumber Co., South Main Street, New Knoxville, 45871

J. B. Knowlton, CKD, The Morgan Company, 5400 Oakhill Drive N.W., Warren, 44481

A. J. Boczonadi, CKD, Ohio Maid Sales Co., 1529 Lemcke Road, Xenia, 45385

Oregon

V. R. Greb, CKD, J. Greb & Son, Inc., 5027 N. E. 42nd Avenue, Portland, 97218

Pennsylvania

R. Wieland, CKD, Kitchens by Wieland, 4210 Tilghman Street, Allentown, 18104

M. F. Weiss, Jr., CKD, M. F. Weiss, Inc., P. O. Box 97, Brodheadsville, 18322

R. M. Carlson, CKD, Madsen, Inc., 2901 Springfield Road, Broomall, 19008

J. H. Stefanide, CKD, Chester Woodworking, Inc., 503 E. 7th Street, Chester, 19013

D. R. Oberholtzer, CKD, R. R. Oberholtzer, CKD, R. G. Snyder, CKD, Oberholtzer Kitchens, Inc., Route 309, Coopersburg, 18036

G. M. Nicolaisen, CKD, Kapri Kitchens, Inc., Div. of Cordal, Corner of Broad & Park St., P. O. Box 100, Dallastown, 17313

G. R. Polachek, CKD, Town & Country Kitchens, Inc., 761 Meldon Ave., P.O. Box 304, Donora, 100069

J. F. Glunt, CKD, Aaron Kitchen Design Center, 1603 3rd Avenue, Duncansville, 16635

J. J. Karner, CKD, Merritt Lumber Co., Inc., 518 Chestnut Street, Emmaus, 18049

W. Z. Peterson, CKD, Peterson Cabinet & Supply, 503 New Alexandria Road, Greensburg, 15601

R. M. Fromme, CKD, D & H Distributing Co., 2525 N. 7th Street, Harrisburg, 17105

R. L. Selder, CKD, Selders Cabinet Shop, R-784 Cooper Avenue, Johnstown, 15906

G. R. Callender, CKD, C. H. Lemmerman, CKD, Wood-Mode Kitchens, Snyder County, Kreamer, 17833

G. D. Lucci Jr., CKD, M. A. Lucci, CKD, R. J. Lucci, CKD, Lucci Kitchens, Inc., 1271 North Brodhead Road, Monaca, 15061

J. W. Brady, CKD, J. W. Brady, Inc., 723 Montgomery Avenue, Narberth, 19072

T. Lamont, CKD, Lamont House of Kitchens, 1990 W. Main Street, Norristown, 19401

D. C. Broscious, CKD, Broscious Lumber Company, 4th & Duke Street, Northumberland, 17857

L. G. Ciliberti, CKD, Sam Donze Kitchens, Inc., 1834-36 E. Passyunk Avenue, Philadelphia, 19148

B. Fleet, CKD, S. Kulla, CKD, J. B. Wagner, CKD, Mayfair Kitchen Remodeling Center, Inc., 7400 Frankford Avenue, Philadelphia, 19136

T. R. Moser, CKD, U. L. Tomassone, CKD, Moser Corporation, 5702 N. 5th Street, Philadelphia, 19120

F. R. Boyd, CKD, Style-Rite Kitchens, 12248 Frankstown Road, Pittsburgh, 15235

L. J. Frey, CKD, Frey Cabinet Co., 510 S. Main Street, Pittsburgh, 15220

J. J. Molek, CKD, R. Morra, CKD, Morr-Craft Products, Inc., 1414 Spring Garden Avenue, Pittsburgh, 15212

C. P. Morrison, CKD, 4871 Clairton Blvd., Pittsburgh, 15236

G. R. Scull, CKD, Kitchen Sales, Inc., 622 Washington Road, Pittsburgh, 15228

S. Z. Stein, CKD, Steins Custom Interiors, 3559 Bigelow Blvd., Pittsburgh, 15213

J. G. Heffleger, CKD, J & J Heffleger Custom Kitchens, R. D. #2, Reading, 19605

C. K. Battram Jr., CKD, Charles Associates, Inc., 113 N. Market Street, Selinsgrove, 17870

A. L. Donze, CKD, S. J. Donze, CKD, Sam Donze Kitchens, Inc., 502 Baltimore Pike, Springfield, 19064

C. J. Walsh, CKD, Wall & Walsh, Inc., 8320 West Chester Pike, Upper Darby, 19082

L. A. Scarf, CKD, Rich Maid Kitchens, Penn Avenue, Wernersville, 19565

H. R. Hurlbrink, CKD, Hurlbrink House of Kitchens, 701 Westtown Road, West Chester, 19380

C. E. Muhly, III, CKD, Conrad E. Muhly Co., 5 Westtown Road, West Chester, 19380

L. Platsky, CKD, M. L. Weisberger, CKD, Betterhouse, Inc., 1140 Wyoming Avenue, Wyoming, 18644

R. D. Botterbusch Jr., CKD, Robert's Kitchens, 790 Carlisle Avenue, York, 17404

H. B. Murray, CKD, Murray Equipment Co., Inc., 1228 E. Philadelphia Street, York, 17405

Rhode Island

J. A. McClure, CKD, American Custom Kitchens, Inc., 145 Chad Brown Street, Providence, 02907

South Carolina

J. A. Clarkson, CKD, Clarkson Kitchens, 946 Harden Street, Columbia, 29205

Tennessee

M. L. Robinson, CKD, Modern Supply Company, Western Avenue at Dale, Knoxville, 37921

J. R. Henry, CKD, C. M. Nixon, CKD, Henry Kitchens, Inc., 1808 Broadway, Nashville, 37203

Texas

G. H. Gerdes Jr., CKD, St. Charles Kitchens of Houston, 2221 Pease (P.O. Box 45005), Houston, 77045

D. B. Steffan, CKD, Kitchens of Houston, 4100 Southwest Freeway, Suite 301, Houston, 77027

Utah

G. N. Sheffield, CKD, Craftsman Cabinets, Inc., 2200 S. Main Street, Salt Lake City, 84115

Vermont

W. H. Huttenlock, CKD, P. W. Meacham Sr., CKD, Vermont Structural Steel Corp., 207 Flynn Avenue, Burlington, 05401

P. L. Hackel, CKD, Vermont Electric Supply Co., Inc., 299 N. Main Street, Rutland, 05701

Certified Kitchen Designers

Virginia

R. F. Bartholomew Sr., CKD, Deavers Appliances & Kitchens, 7960 Columbia Pike, Annandale, 22003

W. A. Dembo Sr., CKD, Kitchen Classics, Inc., 6023 Wilson Blvd., Arlington, 22205

West Virginia

C. H. Coles, CKD, Save Supply Co., Inc., 514 Virginia Street East, Charleston, 25321

Wisconsin

G. F. Soik, CKD, W. Thomas, CKD, Green Bay Kitchen Mart, Inc., 2680 So. Ashland Avenue, Green Bay, 54303

A. B. Mather, CKD, A. Mather Co., 1002 Indiana Avenue, Sheboygan, 53081

Canada

Alberta

G. A. Dreger, CKD, L. D. Dreger, CKD, Dreger's Kitchen Corner Ltd., 10442 Whyte Avenue, Edmonton

Appendix 6

**Addresses of all Firms
Mentioned in Text and
Photo Captions**

Adler-Kay Co., Box 639, Wayne, Mich. 48184

Ajax Hardware Corp., 825 S. Ajax Av., City of Industry, Cal. 91747

Amana Refrigeration, Sub. Raytheon, Amana, Iowa 52203

American Institute of Kitchen Dealers, 114 Main St., Hackettstown, N.J. 07840

Armstrong Cork Co., Liberty & Charlotte, Lancaster, Pa. 17604

Amtico Flooring, Div. American Biltrite Rubber, 3 Assumpink Blvd., Trenton, N.J. 08607

Bailey's Kitchens, 530 N. Tejon St., Colorado Springs, Colo., 80902

Barmark, 198 Central Av., East Orange, N.J. 07018

Betterhouse, 1150 Wyoming Av., Wyoming, Pa. 18644

Bisulk Kitchens, 295 Nassau Blvd., Garden City South, N.Y. 11530

Broan Mfg. Co., 926 W. State St., Hartford, Wis. 53027

Caloric Corp., Sub. Raytheon, Topton, Pa. 19562

Charlotte Clark Kitchens, 18932 W. MacNichols Rd., Detroit, Mich. 48219

City Lumber Co., 75 Third St., Bridgeport, Conn.

Congoleum Industries, Kearny, N.J. 07032

Connor Forest Industries, Box 847, Wausau, Wis. 54401

Coppes, Inc., Nappanee, Ind. 46550

Corning Glass, Major Appliance Dept., Consumer Products Div., Corning N.Y. 14830

Coronet Imperial, 6755 Southwest Av., St. Louis, Mo. 63143

Dacor Mfg. Co., Armory St., Worcester, Mass. 01601

Del-Mar, Div. U.S. Plywood/Champion Papers, 2865 Gordon Rd. N.W, Atlanta, Ga. 30311

Dixie Cabinet, Box 457, Morristown, Tenn. 37814

Durabeauty, Consoweld Corp., 700 Hooker St., Wisconsin Rapids, Wis. 54494

Elkay Mfg. Co., 2700 S. 17 Av., Broadview, Ill. 60153

Enjay Fibers & Laminates, Enjay Chemical Co., Odenton, Md. 21113

Faultless Div., Bliss & Laughlin Industries, 1421 N. Garvin, Evansville, Ind. 47717

Formica Corp., 120 E. Fourth St., Cincinnati, Ohio 45202

General Electric, Appliance Park, Louisville, Ky. 40225

General Electric, Large Lamp Div., Nela Park, Cleveland, Ohio 44112

Grabill Cabinet Co., Box 146, Grabill, Ind.

Gulf Corp., 615 Tchoupitoulas St., New Orleans, La. 70130

Halbeisen, Hen, Inc., 935 Penn St. Reading, Pa. 19601

Home Ventilating Institute, 360 N. Michigan Av., Chicago, Ill. 60601

Honeywell, 2701 Fourth Av. S., Minneapolis, Minn. 55408

Hotpoint, General Electric Co., Appliance Park, Louisville, Ky. 40225

Housing & Urban Development Dept., Washington D.C. 20410

Imperial Cabinet Co., Box 427, Gaston, Ind. 47342

In-Sink-Erator, Div. Emerson Electric, 4700 21st St., Racine, Wis. 53406

IXL Furniture Co., Elizabeth City, N.C. 27909

Jenn-Air Corp., 3035 Shadeland, Indianapolis, Ind. 46226

Karpy Kitchens, Rte. 17A, Florida, N.Y.

Kemper Div., The Tappan Co., 901 S. N St., Richmond, Ind.

Kennedy Kitchens, 727 Fox St., Horseheads, N.Y. 14845

Kich-n-vent, Div. Home-Metal Products, 750 Central Xway, Plano, Texas 75074

KinZee Industries, 259 Second St., Saddle Brook, N.J. 07662

KitchenAid Dishwasher Div., Hobart Mfg., Troy, Ohio 45373

Kitchen Concepts, 750 N.W. McNab Rd., Ft. Lauderdale, Fla. 33309

Kitchen Kompact, KK Plaza, Jeffersonville, Ind. 47130

Kitchen Originals, 5300 Merrick Rd., Massapequa, N.Y.

Kitchens by Krengel, 1688 Grand Av., St. Paul, Minn. 55105

Kitchens by Wieland, 4210 Tilghman St., Allentown, Pa.

Kitchens Inc., Narrowsburg, N.Y. 12764

Kitchens Unliminted, 320 S. Robertson Blvd., W. Los Angeles, Cal.

Kohler Co., Kohler, Wis. 53044

Koss Corp., 4129 N. Port Washington Av., Milwaukee, Wis. 53212

Lightolier, 346 Claremont Av., Jersey City, N.J. 07305

Long-Bell, Div. International Paper, Box 579, Longview, Wash. 98632

MarVell Kitchens, 1150 Wyoming Av., Wyoming, Pa. 18644

Melamite Corp., Div. Johns-Manville, Canal St., Lawrence, Mass.

Merillat Industries, 2895 W. Beecher Rd., Adrian, Mich. 49221

Micarta, Div. Westinghouse Electric, Hampton, S.C.

Miami-Carey, Div. Panacon Corp., 203 Garver Rd., Monroe, Ohio

Modern Kitchens of Syracuse, 2380 Erie Blvd. East, Syracuse, N.Y.

Modern Maid, E. 14 St., Chattanooga, Tenn. 37401

Mutschler Kitchens, Madison at Randolph, Nappanee, Ind. 46550

National Industries, Div. AVM Corp., Odenton, Md. 21113

National Kitchen Cabinet Assn., 334 E. Broadway, Louisville, Ky. 40202

Noblecraft Industries, Box 88, Hillsboro, Ore. 97123

NuTone, Div. Scovill Mfg. Co., Madison & Red Bank Rds., Cincinnati, Ohio 45227

Owens-Corning Fiberglas, Fiberglas Tower, Toledo, Ohio 43659

Panelyte (See Reliance Panelyte)

Parkwood Laminates, Industrial Av., Lowell, Mass. 01854

Pioneer Craftsman, 330 Rose St., Reading, Pa. 19601

Pioneer Plastics Corp., Pionite Rd., Auburn, Me. 04210

Progress Lighting, Erie Av. & G St., Philadelphia, Pa. 19134

Quaker Maid Kitchens, Div. The Tappan Co., Leesport, Pa. 19533

Raygold Div., Boise Cascade, Box 1028, Winchester, Va. 22601

Rangaire Corp., Roberts Cobell Div., Box 177, Cleburne, Texas 76031

Reliance Panelyte, Box 1667, Tupelo, Miss. 38801

Remington Rand, Systems Div., Home Products Dept., Box 171, Marietta, Ohio 45750

Reynolds Enterprises, 2936 River Rd., River Grove, Ill. 60171

Ronson Corp., 1 Ronson Rd., Woodbridge, N.J. 07095

Rutt-Williams, 1536 Grant St., Elkhart, Ind. 46514

Saint Charles Mfg. Co., 1611 E. Main St., St. Charles, Ill.

Scheirich, H. J. Co., Box 21037, Louisville, Ky. 40221

Southern Cal. Assn. Wood Cabinet Mfrs., 9126 S. Western Av., Los Angeles, Cal.

Springfield Cabinet, 932 Dayton Av., Springfield, Ohio 45506

Sub-Zero, Box 4130, Madison, Wis. 53711

Swearingen, Ray Co., 4625 41st St. NW, Washington, D.C.

Tappan Div., The Tappan Co., 250 Wayne St., Mansfield, Ohio 44902

Textolite Div., Laminated Products Dept., General Electric, Coshocton, Ohio 43182

Thermador Div., Norris Industries, 5119 S. District Blvd., Los Angeles, Cal. 90022

Trade-Wind (See Thermador)

Union-Carbide, 270 Park Av., New York, N.Y. 10017

Vaughan, Geo. & Son., 223 S. Frio St., San Antonio, Texas 78207

Waste King Universal, Sub. Norris Ind., 3300 E. 50 St., Los Angeles, Cal. 90058

Wehco Plastics, Box 26, Bloomsbury, N.J. 08804

Westinghouse Electric, 1 Allegheny Sq., Pittsburgh, Pa. 15212

Whirlpool Corp., Benton Harbor, Mich.

Whitehall Cabinets, Whitehall Bldg., E. Rockaway, N.Y. 11518

White-Meyer Industries, 141 & Rte. 45, Orland Park, Ill. 60462

Wilson-Art, Ralph Wilson Plastics, Div. Dart Industries, 600 Gen. Bruce Dr., Temple, Texas

Wilson Cabinet Co., Box 489, Port Clinton, Ohio 43452

Wood-Mode Cabinetry, Kreamer, Pa. 17833

Yatron Bros., 3000 Penn Av., West Lawn, Pa.

Index